Political Philosophy, Educational Administration and Educative Leadership

In this book, Reynold Macpherson initiates a politically critical theory of educative leadership as a fresh line of inquiry in the practice, research and theory of educational administration and educational leadership.

Divided into four parts, the book introduces the subdiscipline of political philosophy to the field of educational administration, management and leadership. It does this by clarifying the knowledge domain of each and identifying how four political ideologies, specifically pragmatism, communitarianism, communicative rationalism and egalitarian liberalism, have primarily informed and surreptitiously provided contestable justifications for power in the development of practice, research and theory in the field of study.

The book goes on to offer three case studies illustrating how political philosophy can be used to interpret how people become leaders and administrators of educational institutions and systems. Additional case studies then demonstrate how crises in governance in educational institutions and systems can be analyzed and improvements made using the tools of political philosophy. The final part uses the subdiscipline to critique the author's decades of research into educative leadership and concludes the book by both establishing the relativity of politically critical critique and the ideology it favors: neopragmatism.

Political Philosophy, Educational Administration and Educative Leadership provides practitioners, researchers and theorists in educational administration, management and leadership with a deeper appreciation of power by formally introducing them to the assumptions, limits and tools of political philosophy.

Reynold Macpherson is a consultant evaluator and capacity builder in educational administration, management and leadership, based in New Zealand.

Routledge Research in Educational Leadership series

Books in this series:

Political Philosophy, Educational Administration and Educative Leadership
Reynold Macpherson

Political Philosophy, Educational Administration and Educative Leadership

Reynold Macpherson

R Routledge
Taylor & Francis Group

LONDON AND NEW YORK

First published 2014
by Routledge
2 Park Square, Milton Park, Abingdon, Oxon OX14 4RN

and by Routledge
711 Third Avenue, New York, NY 10017

Routledge is an imprint of the Taylor & Francis Group, an informa business

© 2014 R. Macpherson

The right of R. Macpherson to be identified as author of this work
has been asserted by him in accordance with sections 77 and 78 of the
Copyright, Designs and Patents Act 1988.

British Library Cataloguing-in-Publication Data
A catalogue record for this book is available from the British Library

Library of Congress Cataloging-in-Publication Data

Macpherson, R. J. S.
Political philosophy, educational administration and educative leadership /
    Reynold Macpherson.
        pages cm. — (Routledge research in educational leadership)
    1. Educational leadership — Political aspects—Case studies.   2. School
management and organization — Political aspects—Case studies.
3. Education—Political aspects—Philosophy.   I. Title.
    LB2806.M2225 2013
    371.2—dc23
    2013016345

ISBN: 978-0-415-71331-3 (hbk)
ISBN: 978-1-315-88335-9 (ebk)

Typeset in Baskerville
by Apex CoVantage, LLC

Printed and bound by CPI Group (UK) Ltd, Croydon, CR0 4YY

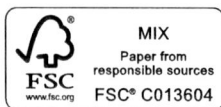

Contents

Dedications

This book is dedicated to three educative leaders. First is my father Guy Macpherson: laborer, soldier, farmer, beekeeper, thespian, politician and educationalist. Second, Dr. Ron Ikin, whose exemplary career in Victoria and New South Wales provided strategic professional development to generations of teachers and educational leaders. Third, Robin Shepherd: fisherman, teacher, principal, and consultant, indeed long-time "Mr. Education" of the Far North of New Zealand, who helped paint the shape of teaching and learning in rural education. Their shared characteristic is that they always spoke truth to power in education.

This book is also dedicated to Nicki, my lady, and our greatest delight—our children Kirsty, Shiona, Ewan and Angus, and our grandchildren, Austin and Olive.

It is dedicated to all of these fine people with thanks, love, and in the hope that they, their children, and their children's children, their host societies and the global community, will increasingly live in polities blessed with power structures and processes that enable education to serve as the most strategic discipline of all—principally by guaranteeing the growth of knowledge and capacity building in problem solving in all other disciplines, people, organizations and peoples.

Acknowledgements

This book acknowledges those practitioners, researchers, and theorists who have given their professional lives to the advancement of knowledge and practices worthy of the term *educative leadership*. In particular, it acknowledges the minds and contributions of the many extraordinary educators I have met and been inspired by over decades, including Paulino de Jesus Araujo, Ibrahim Bajunid, Tom Barnes, John Barrington, Richard Bates, Hedley Beare, Dr. Beeby, Russell Bishop, Jill Blackmore, Lynn Bossetti, Bill Boyd, Karen Brooking, Tony Bush, Brian Caldwell, Paulino de Carralho, Judith Chapman, Jim Cibulka, John Codd, Gary Crow, Frank Crowther, Alan Cumming, Brian Cusack, Peter Cuttance, Raewyn Dalziel, Ali Saaed Bin Harmal Al Dhaheri, Clive Dimmock, Patrick Duignan, Linda Ellison, Colin Evers, John Ewington, Peter Fensham, Patrick Forsyth, Bill Foster, Stanley Frielick, John Fyfield, Paul Gardiner, Viv Garrett, Colin Gaut, Ron Glatter, Gerald Grace, Thom Greenfield, Dan Griffiths, Peter Gronn, Helen Gunter, Richard Harker, Grant Harman, Harry Harris, John Hattie, John Ed Hickcox, Hinchcliff, Chris Hodgkinson, John Hood, Jo Howse, Wayne Hoy, Eric Hoyle, Park Sun Hyung, Larry Iannaconne, Ibrahim, Kerrie Ikin, Ron Ikin, Steve Jacobson, Gabrielle Lakomski, Lee, O. K., Jacky Lumby, Augusto Manuel, Yvonne Martin, Hanne Mawhinney, Keita McIndoe, Ann McKillop, Cheng Kai Ming, Cecil Miskel, David Monk, Claire Morrison, Bill Mulford, Joe Murphy, Peter Musgrave, Roy Nash, Jeff Northfield, Doug Ogilvie, Petros Pashiardris, David Pettit, Elaine Piggot-Irvine, Alan Pritchard, Peter Ramsay, Bill Renwick, Peter Ribbins, Dan Riley, Fazal Rizvi, Vivianne Robinson, Larry Sackney, Twyler Salm, Brian Scott, Dick Selleck, Tom Sergiovanni, Bill Simpkins, Tim Simkins, Robin Small, Don Smart, Jim Spinks, Jerry Starratt, Ken Strike, Ken Sylvester, Margaret Taplin, Angela Thody, Ross Thomas, Helen Timperley, Omar Tofighian, Barbara Vann, Allan Walker, Jim Walker, Charles Webber, John Weeks, John West-Burnham, Norman Wicks, Don Willower, Andrew Wong and Ken Wong.

Irrespective of their many and inspired contributions, the thinking that follows remains solely my responsibility.

Preface

The ancient proverb that to be great is to be misunderstood takes on new and disturbing significance when examined against the background of our modern democracy. To those who like myself had periods of service both in industry and in government, the meaning of this phrase was revealed by a disconcerting experience that invariably came to us. While on duty in Washington we came to have a deep affection and respect for many men who bore great responsibility, and whose names were widely known, but when we visited our home areas and mingled with our old friends we met nothing but harsh criticism for those same men, whom we believed to be devoted servants of our country. Nor was this a matter of politics. It goes on all the time no matter who is in the White House. Administrations come and administrations go, but this general attitude of all but open ridicule of our leaders of our nation remains endemic. Men who not possibly measure up themselves have no hesitancy in condemning those who try to bear those great burdens.

(Randall, 1965)

The problem here, as I see it, is that such commonly covert and occasionally overt ad hominem critique of leaders in education is not just that such criticism might be ill-informed or inappropriate, but that such feedback in a liberal democracy lacks an effective method of informing learning about power and leadership. The wider and parallel challenge is that the academic field of study known as educational administration (or as educational management in the United Kingdom and in many Commonwealth countries, and taken throughout this book to include educational administration, management, and leadership) similarly lacks the subdiscipline of political philosophy in its methods of refining knowledge, research, and powerful practices. The powerful can have weak learning systems about the educative nature of their leadership services and theories.

I came to this view during a career that included leadership at the team, unit, and institutional level in school and tertiary levels of education, and international research into educative leadership. It is only now that I am formally retired that I have the time to lay out a systematic justification for this position, illustrate it with case studies, and then offer a general theoretical remedy: politically critical educative leadership. Be it as teacher in a primary classroom, a mathematics teacher in secondary schools, a senior leader of a school, a professional development officer in an education system, a professor and director of an academic development unit in a research university, a chief executive officer (CEO) of a bicultural institute of technology, a chancellor and CEO of a new university in the Middle East, or as an international consultant assisting with evaluations and post-conflict reconstruction, I learned from experience that leading people in educational organizations is, in considerable part, although not exclusively, an exercise in power.

In essence, like all other leaders I encountered, I used my positional power and authority in order to achieve ends considered valuable by myself and others, such as governors, and the wider policy and societal contexts. At the same time, I was always aware that among my many limitations was that I lacked a sophisticated way of judging the extent to which I (and we) were doing right or wrong.

There were many reasons for this, none of them excuses. Leadership responsibility came to me relatively early, certainly long before I began to appreciate the flaws and limitations in my character, understandings, and skills. Accepting leadership responsibility often meant joining an elite group, a power elite, that tended to assure itself with a myth of dynamic and professional heroism, competence, and worth (Putnam, 1976, p. 73). My terms of engagement as a leader focused on mobilizing action, evaluating outcomes, and achieving reforms in the organizations I was a member of. Yet, oddly, such terms rarely expected me to use systematic methods of collecting data on my own leadership services with a view to understanding and improving their impact in educational terms.

When I undertook postgraduate education about leadership, there was nothing particularly educative or politically critical about the available theories of educational administration, although I did mix with some extraordinary people and gained access to some most remarkable ideas. Foremost was the Master's unit I studied with Bill Simpkins at the University of New England to do with the politics of education, both for its insightful content and stimulating pedagogy which included negotiable assignments.

Curiously, the first and second editions of the seminal text of the field at the time, by Wayne Hoy and Cecil Miskel (1978, 1982), both fine leaders themselves by all accounts, made no mention of how power was being used or might best be used in the leadership of learning, curriculum development, professional development, and governance. This had not changed by the seventh edition nearly 30 years later (Hoy & Miskel, 2005).

It was only when I had been deeply engaged in research for some time did I realize that the branch of philosophy directly concerned with the quality of power, namely political philosophy, was absent from analysis, evaluation, critique, and reform of governance, administration, and leadership in education, and from the preparatory programs for educational leaders offered by universities. Nobody in the field of educational administration used the concepts, tools, and specialist language of political philosophy. The inevitable upshot is that practitioners, researchers, and theorists in our field share a collective blind spot.

Looking back, I was offered instead an ideology of pragmatism and a technology of management, structural-functionalism, that was embedded in systems theory, to deliver on expectations and justify my use of positional power. The component of my leadership most valued by the leaders of organizations and systems was puissance: The ability to get things done. This benchmark of effective leadership did not raise the moral bar any higher than the terms of current policy. Nevertheless, as my leadership responsibilities grew, and I contributed more and more to policy making, the need for the moral legitimation of my leadership services became more acute.

There were many false summits along the jagged ridge of my career. As a team and unit leader in various universities around the world, I was often encouraged by colleagues to adopt an alternative ideology, socially critical collegialism, to justify my use of professorial power. Leadership in schooling and academe were, however, often confused by wider institutional priorities given carriage by a more pragmatic ideology: financially critical corporate managerialism.

Curiously, leaders and interest groups in these institutions and systems rarely clarified or justified their ideologies but appeared to assume and assert that they were right to use political processes to prosecute their ends or the ends they had been given or had adopted. I suspect now that many shared my doubts in their quiet moments. To be sure, we all used the rhetoric and imagery of *rightness* to justify the initiatives we took, used consensus to reinforce our largely intuited sense of rightness, adopted various forms of pragmatism to conjure up justifications when they were required, and then measured our success using the criterion of puissance.

In the course of my career, I made a point of monitoring the development of the conventional wisdom of educational administration as well as edge-cutting research internationally about educational leadership, regularly contributing through the publication of research findings. Along the way, I accrued a BA (Open University) in mathematics and management, an MEdAdmin (University of New England) largely by research into school leadership, a PhD (Monash University) by research into system leadership, and much later, a graduate diploma in business administration (University of Waikato) by coursework. Never once on that learning pathway was I was offered more than the tools pertaining to a given political ideology, never the means of evaluating their justification or relativity. No one offered the means to analyze, arbitrate, or blend ideologies about power reasonably, either in general terms of principle or consequence or for specific purposes and situations.

This should not be taken to imply that I am advocating or denying the place of either normative, deontological, or situational ethics. Instead it should be taken to mean that the field of educational leadership, from my reading, research, and experience, has long lacked a customized philosophical process to reflect ethically on its use and abuse of power.

Two examples can suffice at this point. Consider the widely read and scholarly treatment of *Ethical Leadership and Decision Making in Education* (Shapiro & Stefkovich, 2011), now in its third edition. It offers an approach based on four *paradigms*: an ethic of justice, an ethic of critique, an ethic of caring, and an ethic of professionalism. On my reading, by setting aside procedural issues, the ethic of justice comprises a blend of liberal democratic, communitarian, and egalitarian liberal ideologies. Similarly, the ethic of critique is a blend of critical and liberation-ist socialism. On the same ground, the ethics of caring comprises altruism and humanitarianism. The ethic of professionalism was centered on the best interests of the student with justifications derived from a blend of legal, consequential, humanitarian, and communitarian ideologies.

The four paradigms were clarified by reference to paradoxes in practice. A range of dilemmas, presumably encountered by leaders and decision makers in the United States, were then traced to their origins and presented as contemporary cases with questions for discussion. The dilemmas helpfully included individual rights versus community standards, traditional versus hidden curriculum, personal versus professional codes, cultural rights versus multiculturalism, religion versus culture, equality versus equity, accountability versus responsibility, and privacy ver-sus safety (Stefkovich & O'Brien, 2004). Oddly, the cases offered did not include any dilemmas to do with the nature and use of power in governance, management, or leadership in systems, institutions, and classrooms. By its omission, power was presented as ethically unproblematic, which is simply implausible.

A second example is the classic collection of contributions from some leading and emergent theorists, along with some purported "giants of the field" (Begley, 1999b, p. 2) entitled *The Values of Educational Administration* (Begley & Leonard, 1999). From the outset, the focus was on the "primal concept of power" and how lead-ers use power to achieve "the triumph of the will" (Hodgkinson, 1999, pp. 6–8). Although many authors were excited by and sought to advance Hodgkinson's val-ues hierarchy, which I detail below, and advanced highly sophisticated personal and apparently reasonable theories of what they considered valued and valuable educational leadership and epistemologically sound knowledge production, in the absence of political philosophy, the net effect was aptly described by Begley (1999a) as resembling

> an endless medieval conflict; the champions of each side residing in craggy paradigmatic redoubts, emerging periodically for a skirmish or two on the bat-tlefield of academic journalism. . . . This academic ferment may have seemed almost heroic at times to the academics engaged in it. However, many school practitioners would probably comment that very little has been achieved that has increased the clarity, coherence, and relevance of values to their everyday administrative practice. It has been very much a conversation among academ-ics, far removed from the day-to-day concerns of school administration. As a consequence, a significant relevancy gap has developed between academia and practitioners on matters relating to values and valuation processes in administration. (p. 51)

This criticism was particularly well-justified as regards the analysis of political values and engagement in political philosophy. Confucianism and communitarian-ism were touched on in passing (Evers, 1999, p. 70). The power of language was well-described as follows, echoing Bourdieu and Rorty but failing to evoke and name the ideology of linguistic pragmatism (otherwise known as neopragmatism):

Language is inextricably entangled in a wider social context, and as such, depends on this social context for its power to assign worth. This means that this power does not reside in words alone. Rather all who avail themselves of a form of power that is part of a social institution. Individuals and their linguistic practices will always bear the trace of these various institutions. As a consequence, the power, value, and sense of particular linguistic expressions are as much a product of the (often unequal) relationships between and among groups and individuals as are the various arrangements of symbols and sounds. The power of language to assign or reflect worth then will always depend upon who is speaking, when, where, why, and with whom. In this regard institutional frameworks routinely endow particular individuals (and not others) with the power to assign value. (Ryan, 1999, p. 112)

Political philosophy was briefly educed when Clive Beck (1999, p. 226) distinguished between "*social and political values* [original emphasis] such as justice, due process, tolerance, cooperation, loyalty, citizenship," and other basic, spiritual, moral, intermediate-range, and specific values. It then became the central methodology in Bossetti and Brown's (1999, pp. 234–240) discussion of the future of public education in terms of "three value positions," actually ideologies—egalitarianism, libertarianism, and communitarianism. Although some of the definitions used warrant some refinement, given the literature of political philosophy summarized below, their attempt to evaluate the relativity of political ideologies as expressed in the purposes of public education was a major yet largely unrecognized breakthrough in the field of educational administration.

It was noteworthy that one of the edition's eight themes, specifically "recognizing and critiquing power relationships embedded in language use," and that the first four of the six questions raised for follow-up research in values in educational administration (Leonard, 1999, pp. 247, 252), all require political philosophy to attend to them:

- Is it necessary for all participants involved in collaborative decision making—which often gives rise to value conflicts—to not only arrive at shared values but to begin with shared conceptualizations of the nature of values?
- How do leaders facilitate shared decision making when stakeholders subscribe to different value orientations and hold different and often subconscious interpretations of value theory?
- How can leaders facilitate the process of arriving at the common good?
- What is the nature of the relationship between language and power in the process of achieving common ground?

The voids evident in the edition regarding the articulation of political values needed to describe and evaluate the quality of power structures and practices embedded in educational leadership, and the negligible role ascribed to political ideology in the growth of knowledge about educational administration are two salutary signals to the field. Similarly, it should come as an affront to theorists, researchers, and practitioners that, unlike its twin profession of pedagogy, the field of educational administration does not require training or demonstrable competency in professional ethics prior to appointment, let alone appropriate political ethics. And with regard to practitioner ethics, five years after their careful conceptualization and publication, the field still does not have effective means of governing the quality of professionalism in practice after appointment to comply with its own National Standard 6:

> A. Ensure a system of accountability for every students' academic and social success; B. Model principles of self-awareness, reflective practice, transparency, and ethical behavior; C. Safeguard the values of democracy, equity, and diversity; D. Consider and evaluate the potential moral and legal decision making; and E. Promote social justice and ensure that individual student needs inform all aspects of schooling. (National Policy Board of Educational Administration, 2008)

On reflection, to this point, once appointed as the formal leader of units, institutions, and projects of some significance at various times in my career, I found that I lacked an appropriate method of understanding, evaluating, and improving my use of power to educative ends. Although puissance got me to sleep at night, it was the question of moral legitimacy that woke me again and triggered decades of reflection and research.

As first noted above, a particularly helpful contributor to my learning was Chris Hodgkinson who developed Wittgensteinian propositions about the powerful nature of administration (1978), a neo-Stoic philosophy of leadership that included a method of auditing leadership values (1983), an analytical model of value that enabled him to theorize educational leadership as a moral art (1991), and finally, an axiology linking the technologies of administration to nondogmatic philosophical reflection appropriate for leadership in the postmodern world (1996). Truly, a beautiful mind.

Patrick Duignan and I worked together for some years with some brilliant practitioners in Victoria, Australian Capital Territory and New South Wales (NSW) and stellar theorists from across Australia to advance understanding on what might count as a practical theory of educative leadership (Duignan & Macpherson, 1992). Although I then went on to explore the complexities of educative accountability in education (Macpherson, 1997b), and Patrick carefully unpacked ethical tensions in leadership (Duignan, 2006), the matter of evaluating and justifying the use of power by practitioners in educational administration by applying the subdiscipline of political philosophy was a challenge long unrecognized and left unattended.

This book, therefore, seeks to help practitioners, researchers, and theorists in educational administration, management, and leadership to deepen their appreciation of power by formally introducing them to the assumptions, limits, and tools of political philosophy, as I understand them. Because I am more recent than some to the subdiscipline, it is inevitable that some of my understandings will be corrected and others refuted. So be it. I will have to be comforted by Eric Bell's observation that "Time makes fools of us all."

The aim of this book is to initiate a politically critical theory of educative leadership as a fresh line of inquiry in the practice, research, and theory of educational administration and educational leadership. To this end, the book is in four parts. The first introduces the subdiscipline of political philosophy to the field of educational administration, management, and leadership. It does this by clarifying the knowledge domain of each and then identifying how four political ideologies, specifically pragmatism, communitarianism, communicative rationalism, and egalitarian liberalism, have primarily informed and surreptitiously provided contestable justifications for power in the development of practice, research, and theory in our field of study.

The second part offers three case studies to illustrate how political philosophy can be used to interpret how people become leaders and administrators of educational institutions and systems.

The third part offers case studies of how crises in governance in educational institutions and systems can be analyzed using the tools of political philosophy.

The fourth and final part turns back to review my research over decades into educative leadership using political philosophy, proposes advances to theory, and finally, indicates the ideological relativity of the subdiscipline by advancing other forms of critical reflection on practice.

Part I

Introducing political philosophy to educational administration

1 Political philosophy

> The person who wishes not to be troubled by politics and to be left alone finds
> himself an unwitting ally of those to whom politics is a troublesome obstacle to
> their well-meant intentions to leave nothing alone . . . the establishing of political
> order is not just any order at all; it marks the birth, or the recognition, of freedom.
> For politics represents at least some tolerance of differing truths, some recognition
> that government is possible, indeed best conducted, amid the open canvassing of
> rival interests. Politics are the public actions of free men. Freedom is the privacy of
> men from public action.
>
> (Crick, 1982, pp. 16, 18)

If politics is to be the guarantor of freedom, then political philosophy is needed
to guarantee the quality of politics. Political philosophy is a subdiscipline of
political science, itself a social science discipline. It is an activity. It is thinking
about *how* we think about political analysis. It is meta-analysis that focuses on
how we understand and evaluate the nature, structures and the use and abuse
of power.

Given that leaders hold the levers of power in education, such as the distribution of responsibility, information and communication systems and even how an
organization is conceived, it follows that such politically critical analysis should be
central to scholarship in educational administration. This has not been the case.
However, there is considerable evidence to suggest that political philosophy has
already had a largely unrealized, growing and major potential role in the growth
of knowledge about educational administration.

To be sustained, these introductory claims require relevant definitions and a
summary of the history and conceptual domain of political philosophy; the purpose of this chapter. They also require a brief history of the conceptual domain
of educational administration to interpret the growth of knowledge related to
politics in education, the remit of Chapter 2. The aim of these introductory
chapters in Part 1 is to indicate the potential of political philosophy regarding the
use and legitimacy of power and political structures and processes in education. In
Chapters 3 and 4, I define and introduce the roles played by pragmatism, communitarianism, communicative rationalism and egalitarian liberalism in the growth

of knowledge about educational administration. The first four chapters composing Part 1 culminate into two general propositions:

- The ideological controversies in the theory and practice of educational administration could be attended to much more effectively than in the past by engaging in political philosophy.
- Given the significant agency of educational administrators in the politics of organizations, the growth of knowledge in the field should be enhanced by the systematic development of politically critical practice, research and theory about educative leadership.

Part 2 consists of chapters that explore these two propositions using case studies of becoming an educational administrator in very different jurisdictions and organizations I was once familiar with. The three chapters of Part 3 are all cases where the legitimacy of the distribution of power was challenged, again in settings where I was engaged. The two chapters in Part 4 build on a prior practical theory of educative leadership to suggest an additional line of inquiry that employs political philosophy to understand and evaluate leadership and administrative services in education.

At this point, it is important to define the key term of this text, namely power, hopefully to avoid confusion later. At its simplest, power in educational settings is the capacity to guide the actions of others. And the ethical use of such power is to be evaluated against a meta-value of learning. When this capacity is perceived as appropriate and effective in its cultural or organizational context, it is regarded as legitimate *positional power* and endowed with authority. When power is regarded as lacking in legitimacy and authority, it tends to be described as arbitrary, unjust or evil, and becomes contestable.

Power can be directional in effect depending on the nature of the social system or organization. Where it is exercised through hierarchy, it is termed *downward power*. Where subordinates have influence over their superordinates, it is held to be *upward power*. Power can be exercised by recourse to coercion, which is to use force or the threat of force, or to influence people by using various forms of persuasion, including manipulation (Handy, 1976).

There are many potential sources of power in social and political settings. Power may be held due to delegated authority, law, tradition, electoral mandate, material wealth, social class or standing (mana), exchangeable resources (e.g., ascribed influence, money, property, food, etc.), charisma, celebrity status, persuasion (direct, indirect, or subliminal), knowledge (expertize, granted or withheld, shared or secret), moral and religious persuasion, coercive force and social and interpersonal dynamics. These sources have been summarized in many different ways.

A classic study proposed that the sources of power stem either from personality or leadership, property or wealth, or organization (Galbraith, 1983). It also suggested three types of power: compensatory power in which influence is purchased; condign power in which influence is achieved by making the alternative sufficiently painful; and conditioned power in which influence is gained by persuasion.

Power strategies and tactics have led to another set of definitions. A classic summary of the capacity to implement changes in human systems (Chin & Benne, 1984) employed three categories; empirical or rational, normative or re-educative and power or coercive strategies. Tactics used every day in social and political settings can include the manipulation of rewards, threats and information, including bullying, demanding, disengaging, evading humor, inspiring, negotiating, socializing and supplicating.

These power tactics in interpersonal relationships have been described (French & Raven, 1959) on three dimensions: softness or hardness, rationality or nonrationality, and unilateral or bilateral tactics. Whereas soft tactics are indirect and interpersonal and exploit a relationship, hard tactics tend to be direct, be harsh, be forceful and seek specific outcomes. Rational tactics make heavy use of reasoned examples, evidence and logic and wise judgment, whereas nonrational tactics seek to persuade using the emotions, such a put downs, bargaining, evasions and misinformation. Unilateral tactics rely on the passivity or ignorance of those to be persuaded, such as the use of edicts, disengagement and fait accompli. Bilateral tactics, including collaboration and negotiation, can evoke reciprocity.

The power strategies and tactics used and resultant actions in interpersonal, wider group and organizational settings are also dependent on the wider contexts of time, group, organization and society (Foucault, 1980).

In situations where power relationships are relational and reciprocal, the outcomes usually reflect a fresh balance of power or a new equilibrium that indicates the shift in power currency (McCornack, 2009). In situations where power is motivated by a desire to gain prestige, honor and reputation, power shifts can lead to psychological consequences, such as altering the *empathy gap* in relationships, and lead to strategic responsibilities instead of social responsibilities (Handgraaf, Van Dijk, Vermunt, Wilke, & De Dreu, 2008).

It has been observed (French & Raven, 1959) that professional organizations tend to value expert power over referent power, reward power and coercive power, all of which tend to suffer from diminishing returns over time and offend collegial norms. Even in situations where powers are socially constructed and deconstructed relatively freely, such as in voluntary and professional groups, the charismatic and interpersonal power of individuals to attract loyalty from followers, referent power, tends to be mediated or reinforced by the wider norms of host organizations, polities and societies, and their histories (Foucault, 1980). Because power is both the means of resolving conflicts of interest and determining who wins scarce resources over time, the analysis of sources of power in organizations has increasingly given equal weight to understanding the conditions for current power relations and to the historical forces that shaped the setting in which political actions are played out.

To illustrate the scope of comprehensive political analysis in complex organizations, Gareth Morgan argued (1986, pp. 158–185) that there are at least 14 important sources of power that can be used to shape the dynamics of organizational life: formal authority; control of scarce resources; use of organizational structures, rules and regulations; control of decision processes; control of knowledge and information; control of boundaries; ability to cope with uncertainty; control of technology; interpersonal alliances and networks; control of counterorganizations; symbolism and the management of meaning; gender and the management of gender relations; structural factors that define the stage of action; and the power that one already has.

Further, Morgan (1986, pp. 188–189) proposed that the political analysis of organizations could treat them as mini-states by substituting the relationship between individual and society with the relationship between individual and organization. He used unitary, pluralist and radical views of organizations to contrast how interests, conflict and power would be conceptualized from these perspectives. A unitary view or organization would ignore the role of power in organizational life, with *authority*, *leadership* and *control* used to describe the managerial prerogative of guiding the organization toward the achievement of common interests. A pluralist view would regard power as a crucial variable through which conflicts of interest are alleviated and resolved, with the organization seen as a plurality of power holders drawing their power from different mixes of sources. The radical view would regard power as a key feature of organization, yet unevenly distributed along class divisions, reflecting power relations in society, and closely linked to the wider processes of social control (e.g., control of economic power, the legal system and education).

Space precludes any further attention to the arts of political analysis apart from indicating below some of the tools introduced from political science into the research and theory of educational administration.

Let us now turn to the little elephant in the room whose name is political philosophy. A search of the full text of all articles published in the leading research journal of our field, the *Educational Administration Quarterly*, over 43 years found references to the subdiscipline in seven articles, most made in passing. We might hope that things will be very different in the next 43 years.

To examine the little beast in context, let us assume that the room represented by the *Educational Administration Quarterly*, educational administration, is a hybrid field of practice, research and theory that has been attempting to blend the more trustworthy ideas from education and administration through scholarship. Definitions are important to avoid confusion.

By *scholarship*, I mean the process of advancing knowledge through (1) discovery (disciplined investigation that creates new ideas and understandings, adding to the stock of knowledge), (2) integration (making connections across fields, in a disciplined way, to interpret, draw together and bring new insights to original ideas), (3) application (the responsible and rigorous application of knowledge to problems of consequence to people, institutions and peoples) and (4) teaching (disciplined interaction between learners and teachers intended to build skills, understandings and dispositions, and to interrogate knowledge; (Boyer 1990, pp. 16, 18).

By *philosophy*, I mean "thinking about thinking" in three ways; "rationally critical thinking in a more or less systematic kind about the general nature of the world (metaphysics or theory) . . . the justification for belief (epistemology or theory of knowledge) . . . and the conduct of life (ethics or theory of value)" (Honderich, 2005, p. 205).

These definitions indicate four conditions that are crucial to the organized growth of relatively trustworthy knowledge about educational administration through scholarship. The first is methodical movement toward a rationally critical account of the general nature of the field. Any rationally critical account must remain open to and subject to methodical correction—hence this book and, hopefully, subsequent refutation and improvement.

The second condition is a persuasive process of arbitrating knowledge claims in the field. The approach most convincing to me is that proposed by Evers and Lakomski (1991); a nonfoundational and coherentist epistemology. I only have two quibbles; they understate their apparent support for neopragmatism over pragmatism and favor metaphysical naturalism over the accommodation of plural perceptions of social reality in organizations, key issues I come back to below.

The third condition is a sophisticated method of evaluating the rightness of practice in the field. This was well advanced in a general sense by Chris Hodgkinson (1978, 1981, 1983, 1991), and although there are some technical issues yet to be fully resolved (Bates, 2006,p. 142; Evers, 1985; Hodgkinson, 1986), I focus solely on the use of political philosophy in educational administration to evaluate and improve the quality of political practice.

The fourth condition is an ongoing integration of educational and administrative theories and practices. This has been under active management by the editors of the *Educational Administration Quarterly* who, for example, have long understood that "knowledge and knowledge production are historically and culturally situated" (Pounder & Johnson, 2007, p. 270). They and others have facilitated an international scholarship of integration, as exemplified by the special edition of the *Journal of Educational Administration and History* edited by Peter Ribbins (2006), the themed issues of the *Educational Administration Quarterly* in more recent decades and the recent 40th anniversary edition of the *Educational Management Administration and Leadership* edited by Tony Bush and Megan Crawford (2012b). Because these outlets are among the leading American and British academic research journals of the field, this and the next chapter introduce political philosophy as a means of initiating significant and ongoing corrections to the first condition, often by reference to these special editions.

The correction proposed to the traditional rationally critical account of educational administration can begin with Hodgkinson's axiom that "power is the first term in the administrative lexicon" (1978, p. 217). If this is a reasonable axiom, and my experience and research provided a plethora of supportive examples, it follows that we need an orderly approach to "thinking about our thinking" concerning power, so that we can improve the justifications we use for the use of power, politics and current political arrangements in education at team, institution and system levels.

Without this capacity we can't know what we do with our powers, we can't know what is morally reasonable, and even more important, we can't know how to improve our use of power. If power is the first term and moral dilemmas over power are at the heart of administrative practice, then political philosophy is needed to help create appropriate answers about how we might think more effectively about power. The retarded role of political philosophy in the field has limited its capacity to evaluate justifications for the politics of educational administration in practice. In my time, it was only with Thom Greenfield's (1975) iconoclastic questions did the practices of leaders and the structures they created and sustained in educational organizations begin to be uncovered and questioned using the tools of interpretive and critical sociology. However, before we explore this exciting watershed, we need greater clarity on key terms.

The term political philosophy has two meanings in common discourse that are quite different and often confused. It is, technically, the branch of philosophy concerned with the ethics of and justification for political infrastructure and processes. It is often, however, used informally to refer to a personal credo or ideology that is being used to justify or ingratiate forms of political action or structures. This is most unfortunate. Political philosophy is something you do or you don't do. Rebranding a political ideology, a belief system, as a political philosophy, is verbal trickery and implies that it carries a justification with it. Not so.

The formal meaning, which is limited to a philosophical activity concerned with thinking about the quality of political analysis and practice, is further elaborated below by reviewing the conceptual domain of political philosophy. The latter and informal meaning is particularly evident in Chapters 2 to 4 where selected researchers' contributions and special editions of journals in educational administration are examined to identify how personal political philosophies, or more accurately *personal ideologies*, as well as tentative and often unrealized engagement in political philosophy, are shown to have actually helped advance the growth of knowledge.

Political philosophy, as a subdiscipline, is to be understood as a pragmatic and critical project of understanding, interpreting and then evaluating political analysis and action. When *doing* political philosophy, it is assumed that

> at some level, our political arrangements are subject to rational assessment and choice. These assumptions lie behind the effort to distinguish political practices and forms of political action that can be justified and those that cannot. That effort, more than anything else, defines the general project of political philosophy. (Bird, 2006, p. 4)

This general project is ubiquitous in daily life although typically rather disorganized. Political arrangements are often discussed in ways that focus on selected concepts of power such as authority, rights, responsibilities and representation. In education, we are quick to make judgments about practices that violate our intuitive conceptions of other related concepts, such as freedom, equality and justice. The *legitimacy* of policies, laws and administrative arrangements is often questioned, usually with reference to vested interests, the public interest or the common good. I discuss different approaches to justification below.

Most interesting, whereas ideals and practices are often bundled, they tend to be treated quite differently. Some of the concepts that are used to justify or criticize political behaviors, such as freedom, equality, justice and the common good, are ethical ideals or principles and can have unwarranted success in arguments as unexamined absolutes. Others, such as authority, rights, coercion and obligations tend to be regarded as much more arbitrary, and attract much more comment. To avoid confusion over the differences between what people say they do, say what they intend to do and what they actually do, political philosophers usually find it more helpful to focus on practices and outcomes to uncover the values in use and then evaluate how well these embedded ideals or principles justify current political arrangements. Where they fall short, reasoned proposals then have to be developed, justified and defended.

This helps explain why higher education courses in political philosophy tend to focus on questioning and developing justifications for political actions and structures:

> A course in political philosophy usually takes as its subject matter general justifications for the state and for other political institutions, and for particular actual and imagined ideal forms of these; it all tends to be the abstract politics of quarterlies rather than the concrete politics of the dailies. Besides the state, such other institutions as property, the family, the legal system, government and public administration, international relations, education, class structure, religion and individual rights, duties, and obligations are discussed. (Flew, 1984, p. 279)

The growth of trustworthy knowledge through political philosophy requires appropriate research methods sustained by a justification for the discovery process used. In general, the research methodology typically employed by political philosophers is to analyze the nature of organization to reveal dominant political values, and then to use ethics to evaluate the quality of political organization. In more detail, this methodology uses a range of descriptive-explanatory and ethically normative approaches, concepts, data and tools of analysis to propose improvements to political arrangements or key concepts. Given the obviously close relationship to political science, which focuses on understanding and interpreting the practice of politics, the concepts researched are the bases for justifying the use of power, such as autonomy, authority, ideology, sovereignty and justice.

The most troublesome of these concepts in political philosophy related to educational administration is probably ideology. An ideology is technically "any system of ideas and norms directing political and social action" (Flew, 1984, p. 162), which gives it the same meaning as a personal political philosophy, or more accurately, a credo for action (yet another term for ideology), as noted above. Knowing this hints at another potentially powerful benefit of normalizing political philosophy as a leading subdiscipline in educational administration. It could provide a pathway around the counterproductive ideological battles in theory building that have plagued the field of educational administration.

Whatever the organizational unit of analysis focused on while using political philosophy, it is generally expected that description and evaluation "must be combined coherently into an account of a properly structured and functioning community . . . with its main constitutive institutions and values" (Sankowski, 2005) prior to comparisons in related settings, indicating the importance of coherentism in epistemic practices. Case studies in later chapters illustrate this point and remind us that political science is a social science discipline concerned with the study of the state, government and politics that has three interconnected subdisciplines: political philosophy, comparative politics and international relations.

This means that political philosophy is a form of philosophical reflection on how best to arrange collective affairs, both political institutions and social practices, such as economic systems, family life and educational organizations. The intended outcomes can, of course, vary. Political philosophers, for example, can strive to identify basic principles that will,

> justify a particular form of state, show that individuals have certain inalienable rights, or tell us how a society's resources should be shared among its members. This usually involves analyzing and interpreting ideas such as freedom, justice, authority and democracy and then applying them in a critical way to social and political institutions that currently exist. (Miller, 1998, p. 687)

Although the outcomes of political philosophy tend to reflect the pressing political issues of the day and change as the assumptions and tools of epistemology and ethics have developed, three unresolved questions have persisted concerning the production of principles. They are the extent to which the principles established by political philosophers may be regarded as (a) universal, (b) reflecting the assumptions and values of a particular political community, or (c) reflecting the nature of human beings, their needs, capacities and limitations. These questions remain stubbornly unresolved in educational administration where, as I noted above, the deployment of personal political ideologies have led to fierce ideological disputes over theory, in lieu of political philosophy. More, the persistence of these unresolved questions points to the problem of using foundational beliefs when creating principles, and therefore to consider testing truth claims for their coherence with other statements and discourses using a nonfoundational epistemology.

This is not to denigrate the role of ideology in political philosophy. Given a particular and contested policy context, political philosophy can be an ideologically constrained evaluation of the nature and justification for selected political values leading to a philosophically informed reconciliation. To be worthy of the name political philosophy, however, the evaluation would have to be politically critical of the ideologies at work, especially so in theory building, and avoid giving privileged status *a priori* to a foundational set of beliefs.

This process may be less pejorative than as first imagined. An example not irrelevant to leaders in education is analysis that tests the justification for having coercive institutions or degrees of coercion in institutions, and what these arrangements do for their legitimacy as educational organizations. Another is an analysis of the blend of ideologies evident in the perceptions of organization and leadership styles seen on a daily basis in preschools, schools, polytechnics, universities and administrative systems.

Such an analysis of coercion would proceed on the assumption that while educational institutions and systems may range in size from groups to global organizations, a common feature is that they either employ force or use the threat of force to control the behavior of members. Hence, justifying such coercive institutions requires showing that the authorities within them have a right to be obeyed and that their members have a corresponding obligation to obey them, i.e., that these institutions have legitimate political authority over their members. (Sterba, 2000, p. 718)

Such an analysis of organization and leadership proceeds on the assumption that, while purposes may vary quite legitimately, a common feature is that they use structure and administrative processes to regulate the making and implementation of policy. Political philosophy is a method of examining the legitimacy of such structures, criteria and processes.

As touched on earlier, another intended outcome of political philosophy can be the explication of a single concept or principle, such as justice. A contemporary example of adopting this approach follows:

Political philosophy, as I understand it, is a matter of moral argument, and moral argument is a matter of appeal to our considered convictions. In saying this, I am drawing on what I take to be the everyday view of moral and political argument; that is, we all have moral beliefs, and these beliefs can be either right or wrong, and these reasons and beliefs can be organized into moral principles and theories of justice. A central aim of political philosophy, therefore, is to evaluate competing theories of justice to assess the strength and coherence of their arguments for the rightness of their views. (Kymlicka, 2002, p. 6)

This growing range of intended outcomes that political philosophy can be used to address reflects the evolution of description and explanation for politics and the rigorous evaluation of political arrangements since ancient times. A sample was selected from antiquity (Plato, Aristotle and Cicero), the Middle Ages (St. Augustine), the Renaissance (Machiavelli), the Enlightenment (Hobbes, Locke, Burke, Rousseau), industrialization (Bentham, Mills, Hegel, Marx), modernization and postmodernism (Dewey, Mosca, Bakunin, Lyotard) and more contemporary works (Nozick, MacIntyre, Habermas, Rawls). Many outstanding contributors are necessarily excluded, such as the contributions of ancient Chinese and Indian political philosophers, the Islamic scholars from the seventh to the fourteenth century, scholars from indigenous civilizations and those who place questions of cultural and gender identity central to politics.

Table 1.1 is therefore an introductory and modest summary intended to illustrate the scope of political philosophy and to provide the basis for a preliminary evaluation in coming chapters of the contribution that the subdiscipline has already made to the field of educational administration. It is a compilation informed by general sources in Sankowski (2005), Hampsher-Monk (2000, p. 691), Flew (1984, pp. 279–281), Plant (2000, p. 693) and by other sources cited in the table.

This summary locates political philosophy alongside moral philosophy, social philosophy, philosophy of economics and philosophy of law, in addition to its symbiotic

Table 1.1 A summary of the growth of knowledge in political philosophy[1]

Significant positions	Focus of description and explanation	Focus of ethical or normative evaluation
Utopianism (Plato, 1974)	The alignment of reason, spirit and appetites. The philosopher king who identifies and applies universal principles such as justice and goodness.	The development of just action, the just individual and the just state.
Perfectionism (Aristotle, 1912)	Moral education, reason, describing and perfecting the institutions and constitutions of city states (*polis*).	The development of persons of excellence as statespersons.
Cicero's republicanism (Gaskin, 2005, p. 142) (White, 2000, p. 141)	Peace, unity, human rights, brotherhood of man, the equality of all men, active citizenship and binding universal laws based on the common nature of man. Divine reason and order that permeate all that is.	The development of a mixed and balanced constitution that subordinates different interests to the interest of all citizens, preventing the capture of government by power sharing, checks and balances, and the redistribution of resources.
St. Augustine's Christian religionism (Flew, 1984, p. 279; (Mathews, 2000, p. 63–65)	The temporal political order and the hereafter. The divine right of kings to rule and the relative jurisdictions of secular and religious authorities.	The development of Christianity-compliant governments in Medieval Europe.
Realism (Machiavelli, 1886)	Detached political science, Roman republican virtues and the economic use of violence to achieve political ends. *Realpolitik*—purely practical politics to achieve the interests of the state, however coercive or amoral.	The development of an institutional balance between the nobility and the common people where the ends of reinforcing the state justify the means.
Natural contracturalism (Hobbes, 1914)	The nature of man, the laws of nature underpinning the reason of law and the pooling of individual rights to self-preservation into national security.	The development of sovereignty as part of the social contract that underpins the modern secular nation state.
Lockes' individualistic contracturalism (Wootton, 1993)	Constitutional rule, the rights of the individual and the legitimacy of government derived from natural rights, the consent of the governed and a constitution—with the right of revolution.	The development of a positive freedom through an individual's social contract with civil society, requiring government, law, property rights and toleration.

Burke's traditionalism (Kramnick, 1999, pp. 108–109)	Appreciate the subtleties of social and political institutions that developed incrementally in a particular context, beyond the comprehension of rational theorizing.	Custom and tradition are to take precedence over any doctrine of what is natural or universal for man when developing institutions.
Collectivism (Rousseau, 1987)	The general will as the sole source of legitimate sovereignty, inevitably in the common good, resulting in a moral obligation to obey the law and reconciliation of autonomy and authority.	Direct participation in the development of, and the total and voluntary subjugation to, the general will, with little allowance for individual conscience, private life, freedom of religion and political dissent.
Utilitarianism (Bentham, 2002)	The degree of pleasure achieved over pain for individuals (act utilitarianism) or for all (rule utilitarianism).	A hedonic calculus intended to measure the degree of pleasure over pain, with rightness or wrongness judged by the degree of utility or welfare achieved.
Classical liberalism (Mill, 1972)	Freedom and other rights of the individual, social controls only legitimate to prevent harm to others and when violation of other's rights have occurred, rejection of paternalism and religious authority in politics, fear of "the tyranny of the majority."	Respect for the rights of the individual and the greatest welfare for all when striking a balance between the democratic state and its constituent institutions in a properly functioning community.
Hegel's idealism (Pippin, 1999, pp. 365–370)	Society is more real and more fundamental than the individual, making the state and its claims primary in comprehensive and integrative analyses using a coherence theory of truth—thought governing reality.	The development of a state's political systems using social and political concepts to advance consciousness of freedom through projection and transcendental thinking, and thus control history.
Marx's historical materialism (Tucker, 1978)	History as struggles between classes, state as an instrument of oppression by one class over another, with changes in the economic infrastructure causing changes in the institutional and ideological superstructure.	The development of a proletarian revolution that will replace the capitalist state with a dictatorship of the proletariat, followed by a withering of the state.
Dewey's democratic and educative pragmatism (Campbell, 1995)	Scientific experimentalism, rejecting dualisms in favor of mediating ideas. Combining fallibilism and optimistic progressivism.	The development of a democratic community committed to growth through inquiry-based learning.

(*Continued*)

Table 1.1 Continued

Significant positions	Focus of description and explanation	Focus of ethical or normative evaluation
Mosca's elitism (Finocchiaro, 1999, p. 591)	The nature of human social life makes true democracy impossible to attain and may enable anarchy; political decisions are inevitably in the hands of an elite, how organized minorities rule host societies.	The development of democratic political systems that use the principle of *juridical defense* to prevent any person, class, force, or institution from dominating others.
Bakunin's anarchism (Miller, 1984)	The individual is sovereign, authority is an unjustified repression of will and attempts to resolve individual and common interests through institutions using the threat of force are futile.	The resistance of coercion and the development of nongovernmental collectivism based on voluntary cooperation without private property or religion and reward according to contribution.
Postmodernism (Lyotard, 1979)	The collapse of grand narratives, the open multiplicity of incommensurable language games, rejection of the values of enlightenment, critique and rational consensus.	The development of many first order, natural and pragmatic narratives as the touchstone of democratic freedom.
Libertarianism (Nozick, 1974)	Individual will and initiative create the economy and social life, protection of the rights of individuals and process theories that demonstrate the rightness of piecemeal actions independent of final outcomes.	The development of a minimal state in support of self-determining individuals in free-market capitalism.
Communitarianism (MacIntyre, 1984)	Social life, identity and relationships, the collective providing rights and obligations to individuals and the integrity and value of traditional practices, such as the social construction of meaning.	The refinement of institutions and practices that promote and serve the community, the public good and cooperative practices and values such as reciprocity, trust and solidarity.
Communicative rationalism (Habermas, 1992)	Control, understanding and emancipation, communicative as opposed to instrumental rationality, disruptive effects of market and bureaucratic systems, intersubjective notions of practical reason, the discursive procedures used to justify universal norms.	The development of an open, participative and deliberative democracy for a complex modern world that uses the values of the Enlightenment, legitimate law and discourse ethics to provide a defense and critique of institutions using public practical reason.

Egalitarian liberalism (Rawls, 1993)	A new hypothetical social contract derived from an original position of not knowing socially significant facts or what a good life is—this *veil of ignorance* leads to an equal concern for everyone and distributive justice.	The development of justice as fairness; equal liberty and equal opportunity, with inequalities only justified if they benefit the worst off.

[1] More comprehensive introductions and guides are available at http://en.wikipedia.org/wiki/Political_philosophy, http://lgxserver.uniba.it/lei/filpol/filpole/homefpe.htm, and at http://lgxserver.uniba.it/lei/filpol/filpole/lintexe.htm.

relationship with political science already noted. Despite these intimations of common ground, the concepts that are intrinsic to the subdiscipline of political philosophy have been identified.

Two general approaches to justification have traditionally dominated the subdiscipline of political philosophy; *common good* and *social contract* justifications, with a range of more critical forms of justification emerging in recent decades. They are each now briefly introduced and related to the field of educational administration.

So-called common good justifications include the utopianism proposed by Plato (Nettleship, 1935), the perfectionism wished for by Aristotle (Burnett, 1936) and the modern utilitarianism initiated by Jeremy Bentham and John Stuart Mill (Brown, 1986). Utopianism, perfectionism and utilitarianism each, of course, evolved to reflect particular contexts. For example, utilitarianism was used over 80 years ago by the U.S. Supreme Court to justify the ruling that parents should have the right to educate their children in nonpublic schools. A more recent review found that the Court sought to maximize educational opportunities in the common good using both economic utilitarianism and "egalitarianism, the apparent political philosophy [*sic*, ideology] of the day" (Murphy, 1979, p. 120).

In sharp contrast with appealing to the common good, social contract justifications are expected to clarify the extent to which they satisfy voluntary agreements entered into between the state and the people, however defined, including agreements the people supposedly would have freely agreed to. This approach was developed in the 17th century by Thomas Hobbes and John Locke, advanced in the 18th century by Jean-Jacques Rousseau and Immanuel Kant (Kant, 1991), and in the 20th century by John Rawls (1999). They all focused on how well the state was delivering on implicit or explicit social contracts to their polities, and the resultant legitimacy of the state. Figure 1.1 overleaf maps the major concepts of the sub-discipline.

This is not a million miles from school leadership. Research into the influence of social contract theory on American institutions identified the strong felt need for (a) due process where liberty and property were involved and for (b) greater clarity over the nature of the individual's responsibility to the government whenever social contract theory impacted public education. It also found "an unawareness or conscious disagreement among some leadership personnel with Social Contract Theory, a political theory on which many agree our country is based" (Morte, 1997, pp. 31–32).

Political Philosophy

- Questions of Analysis for Description and Explanation
  - Authority and Obedience
  - Ideology
  - Sovereignty
    - Its location
    - Its nature
  - Justice
    - Punishment
  - Nature of state / Types of constitution
    - Democracy
    - Oligarchy
    - Timocracy
    - Plutocracy
    - Monarchy
    - Tyranny (dictatorship)
    - Totalitarian regime
- Questions of Justification for Ethical and Normative Evaluation
  - Justifications for property
  - Justifications for existence of state or for type of state
    - Purpose of State
    - Basis of state
      - Respecting civil liberties
      - Rights of citizenship
      - Punishment
      - Emigration
  - Justifications of behaviour
    - Of state
      - To citizens
      - To foreigners
        - To foreign states
          - Commercial relations
          - War
          - Right to a homeland
          - International law
        - To foreign individuals
          - Immigration
          - Rights of citizenship
          - Extradition
          - International law
    - Of citizens
      - Justification of rebellion or political violence

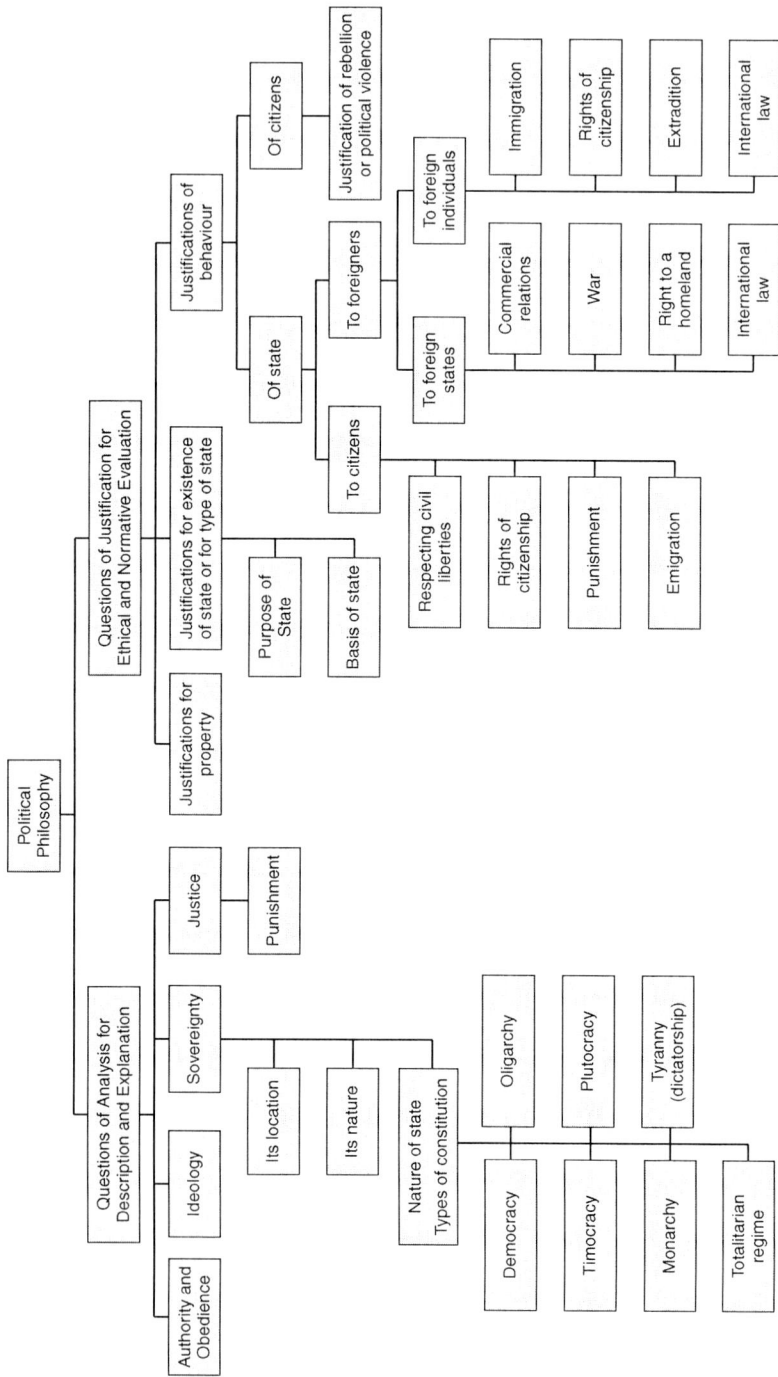

Figure 1.1 A concept map of political philosophy (Honderich, 2005, p. 983)

In particular, the study revealed uncertainty or ambivalence by school authorities over the role they should play in maintaining the order required to educate students, partly because their attempts to exclude students or dismiss employees reportedly ran into serious constitutional difficulties whenever school systems' leaders assumed they could act as instruments of the state. Diverse local interest groups instead and variously saw their schools as instruments of community or the Enlightenment, of which they believed that they were guardians.

In addition to common good and social contract justifications, other forms of justification have been derived from the radical critiques offered by other political philosophers. One general reason often cited is that Marx, Rousseau, Lyotard and others deconstructed the many forms of political reality in social situations and revealed the relativism of concepts associated with institutions of state and Enlightenment principles.

Three potent implications of their works, for the field of educational administration, have been the importance of (a) maintaining a critical distance from the institutions of state and political processes being described and evaluated, (b) giving voice to those traditionally silenced by the distributions of power and (c) employing critically orientated theories, including socially critical, feminist, race and queer theories, as well as critical pragmatism and feminist poststructuralism, to develop understandings and proposals for reform (Capper, 1998). My strong sympathy for these implications, reinforced by ethnographic and evaluation research experiences over decades, has undermined any absolute belief in naturalism, otherwise known as metaphysical naturalism, wherein only the laws of nature operate in the universe. I am much more comfortable with methodological naturalism whereby I can examine and weigh up multiple and simultaneous perceptions of social reality, especially of power, without necessarily considering naturalism as an absolute truth with philosophical entailments.

In sum, to this point, political philosophy has been defined formally as a subdiscipline used to evaluate justifications for political arrangements, in direct contrast with its misnamed use as a personal credo for taking political action. As a form of scholarly activity, political philosophy requires a general account of its own nature, an argued methodology of discovery to provide convincing knowledge claims and systematic moral evaluation that leads to proposals for the improvement of political arrangements. Hence, as a research methodology, political philosophy uses descriptive-explanatory and ethically normative methods to understand and then appraise the nature and use of power in the context of structured organizations and functioning communities. The purposes of political philosophy can range from critical reflections on the quality of collective affairs, using general principles such as justice to focusing sharply on the means and ends of justifiably exercising power, such as the legitimacy of coercion or organization. Common good, social contract and critical justifications are available.

In the next chapter, I examine educational administration more closely assuming it to be an emergent and hybrid field of scholarship and practice. The section begins with a working definition and then offers an introductory history of the development of its knowledge base and conceptual domain prior to uncovering the extent to which political philosophy has already played a hidden hand.

2 Educational administration

> Administration is philosophy-in-action. Philosophy, whether it be in the mode of articulated policy utterances of inchoate or unuttered values, is daily translated into action through the device of organisation. How? In a two-fold way. By means of administrative processes which are abstract, philosophical, qualitative, strategic, and humanistic in essence, and by means of managerial processes which are concrete, practical, pragmatic, quantitative, technical and technological in nature.
>
> (Hodgkinson, 1981, p. 145)

I understand the phrase *educational administration* to have two general meanings: an embryonic and blended field of study with a growing corpus of knowledge concerning the leadership and management of institutions or systems in education; and the practices of those responsible for advising and implementing the policies of organizations with educational purposes as depicted in discourses.

This is consistent with Hodgkinson's view of philosophy of administration and the nature of my experience, as conveyed by language. His two-part set of assumptions was empirically ratified by reference to the processes of system reform level (Macpherson, 1990). It endured as an explanatory framework throughout my experience of team and institutional leadership service over decades. Nevertheless, to acknowledge the axiomatic and therefore provisional nature of this definition, I also regard educational administration as a field of scholarship, which gives its scholars the responsibility of improving understandings through discovery, integration, applications, and teaching (Glassick, Huber, & Maeroff, 1997). Fortunately, the outcomes of research in the field are recorded in a corpus of published literature that enables synthesis, critique and thus systematic theory building. Most notably, however, I now see that the access we have to the empirical realities of educational administration is primarily through language, be it via first-hand description, second-hand ethnography, third-hand empirically verified reports and other discourses, and so on through our corpus of literature.

An alternative to systematic scholarship assumes that the growth of knowledge in educational administration is, in essence and inevitably, a compilation of, and competition between, ideologies and doctrines (Button, 1966). Although there is some evidence available to support this proposition, and some of it is reviewed below, it might be preferable to aim for evidence-based practice and theory, as far as that is possible and fruitful, if we prefer a rationally critical account.

Hence a key purpose of this text is to introduce political philosophy to the field so that researchers, theorists, and practitioners will be better able to identify and arbitrate the ideological components of their knowledge claims related to power. I trust that by now that they will find it difficult to understand how a field so intimately implicated in the use of power could advance the quality of its knowledge systematically without the subdiscipline of political philosophy.

To start at the beginning, the history and the orthodox conceptual domain of educational administration can be understood as the result of an unfolding attempt to understand, interpret, evaluate, and improve the knowledge and practices of both administrators responsible for organizing institutions and systems with educational purposes, as well aseducationalists responsible for the organization and management of groups, units, institutions, and systems.

This approach makes the assumption that administrative arrangements in education are and should be subject to systematic evaluation and choice, and that they can be found to be justified or not. This assumption also requires the development of a philosophy of educational administration, rather than simply adopting and uncritically applying a philosophy of education or administration. Whereas a particular philosophy of education and a particular philosophy of educational administration might be commensurable to a satisfactory degree, this needs to be argued systematically, as exemplified by Hodgkinson's pioneering contributions. The problem here is that the relationship between philosophy of education and philosophy of administration has not been clear for most of the history of educational administration and the need for this has not been widely appreciated.

Administrative arrangements intended to achieve educational purposes are discussed by educational professionals in ways that recognize key administrative concepts, such as policy, strategy, structures, leadership, management, and evaluation. This typically occurs in a context of educational philosophy, sometimes unrelated to administrative priorities. Leaders in education who wish to be successful at levels more complex than team leadership will need a philosophy of educational administration to arbitrate the relevance and significance of concepts, and to evaluate the actual values, embedded ideals, or principles being served by current administrative arrangements.

As implied by the two-part definition above, the arrangements include those used to support policy making and policy implementation at institutional and system levels of complexity, and to evaluate structures and practices with a view to making improvements in systems and in the growing plethora of knowledge organizations (including other institutions of the state), not just schools. Practitioners may find Hodgkinson's (1981) taxonomy of the administrative process helpful in distinguishing the components of their own leadership responsibilities.

This model traces how an abstract idea created by philosophical analysis and strategic planning is transformed by political and cultural processes into a cultural artifact, and then implemented as a fact using managerial and evaluative tools. Hodgkinson also theorized the value types likely to be evident in administrative practice, an issue of great interest to political philosophers. I revisit his analytical model of the value concept (Hodgkinson, 1978, p. 111) in the final chapter. The point here is that his pioneering model was proposed to help audit values in practice, but there was very limited use made of it in educational administration. I found it remarkably effective for conducting a values audit of social issues in technology-based distributed learning (Macpherson, 2000).

It is, however, one thing to project likely values in administration, yet it is quite another to uncover the actual political values in use in educational administration and, moreover, to reveal the long-unrealized role of political philosophy in the history of knowledge production in educational administration in the United States.

This remarkable feat was first achieved, probably unintentionally, by a well-designed content analysis, or more precisely, discourse analysis of the field's textbooks (Glass, Mason, Eaton, Parker, & Carver, 2004). It was found that the major textbooks used in courses in educational administration in the United States have justified orthodox knowledge claims about school leadership, and therefore implicitly claims about the use of power, in four general ways since 1840: as an applied philosophy of virtue; as executive action; as applied behavioral science; and most recently, as standardized professionalism. It also found that the textbooks used in the 1800s showed that the field first developed and continued to be conceived primarily as the leadership of public schools.

The narrowness of this definition can be attributed to the well-intentioned practice of powerful and retiring practitioners who wanted to assist their successors. In so doing, these senior practitioners revealed an earthy commitment to the values of the Founding Fathers of the United States who stressed e pluribus unum (unity in diversity), meaning unity without uniformity and diversity without fragmentation. Their sense of diversity appreciated the plural religious commitments brought to the New World, yet the requirement to be unified by their interpretation of the values of the Enlightenment: That reason enables people to think and act correctly; people are naturally rational and good; individuals and humanity can progress toward perfection; all people are equal before the law and in individual liberty; tolerance of other creeds and ways of life; beliefs accepted only on the basis of reason; reason is a global resource; and, the lesser importance of the nonrational (Honderich, 2005, p. 253).

These values were mediated in public education by the ideology of American pragmatism. The systematic formulation of pragmatism was initiated in the late 1800s by C. S. Pierce, popularized by William James, and then applied in education by such as John Dewey. American pragmatism holds that "the validity of standards of meaning, truth, and value as ultimately rooted in considerations of practical efficacy—of 'what works in practice'" (Rescher, 2005, p. 23).

This begins to explain why American pragmatism served early as a political ideology in educational administration and persisted as knowledge was elaborated in practice and by research, and as sister fields and disciplines provided fresh tools for analysis. It also suggests that the more recent and fashionable use of *managerialism* as an epithet is at odds with American history, and that its continued employment as an epithet signals the presence of alternative and undeclared political ideologies that await identification and justification.

To illustrate, when the best practice textbooks written in the 1800s were gradually displaced during the early 1900s with management prescriptions, and justifications were drawn from the early management science developed in the private sector, they were driven by pragmatism that was later described pejoratively, and echoed uncritically over the decades, as part of a "cult of efficiency" in education (Callahan, 1962). Despite technically accurate descriptions of the neo-Taylorist legacy in the theory of educational administration (Gronn, 1982), such judgments can now be seen to employ historicism.

Efficiency is not so much a cult in the United States, with all the derogatory meanings attached to the word, but as evidence of a mainstream American ideology with a particular blend of democracy and capitalism. Efficiency is also an obligatory component of any theory in educational administration that recognizes that limited resources are a matter of empirical fact in education, and further, that educational administrators are commonly obliged by their line managers and governors to "square the circle" with "creative resource management."

The key point here is that there needs to be a distinction made between inappropriate degrees of ideological absolutism and the advanced and critical use of managerial technique during policy making and implementation. An example would be the wise and skilled use of information and communication technology (ICT) in strategic evaluation and planning at the system level to educative ends.

Another point is that pragmatism is not necessarily inevitable when facing the challenge of providing leadership services in education in a context of a multiethnic society. To illustrate, Rizvi, Duignan, and Macpherson (1990) demonstrated that educative leadership should champion interculturalism and thus boost the degree of communicative rationalism in Australia's multicultural society. But I jump ahead.

From the mid 1900s, the best practice literature from early management science was steadily displaced in the United States by other pragmatic ideas from the "Theory Movement" that offered explanations and techniques from the social and behavioral sciences. And more recently, the evidence offered by Glass et al. (2004) is that the Theory Movement literature is now being displaced by textbooks that justify best practice either using "professional standards" or specialist expertise in administrative support areas, such as finance, law, policy, public relations, and personnel.

The resultant structure and scope of substantive knowledge in educational administration is evident in the categories used by its leading research journal, the *Educational Administration Quarterly*, to classify research publications in the field, as indicated in Figure 2.1 (*Educational Administration Abstracts*, 2001).

This concept map indicates the scope of orthodox knowledge production in educational administration, until more recent times as I show below. It is interesting that the process of knowledge production has long been limited to the development of an understanding of effective public school leadership practices in the United States. It was apparently relatively unconcerned with political arrangements and took the political order in education and in the wider context for granted. It seems reasonable to attribute this unconcern to the pervasiveness

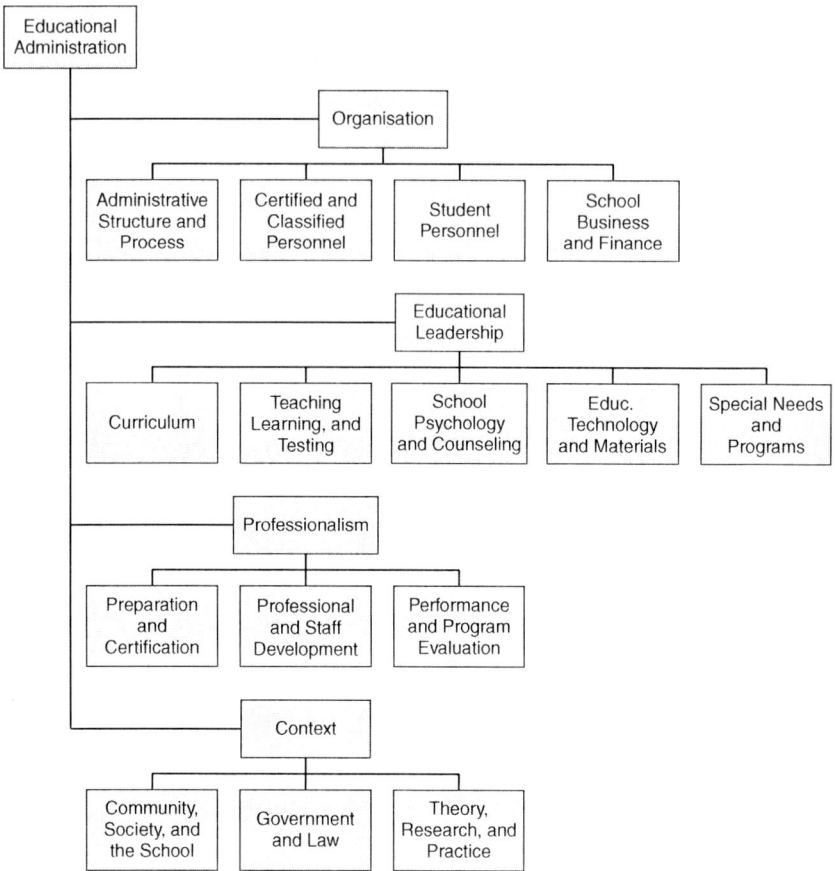

Figure 2.1 A concept map of educational administration

of American pragmatism. On the other hand, the development of a more active concern over current political arrangements in educational administration has brought political philosophy into play, albeit unnamed, and helpfully advanced the growth of knowledge.

Particular scholars have made significant contributions to the growth of knowledge in educational administration through the agency of political philosophy, commonly without evoking its presence or utility. Corrections to my understanding of each individual's position are welcomed, especially so to help advance politically critical scholarship. The approach I use replicates that used above in Chapter 1; that is, I examine how the foci of description, explanation, and evaluation of practices have assisted with the growth of a more critical account of educational administration. In so doing, I highlight how seven political ideologies have impacted unevenly on educational administration since 1900: democratic utopianism; perfectionism; pragmatism (through sociological functionalism, behavioral functionalism, and standardized professionalism); scientific humanism; communitarianism; communicative rationalism; and egalitarian liberalism. Many other outstanding contributions could not be included.

An excellent place to start is with the first woman to be appointed as the superintendent of a large city system in the United States, Ella Flagg Young (Webb & McCarthy, 1998). She lived a political ideology of democratic utopianism and perfectionism. With regard to power, she helped pioneer teachers' councils to advise school administrators, collaborated with John Dewey in experimental education, objected to the uncritical application of "scientific management" in education, and campaigned remorselessly for education as a city development strategy—until, ironically, she was brought down by city hall politics.

Another application of democratic utopianism and perfectionism was the complex taxonomy of administrative processes for democratic schools developed by William Reavis (Peckenpaugh, 1968). His aim was to create schools as model democratic cultures through stakeholder participation in policy formulation, organization, leadership, decision making, curriculum development, pedagogy, and evaluation. It is interesting that, even here, pragmatism played a major role. Reavis justified the use of democratic processes as providing the most efficient procedures for managing the affairs of a community school.

In passing, political philosophers might note that this justification based on management efficiency contrasts sharply with (say) basing a justification for greater democracy in leadership on sweeping away hierarchy on the promise of distributed leadership in networks and partnerships (Woods, 2005, pp. 21–23) or for greater democracy in school governance on the promise of innovative entrepreneurialism (Woods, 2011, pp. 40–44). Such justifications tend to be promissory, in that they rely on a belief in the eventual triumph of hope over experience, or dualistic, in that they back up into an array of contrasted absolutes about fixity and openness regarding the sharing of power, hope, and the fruits of society (Woods, 2005, p. 139). I return to this interesting and recent strand of scholarship on democracy below.

Pragmatic political ideologies came strongly to the fore from the 1950s when they were embedded in social systems functionalism, thus legitimating the explicit use of positional power by school leaders. Leadership was explained and evaluated as the management of a formal and closed social system that comprised nomothetic phenomena (institutions with roles and expectations regarding system goals) and idiographic phenomena (individuals with personalities and needs-dispositions; Getzels & Guba, 1957). The interactions between these two sets of phenomena were assumed to create the social behavior observed. Hence, leaders alone were empowered to manage the intervening variables of organizational behavior; that is, to modify the incentive systems and reference group norms in order to adjust cognitive and affective orientations to role, and thus better achieve school goals (Abbot, 1965).

This social systems functionalism was challenged in the 1960s by behavioral functionalism, although it was driven largely by a similarly pragmatic political ideology (Griffiths, 1964, 1977). As a highly experienced, successful, and reflective practitioner of educational administration in higher education, Griffiths encountered little empirical evidence that supported the notion that educational organizations operated as well-ordered social systems. Instead he found that he was held responsible for the actions of willful individuals in internally focused "organized anarchies" that (a) used "Garbage Can" decision making, (b) reacted to environmental conditions by generating various forms of informal organization, (c) participated in both loosely and tightly coupled organizational units, and (d) regularly defaulted to bargaining behavior. He recommended research into how educational organizations actually function and use concepts from organization theory (that originated in turn in sociology, psychology, economics, and anthropology), from management science, and potentially, from phenomenology.

Blends of social system and behavioral functionalism were then developed into more comprehensive accounts of educational administration as an applied behavioral science—that, in one outstanding case, as I noted above, ran to at least seven editions (Hoy & Miskel, 2005). Such accounts were supported by a sophisticated management technology of "organizational development" for schools (Miles, 1993; Schmuck & Miles, 1977; Schmuck & Runkel, 1985).

These social system and behaviorist approaches commonly assumed that the legitimacy of the positional authority of school leaders backed up into the interests of students, and therefore, justified leaders modifying administrative systems and processes, cultural norms, and the distribution of power. The most recent elaboration of these approaches in the United States has been to standardize the professionalism of school leadership as the Interstate School Leaders Licensure Consortium's (ISLLC) standards, with the implicit American pragmatism justified by vague appeal to "the success of all students" (Council of Chief State School Officers, 2003). I mention the equivalent standardization process in England below.

The danger here is not, therefore, the nature of managerialism per se, because practices can back up into reasonable pragmatism in a balanced philosophy of educative administration, but the possibility of doctrinal capture of knowledge production. Joe Murphy, the father of the ISLLC standards, has conceded that the knowledge base of the field is increasingly being defined by the standards (Murphy, 2005).

There are good reasons to be concerned (cf. English, 2007). The ISLLC project cut corners on its prior contextualization and was driven by political priorities rather than by educational priorities and constrained by methodological niceties. Outcomes included degrees of reductionism in the preparatory program curriculum and partial disconnection from knowledge creation activities in universities. These outcomes imply the presence of a political ideology that is against change and democracy informed by research.

Educational administration was even blamed by those in a sister field of study for its own slow uptake of political philosophy, albeit embedded in a socially critical agenda:

> The politics of education as a field of study has historically been closely allied with the field of educational administration, which has tended to use

a management lens to view political phenomena. Because of this connection to educational administration, leadership and policy analysis, it may seem "unhelpful" to analyze from the perspective of the participants in educational institutions. Taking the side of institutional resisters—both active and passive—like those cited above may even seem heretical in a field that seems more interested in impression management and the politics of legitimization and denial than in confronting the causes of persistent social inequities. (Marshall & Anderson, 1995, p. 180)

This critique is about recruitment for a knowledge war on the side of those supposedly oppressed by educational administration. It offers a blunt choice between American pragmatism and an alternative and unspecified socially critical ideology without a systematic justification.

The path to understanding educational administration, management, and leadership has been similarly paved with pragmatism and its contestation without the check of political philosophy in Britain and in the Commonwealth, almost from the time it emerged as a field of study sometime after it had in the United States (Baron, 1980; Glatter, 1980; Hughes, 1980). And while what I term *English pragmatism* is significantly more understated than its counterpart in the United States, it was evident in early research in educational management that "has been directed away from the dynamics of interpersonal and intergroup relationships towards the structure and functioning of institutions, resource allocation and use, and policy-making and its implementation" (Baron, 1980, p. 11). It was also seen in attempts to reconcile professional and administrative concerns in large educational organizations (Hughes, 1980) and in a rejection of attempts to

> create two and separate fields of study of educational "policy" and "management." . . . [as being] . . . unjustified both conceptually and empirically . . . [since it may] . . . represent a further manifestation of our strong tendency in Britain over more than a century to devalue "the culture which is concerned with doing, making and organizing" . . . [which is] . . . part of a wider debate about the purposes and direction of education in Britain . . . [especially] . . . towards education for capability, which is sorely needed. (Glatter, 1980, pp. 35–36)

This should not be taken to imply that English pragmatism was unconcerned with the nature and role of politics in educational management. Hoyle (1982) differentiated between personal, professional, and political interests and the role of temporary coalitions and interest groups in micropolitical processes. He introduced a classical distinction between micropolitics, which refers to how individuals and groups in organizations use formal and informal power to achieve their purposes, while macropolitics occurs in the wider community and society when leaders of interest groups and political parties discuss and determine education policy and allocate scarce resources.

Bush (1986) drew on the work of J. V. Baldridge (1989) to offer a blended framework for political analysis that addressed central features of politics (groups, interests, conflict, goals, bargaining, external influences, and the distribution of resources), sources of power in education, compliance and exchange, and how political processes might be modeled using goals, structure, environment, and leadership. It was predicated on a functionalist view that "management is directed towards the regulation of political behavior" (Bush, 1986, p. 68) and used English pragmatism to privilege the head teacher with a dual role of participant and mediator (p. 130) in a four-phase model of policy formulation (p. 135). In response to criticism that such "management theory is pragmatic and expedient," John West-Burnham's (1994, p. 23) rebuttal was directed solely against the charge of expediency, principally on the grounds that it was based on a misreading of contingency theory, perhaps thereby conceding that management theory was underpinned by an undeclared English pragmatism.

The shadowy presence of English pragmatism in the field has also been evident over decades in the practical nature of most problems researched (Bush & Crawford, 2012a, p. 540), the recurrent practical challenges faced to do with consensus and centrism in national policy making (Ribbins & Sherrat, 2012), and school accountability (Glatter, 2012). Finally, it is also seen in the high degree of functionalism whereby leadership and management development is explored "in terms of objective realities between actions and outcomes that enable causal consequences to be understood, planned for, and controlled. It assumes that the agreed purposes of leadership and management development can be specified and research can determine how these purposes can best be achieved" (Simpkins, 2012, p. 627). This limitation has been demonstrated to be an international problem (Lumby, Crow, & Pashiardis, 2008).

In sum, the history of the growth of knowledge in educational administration, and the standardization of training of school leaders in the United States and United Kingdom in recent decades in particular, illustrate a general problem in the field. The justification for knowledge claims about power in education has rarely been supported by a hybrid philosophy of education and administration, yet sailing on under a flag of convenience, American or English pragmatism. This continued the tradition of taking for granted the legitimacy of political arrangements at system and institutional levels, while retaining power over evaluating and improving the political arrangements in classrooms and staffrooms, ostensibly in the students' interests. In the next chapter, I describe the shrouded emergence of politically critical philosophical activity in the field.

3 Intimations of communitarianism

It was clear that something rather extraordinary was happening. Even before the session the atmosphere was electric. It was like a time-bomb waiting to go off, and I walked into to the session with many doubts and uncertainties. As the paper had been circulated, I didn't read it or even summarize its main points. Everyone, it seemed, wanted to say something. I remember George Baron saying to me afterwards, "Well it had a slow start, but once you got wound up . . ." He recalled an incident where Griffiths interrupted me as I answered a question. I had been saying that the dominant theorists of the field were systems thinkers— I may have added that most were Americans . . . Griffiths interrupted at that point. "Name one," he demanded in his stentorian voice. "Talcott Parsons," I shot back. I might have added "Daniel Griffiths." Baron said he was in admiration of that exchange. Certainly from that point the gloves were off; I have come to be deeply grateful to Daniel Griffiths for his latter day views, but it was another case in the beginning.

(Thom Greenfield in Greenfield & Ribbins, 1993, pp. 244–245)

The largely pragmatic and undeclared narratives of political philosophy in educational administration were confronted in 1974 by Thom Greenfield (1975, pp. 64–65). He challenged the ideological hegemony based on systems theory in the study of educational administration. He pointed out that the hegemony assumed that social reality was a natural system (using metaphysical naturalism I would add); that educational organizations were real, had a life of their own and were instruments of order in society, serving both society and the individual. According to this hegemony, organizational pathologies indicated the need to adjust internal structure or external relationships with entities or factors in the environment.

Greenfield argued instead that organizations were social creations, perceived very differently by participants and governed by the values of people with access to power. Because perceptions of organizational pathology actually reflected contested values, he argued, leaders should map the values in conflict and either change the people or change their values if possible. My PhD thesis reported research into "Being a Regional Director of Education" (Macpherson, 1984a, 1984b) and found substantive support for his theoretical propositions about how administrators create and control knowledge about being organized, principally through talk (Macpherson, 1988).

Like Dan Griffiths, Greenfield's primary focus was ontological, ontology being the branch of metaphysics concerned with the nature of being, in this case, being an educational administrator. Unlike Griffiths, however, his attack in part reflected his personally injurious and short-lived experience of being a head of department in academe who found himself "backed up against a cliff" and forced to relinquish the reins of power. He attacked the assumption that organization was an empirical and morally neutral entity, arguing instead that it was a socially constructed artifact that reflected the values of those with the power to manage perceptions of being organized and to change organizational cultures. In a conversation with Peter Ribbins, he explained why he sought a humane approach to politics in educational administration (Greenfield & Ribbins, 1993, p. 262):

> [Boethius was a] Christian who stood at the hinge between the Roman World and the Middle Ages. He is an administrator; one caught between the Emperor and the Pope, or as it turned out, the wrong Pope. He is condemned, and as he awaits his death he thinks back on his career and writes, thus bringing us new insights into the administrative task. Few of us will face the horror that Boethius did, but I am convinced that potentially there is the same dimension in all administrative rule, a kind of horror. The wielding of power is terrible, and the more power, the more terrible it becomes. If there is to be some kind of humanizing of that power a contemplative, philosophical dimension must and should be brought to it.

Curiously, Greenfield never developed a systematic appreciation of political philosophy as a means of auditing the values of interest groups, their interaction and the effect of wider political conditions and arrangements. Further, he persisted with a simplistic dualism of organization as either a natural system or a human invention long after other organizational theorists such as Morgan (1980) had developed plural paradigms and metaphors for puzzle-solving in organizations. Indeed, Morgan (1986) went on and offered a range of metaphors for organizational analysis; organizations as machines, organisms, brains, cultures, political systems, psychic prisons, flux and transformation, and instruments of domination.

Nevertheless, Greenfield's iconoclastic style and reactions by his opponents helped create the conditions for political philosophy to emerge in the field, albeit it unnamed and often unappreciated. Practitioners, researchers and theorists internationally began to consider approaches in addition to systems theory. Greenfield's final and collaborative work with Peter Ribbins (1993) proposed a graceful "humane science" of educational administration that was largely bereft of socially critical or politically critical dimensions. As Greenfield put it, "When I was in England, British sociologists like Beryl Tipton wanted me to become 'structural', but I have always resisted the ethno-Marxist or critical perspective" (Greenfield & Ribbins, 1993, p. 241).

Greenfield's pioneering challenge triggered interpretive (Gronn, 1983, 1984) and socially critical (Bates, 1980) approaches to research in educational administration first in the Commonwealth and then in the United States (Capper, 1998; Foster, 1986a). Most initially focused on the consequences of the values and characters of educational administrators, and then elaborated accounts of being leaders in specific contexts, with many exemplars available today (e.g., Ribbins & Sherrat, 2012). It has also endured as a constructivist perspective in leadership and management development where it was seen in efforts to personalize role socialization, coconstruct preparatory programs and mentor the cocreation of personal narratives about leadership identity (e.g., Cowie & Crawford, 2009; Simpkins, 2012), ultimately as forms of "designer leadership" (Gronn, 2003) intended to prepare head teachers to be "completely in control of everything that made policy implementation possible" (Gunter & Thompson, 2009, p. 473).

Yet, remarkably, none of these researchers, including myself, ever evoked political philosophy as a subdiscipline to critique the deliberate construction of power relations. Some moved on to consider the structural impediments to social justice being sustained by the actions and inactions of powerful educational administrators, and gradually developed unstated but identifiable political ideologies.

To illustrate, Richard Bates, a long-time and successful administrator of a university school, responded to Greenfield's challenge by advancing a socially critical critique with colleagues at Deakin University. It was intended to create a new model of practice centered on "the problem of the justice and fairness of . . . social and educational arrangements" (Bates, 1983). He had claimed earlier (1980, p. 1) that one of the four reasons that educational administration as a field of study was held in low regard in the academic community was the overtly political yet unreflective nature of the field. Curiously, he recommended critical reflection, not using political philosophy as he might have done, but the priorities and assumptions imported from British New Sociology:

> The processes through which learning is organized in society are of central importance in . . . the production of knowledge, the maintenance of culture, and the reproduction of social structure. Educational administration is a key element in these processes of structuring knowledge and society. It is concerned very much with the management of the structures of knowledge and the structures of control. It is a human activity of major importance in the reproduction of culture and society. (Bates, 1980, pp. 1, 2)

Although these priorities and assumptions were explicitly concerned with political arrangements, the potential utility of political philosophy in the growth of knowledge in the field was again overlooked, although he came very close. By this, I mean that Bates focused on the concept of "ideology" to explain how the use of power in education systems is typically justified, rather than how the ideology he selected to conduct the evaluation was justified and to what extent. He argued that it is

> ideology which either justifies or significantly limits the arbitrary exercise of power in education systems. Ideology specifies the nature of the relationship between

structures of knowledge and structures of control which are acceptable as a basis for particular forms of educational administration. (Bates, 1980, p. 16).

This was to repeat Greenfield's error in not taking the step from ideology into political philosophy to evaluate justifications for political arrangements.

Compounding this problem is that ideology can have two almost irreconcilable meanings (Freeden, 2000). The first meaning is pejorative and indicates particular and historically distorted forms of political thought that reinforce relationships of domination. When used in this way, ideology can serve as an unmasking concept and/or as a belittling "silver bullet," as I show below.

The second meaning is nonpejorative and indicates families of cultural symbols and ideas that people use to see, understand and evaluate social and political realities in general, often within a systematic framework. These families of symbols and ideas have major mapping and integrative functions. It is important to note that this second meaning has its own internal division:

> Some analysts claim that the study of ideology can be non-evaluative in establishing scientific facts about the way that political beliefs reflect the social world and propel people to specific action within it. Others hold that ideology injects specific politically value-laden meanings into conceptualizations of the social world which are inevitably determinate, and is consequently a means of constructing rather than reflecting that world. This also applies to interpretations undertaken by the analysts of ideology themselves. (Freeden, 2000, p. 381)

The former approach assumes that people act largely within existing organizational structures, reflects traditional systems theory and is therefore categorized as *structuralist* in orientation. The latter approach assumes that structures are themselves being reconstructed by people as they act in an organized world and is categorized as *poststructuralist*. As a sociologist, Bates probably used the term *ideology* in a nonpejorative sense in 1980, and in time, moved steadily to develop a Habermasian form of communicative rationalism. However, his unqualified use of the term ideology at the time allowed the pejorative meaning to be worked into a naturalistic silver bullet:

> Subjectivism, neo-Marxist critical theory, postmodernism, and identity politics are all creatures of the times, the more so because of their lack of intellectual plausibility and the staying power that such plausibility confers. They are views that depend and thrive on relativism and ideology. In varying degrees, they give emotion priority over reason and advocacy priority over problem solving. They typically downgrade science and reject the kind of naturalistic position presented here. (Willower, 1996, p. 344)

Although this near absolute naturalism or metaphysical naturalism can be set aside, with respect and subjectivism, and the various forms of poststructural critical theory can be regarded as legitimate perspectives that helpfully extend understanding, postmodernism poses an almost irreconcilable challenge to political philosophy, unless it is delimited by the use of a nonfoundational epistemology.

Postmodernism is evident in a wide variety of cultural phenomena in many fields and is characterized by two assumptions. The first is that there is no common denominator (such as nature, truth, God, or the future) available that can guarantee the coherence of the world or the possibility of neutral or objective thought. The second is that all human systems act like language, "being self-reflexive rather than referential systems—systems of differential function which are powerful but finite, and which construct and maintain meaning and value" (Ermarth, 2000). Postmodern philosophers typically assert (e.g., White, 1991) that:

- Western modernity uses moral and political concepts in a way that marginalizes, denigrates and disciplines those who do not measure up to prevailing societal criteria of rationality, normality and responsibility.
- The West's self-congratulatory attitude on liberal democracy and traditions obscures this process, and thus the importance of disrupting this attitude as a means of radically improving democracy.

This approach subverts the project of political philosophy unless it is accepted as a form of political discourse about the production of knowledge. A little like the late Don Willower, I find postmodernism unhelpful because it symbolically licenses its followers to employ antischolarly norms and ad hominem techniques that do violence to the systematic growth of knowledge. Its approach to justification appears to be that an ethical system of rationality, normality and responsibility will emerge from the ashes. This is a crude non sequitur and analogous to Pol Pot's theory of community development.

Further, having provided leadership services and researched leadership development in sometimes troubled non-Western settings (Macpherson, 2008b, 2011; Macpherson, Kachelhoffer, & Nemr, 2007; Macpherson, Pashiardris, & Frielick, 2000; Macpherson & Sylvester, 2007; Macpherson & Tofighian, 2007), I have learned that each setting offers opportunities for respectful interculturalism and collaborative interprofessional collaboration around educative leadership and that the Western versus non-Western framework is a simplistic dualism.

On the other hand, the balance of Willower's judgment can be seen in retrospect as primarily concerned with correcting epistemological deviance from metaphysical naturalism, too often an unrealized artifact of American pragmatism and as increasingly obsolete in the light of the proposals advanced by Habermas and Rawls, as summarized above and further clarified below. Indeed, one of the consequences of Bates's edge-cutting work is that the field of educational administration has moved steadily toward accepting that it has a role to play in developing communities and in promoting justice.

Clear evidence of this was seen in the broad acceptance of Bill Foster's critical humanism in the United States to the point where his scholarship was given the singular honor of a special edition by the *Educational Administration Quarterly* on his early death. Parallel evidence, also reviewed below, was also seen in other special editions. Three political ideologies in educational administration are now examined that are beginning to intimate their presence in addition to democratic utopianism and perfectionism and managerial pragmatism: communitarianism, communicative rationalism and egalitarian liberalism.

To recall, the focus of communitarian analysis and description in educational administration is the nature of being organized for educational purposes and the essence of identity and relationships in such organization, and how collectives provide rights and obligations to individuals. Central to this project is the integrity and value of traditional practices, such as the cultural means of socially constructing meaning. The focus of evaluation and reform is therefore the refinement of institutional life and leadership practices so that they will promote community, serve the community and the public good, and develop cooperative practices and values such as reciprocity, trust and solidarity.

The political ideology of communitarianism got its first significant airing in educational administration when Tom Sergiovanni (1980) proposed and justified *social humanism* as an appropriate sociopolitical theory for the field. In the next decade, clearly influenced by MacIntyre (see Table 1.1), Etzioni (1993), and Coleman (1990), he switched the central metaphor of his theory building from organization to community (Sergiovanni, 1994), and the exploration of political arrangements in communitarian terms accelerated. For example, with regard to legitimate authority, he observed that:

> In communities, the sources of authority for leadership are embedded in shared ideas. One source is moral authority in the forms of obligations and duties that emerge from the bonding and binding ties of community. Another source is professional authority in the forms of commitment to virtuous practice.
>
> When bureaucratic and personal authority move to the side and moral, and professional authority move to the center, our understanding of what leadership is and how it works changes. Professional and moral authority are substitutes for leadership that cast principals and teachers together into roles as followers of shared values, commitments, and ideals. This shared followership binds them into a community of mind. (Sergiovanni, 1994, p. 233)

The exact nature of communitarianism in U.S. educational administration was a little confused by a study of career assistant principals (Marshall, Patterson, Rogers, & Steele, 1996). It showed that the ethic of caring favored by many of those surveyed was disrupted in daily enactment by demands from organizational and professional sources. Nevertheless, the coming of communitarianism was then firmly ushered in by a special edition of the *Educational Administration Quarterly* in 1999.

The editor (Furman-Brown, 1999) was prescient in noting that the focus on community was a "signifier of sea change in our thinking about the purposes of public schooling and schools as organizations" (p. 10). Included in her "thinking about our thinking" was reference to the shared assumption that "community" was a rich, complex and dynamic concept that had to be understood in context to improve the "quality of day-to-day life in schools." And while each contributor to this special edition then identified empirical and analytic aspects of the quality of relationships in community schools, they all remained a short step away from evaluating the justifications presented for the changes to power relationships they proposed.

For instance, it was demonstrated (L. G. Beck, 1999), with considerable subtlety, that while current meanings of community in context were complex and coherent enough to sustain research, they were also being reconstructed in the communities as they were being studied. Using an educative form of communitarianism, it was suggested that people seeking to create and sustain communal schools might need guidance to understand the ways of making sense of being in and out of community.

Similarly, a two-year qualitative case study of three rural middle schools wanting to foster professional communities found major tensions between the norms of bureaucracy and professionalism (Scribner, Cockrell, Cockrell, & Valentine, 1999). These tensions had to be resolved through negotiations to achieve a communitarian outcome, and subsequently sustained with double-loop learning. The redistribution of power involved was mediated by four factors; principal leadership, organizational history, organizational priorities and organization of teacher work. The next question not asked was the justification for the new communitarian norms of professionalism achieved.

This question came close to be asked when a potential dilemma was identified (Strike, 1999) in the concept of public community schools, that is, the partially incompatible values that support communitarian and liberal forms of inclusion. Three political ideologies (comprehensive doctrines, caring and democracy) were considered, but it was found that if any one of them became an overly robust aspect of communitarianism, it would lead to inconsistencies with liberalism. The subtle recommendation was to adopt the middle ground using reasonably vigorous variants of each of the three positions and to allow a flexible degree of association, neatly illustrating how political philosophy can be enabled by a nonfoundational epistemology that gives high priority to coherence.

Another related study (Westheimer, 1999) also demonstrated the analytical utility of political philosophy, again without mentioning it by name, by unraveling vague notions of a "teacher professional community." It was shown that current models obscure significant differences in beliefs and practices. A provisional model derived from a number of settings highlighted many subtle distinctions between the unnamed political ideologies of egalitarian liberalism and communitarianism.

Likewise, when seen through the lens of political philosophy, a case study of Navajo high school students' views (Shields, 1999) found an interesting tension between the communitarianism explicit as cultural affiliation and the egalitarian liberalism implied by vocational drivers. Important clues were found about how to create school communities in the interface of competing allegiances, perceptions, and understandings, and by catering for difference rather than just for homogeneity.

The changing rationally critical account of educational administration, and how the field was evaluating political arrangements, was comprehensively revealed in 2004 when the field marked the passing of one of its heroes, Bill Foster. An edition of tributes traced how his critical idealism had impacted on educational administration since the publication of his *Paradigms and Promises* (Foster, 1986a) until his untimely death in 2003. Foster's contributions to the growth of knowledge, it was pointed out (Lindle, 2004), had encouraged engagement in a dialectical construction of education and leadership, generous mentoring, and a scholarship marked by collegial relations.

As regards power, Foster's *posthumous* position (2004) reiterated his assumption that educational leadership too often comprised bureaucratic control over individuals in systemic, rule-bearing institutions. He asked educational leaders to become "virtuous and free" rather than act as agents of the state. He did this by contrasting national and state narratives for disseminating rules and standards against the ethos of local communities and encouraged educational leaders to create communal narratives to resist the domination of the state. His descriptive and evaluative framework primarily used a political ideology of communitarianism without explicit justification, with reviewers also correct in noting hints of postmodernism and more extensive deployments of communicative rationalism.

An insightful analysis showed that Foster's account of school leadership was always located in the intersections of social, economic and political forces of communities and comprised nuanced analyses of the dilemmas of deliberation (Mawhinney, 2004). It also demonstrated that his call for a critical praxis drew on an emerging scholarship on leadership from native and indigenous populations, and that this scholarship highlighted the communicative processes required to mediate ideas and interests and to achieve institutional reforms. Such praxis, it followed, would be more easily achieved by using multidisciplinary scholarship that involved local politics to create a deliberative democracy for a globalized world. This astute conclusion supported the finding above; that Foster's communitarianism was often blended with aspects of communicative rationalism, confirming in my view, his deep respect for Bates's pioneering work.

Another review (Grogan, 2004) added support by noting how Foster had used critical theory to propose reforms to educational leadership, to create fresh interest in social justice, and to call into question the homogenizing effects of national leadership standardization policies. On the other hand, this review also advised those preparing local leaders to conduct research at the community level to find educative means of transcending policy limits on leadership, such as developing a localized application of postmodernism. However, a respondent to Foster's final paper (Anderson, 2004), who discussed the new "technologies of thought" (yet another term for ideologies) that were becoming evident through discourse analysis of the use of language, information, and numeracy during research, concluded that Foster was far more reliant on communicative rationalism than on postmodernism. This conclusion was complemented by Jerry Starratt's (2004a) compelling review that stressed the extent to which Foster's contribution to the growth of knowledge about moral leadership was advanced by a lifelong scholarly dialogue with other scholars, especially about justice in schooling within a humanistic framework.

Empirical research encouraged by Foster's scholarship provided support for the reforms he proposed based on his primary political ideologies of communitarianism and communicative rationalism. A case study of a regional agency (Hoffman & Burrello, 2004) provided an account of superintendents' services that trialed Foster's thinking by shifting their focus from economic effectiveness to teaching and learning, in my terms, to educative leadership. The superintendents' services became critical, transformative, educative and ethical in nature, and sought to achieve schooling with equity for all students. As the superintendents developed a shared understanding of the purpose of their work, and when they began to adjust their work between leadership and "followership" roles by reforming power relationships, an "ethic of community" reportedly emerged.

Finally, an edited collection of tributes from international scholars (McCarthy, 2004) then clarified how many had been engaged in forms of political philosophy with Bill Foster without reference to the subdiscipline. These scholars clarified how the blended political ideologies of critical humanism and communitarianism had driven Foster's concern for social justice, the moral purposes of leadership, the ethical dimensions of practice and deep caring in his personal relationships. He was, they said, an "authentic critical theorist" with "intellectual acuity" and profound "humanity" who had asked the field to justify its practices and the organizations it created and sustained.

Foster's (1986, p. 184) final word on power insisted that "leaders who have vision and spirit can share power. In so doing they release the human potential of the agents in the organization." He believed that educational leaders could help emancipate people and peoples by aiming "toward the gradual development of freedoms, from economic problems, racial oppression, ethnic domination, and the oppression of women" (1986b, p. 49). We can conclude that Foster's communitarianism was significantly mediated by communicative rationalism.

The emergence of communitarianism in British and Commonwealth educational administration took a similar path although many educational leaders remained wary of its saliency in so-called Third Way politics in the United States and the Commonwealth at the time. National leaders, such as Tony Blair in the United Kingdom, Bill Clinton in the United States, Roy Romanov in Canada and Kevin Rudd in Australia, each developed various progressive syntheses of right-wing economic and left-wing social policies when faith in Keynesian interventions fell and the popularity of neoliberal prescriptions started to rise. Tony Gidden's (2010) treatise attempted to take the middle ground in the politics of education by promoting greater egalitarianism in society, through a wider distribution of productive knowledge skills and understandings, and yet argued for balanced budgets, equal opportunity, personal responsibility, subsidiarity, public-private partnerships, investment in human development and the protection of social capital and the environment.

Communitarianism almost surfaced in socially critical studies of school leadership in Britain that were concerned with the more limited development of schools as the "cradles of democracy" and school leadership as a form of democratic agency, especially when confronting contemporary challenges like accountability. Gerald Grace, for example, opined that:

> Democratic accountability in schooling, when taken seriously, is a far more radical conception than market accountability. Its organizing concepts are communities, citizens and democratic leadership, and the model for the school is not that of a commercial enterprise but that of a democratic community itself. (1995, p. 201)

Communitarianism was nearly exposed by a comprehensive review of research into cultural leadership in the United Kingdom with special reference to power and equity at four levels of cultural activity; the cultural context created by global phenomena, the cultures of local communities, the organizational culture and the sub- and countercultures within the organization (Lumby, 2012). The review set the scene for a communitarian agenda for leaders when it noted the

> relentless persistent negotiation of culture and community . . . [instead of] . . . a creating a strong culture or for re-culturing . . . [and concluded that] . . . integrationist [ideological] perspectives embedded in normative encouragement to action are likely to perpetuate the kind of inequities that currently exist in education. Rather than focusing on changing others, the goal is changing oneself, and understanding more fully one's own culture and its relationship with the alternative and oppositional cultures that exist in each organization. (Lumby, 2012, p. 587)

A review of leadership and diversity literature in Great Britain (Coleman, 2012) showed that the heavy focus on gender issues had broadened into the wider concept of diversity from 2000, including ethnicity, religion and sexual orientation, and stressed the moral imperatives of establishing an inclusive culture without reference to the hosting ideology of communitarianism. Similarly, it appears from the decades of research into the merits of sole and distributed leadership (Crawford, 2012) that the latter has been conceptualized as structure, as agency, as cooperative professionalism (Corrigan, 2000), or even as interprofessional collaboration (Salm, 2009), but oddly, hardly ever as an outcome of sharing power according to a particular political ideology with an explicit justification.

An important exception that illustrates the point is Philip Woods's (2011, pp. 10–11) proposals regarding holistic or developmental democratic leadership. He conceptualized a model of four dimensions; holistic meaning (pursuit of truth and meaning), holistic well-being (social belonging, connectedness and feelings of empowerment embedded in democratic participation), power sharing (active contribution to the creation of the institutions, culture and relationships people inhabit) and transforming dialogue (exchange and exploration of views, open debate and transcendence of narrow interests). The model benefits from drawing its justification from a specific political ideology; the ethical socialism of British idealism (Green, 1999). On the other hand, this position brought with it the limitations of absolute idealism because it imagines a single and comprehensive reality where thought-and-object compose a system with strongly coherent unity. Green's position was that the existence of the state was only justified to the extent to which it made valuable contributions to the lives of individuals. There are, in my view, better justifications for democratic leadership available that are more suitable to the modern and diverse governance conditions seen in school education systems and emergent networks. For example, as introduced above in an English setting, Woods argued that

> the point of democratic leadership, grounded in the conception of [holistic democracy], is only partially to enable equal participation by all in decisions that affect them. The primary point is to strive towards a way of living—in and through relationships—which is orientated towards values that ultimately present human progress and goodness. (Woods, 2005, pp. 137–138, 2011, p. 12)

This suggests that there may be a serious deficit in such capacity at national levels where the authoritative knowledge of educational leadership is replicated as a matter of national policy. The Leadership Programme for Serving Headteachers in England has been described as using impoverished spiritual assumptions and an unacceptably narrow version of communitarianism. Luckcock (2012a, p. 545, 2012b) concluded that the Leadership Programme for Serving Headteachers:

> would appear to legitimate an approach to leadership development that values the interior life of the headteacher as long as this is exclusively oriented to a psychology of personal achievement and organizational effectiveness . . . there appears to be little interest in other philosophical approaches to community leadership, for example, the quest for wisdom, a flair for originality and authenticity, caring for the well-being of others or peaceful mediation in times of strife and conflict.

In the next chapter, I report the coming of two other ideologies to the practice, research and theory of educational administration, management and leadership.

4 Intimations of communicative rationalism and egalitarian liberalism

> A political myth which is contrary to the fact may serve a group best in a political struggle when: (1) the group which created it uses it, (2) others have come to believe it, and (3) the group itself does not itself believe in it as a description of reality.
>
> (Iannaccone, 1967, p. 8)

Larry Iannaconne's astute observation reminds us that the purpose of political mythmaking is to create and shape social reality, but that it is not the same thing as altering empirical reality. As noted in Chapter 1, description and analysis using a political ideology of communicative rationalism focuses on the nature of control in organizations, how participants' understandings related to emancipation develop, the nature of communicative rationality (as opposed to instrumental rationality) and the disruptive effects of market and bureaucratic systems. Communicative rationalists seek to map the intersubjective notions of practical reason and the discursive procedures used to justify universal norms.

How might this be evident in day-to-day leadership practice? One example would be a communicative rationalist leader facilitating a workshop of stakeholders and executives to solve problems in a way that also develops more open, participative and deliberative democratic processes appropriate for a complex modern world. In its purest form, this leader would suspend positional authority and allow power to move and become a group resource. Such an approach would tend to use the values of the Enlightenment as well as legitimate law and discourse ethics to provide a defense and critique of subsequent organization using public practical reason. There are potential limitations to this approach; it can ingratiate influence achieved through charisma, give undue weight to consensus, reiterate the social priorities of the group, make an unsystematic appreciation of relevant evidence, downplay concerns and values in wider politics and limit consideration of ethical principles and longer-term consequences.

There are also potential strengths to this approach. In earlier chapters, it was indicated that Richard Bates's pioneering socially critical research program developed into the most comprehensive and sustained development of Habermasian communicative rationalism yet seen in educational administration. He and his colleagues' political ideology, despite never being explicitly clarified as such, insisted on (a) the integration of educational and administrative principles in the interests of students and (b) research unmasking the managerialist ideology embedded in policies, practices and outcomes. It called on educational administrators to trace the links between the moral and social order to justify interventions into the repro-duction of inequalities, poverty and discrimination, and to install a pedagogy of liberation. Bates's evaluation of administrative practice has long expected the development of communicative practices that will improve social and administra-tive practices and prevent educational administration from becoming a substitute for politics.

Conceptual research inspired by Bates's scholarship in communicative rational-ism was initially much more extensive in the Commonwealth than in the United States and more concentrated at Deakin University than at sister universities in Australasia. To illustrate, early examples examined agency and structure (Watkins, 1985), multiculturalism as an educational policy (Rizvi, 1985), administrative leadership and the democratic community as a social ideal (Rizvi, 1986a), ethnic-ity, class and multicultural education (Rizvi, 1986b), a (socially) critical review of leadership concepts and research (Watkins, 1986) and the reconstruction of leadership (Foster, 1986b). Later examples examined gender and education policy (Kenway, 1990), gender, knowledge and education (Yates, 1990), feminist research in education (Lather, 1991) and feminism in the making of educational history (Blackmore, 1992).

This burst of abstract scholarship sustained its focus on advancing socially critical theory, that is, a political ideology of communicative rationalism often with elements of communitarianism. For example, it was argued that the suppos-edly irreconcilable differences between technical/managerial and participative/professional approaches to educational organization led into a case for democ-ratized governance and communitarian leadership for schools (Angus, 1994). In another example, historical sociology was employed to relate the concepts of leadership, social justice and feminism to propose a theory of practice in educa-tional administration (Blackmore, 2006). This analysis linked the limited power of marginalized groups to their claims on the state with regard to social justice and noted the extent to which educational administrators have sidelined their interests, principally by not focusing on teaching and learning. This *is* then became an *ought* when feminist and critical theorists' ideas of democratic leadership were proposed as means of dissolving the differences between formal and informal leadership and to construct a notion of leadership that more explicitly valued social justice.

This ideology-driven approach to theory building tended to be light on empiri-cal evidence, strong on assertion and heavy on projection in order to promote a political ideology, and proceeded largely without the benefits of political phi-losophy as a disciplined process. When the members of the Deakin School gave near-absolute standing to social justice for fairness as a purpose in theory building and improving practice, the justification appeared to be primarily a projection of their shared personal educational ideologies. It is also an approach that defied political gravity; people tend to be socialized or radicalized into political com-mitments (Putnam, 1976, pp. 42–43), for example through the articulation and servicing of common interests, rather than by an abstract logic that expects prior commitment to a theoretical political ideology.

The assertions of avowedly poststructural Marxist social theorists such as Michael Apple have, in my view, both helped and hindered the process of advancing the idea of social justice for fairness. They have helped by clarifying possible lines of inquiry regarding the dynamics of structuration and resistance to unequal power relations, but served the process of scholarship badly by reiterating propositions to the point where they pose as knowledge claims. To illustrate, it was asserted in the latest edition of *Education and Power* that:

> A central thrust of radical criticism of our institutions during the last decade or so has been on the school. It has become increasingly obvious over the same time period that our educational institutions may serve less as the engines of democracy and equality than many of us would like. In many ways, the criticism has been healthy since it has increased our sensitivity to the important roles school—and the overt and covert knowledge play within them—play in reproducing a stratified social order that remains strikingly unequal by class, gender and race. . . . The educational and cultural system is an exceptionally important element in the maintenance of existing relations of domination and exploitation in these societies. (Apple, 2012, pp. 8–9)

Limited evidence and poor methodology in the edition aside, this approach highlights to me the importance of educators being clearer about how politics actually works, the blend of many purposes that can reasonably be served by schools and, in particular, who should decide this crucial matter in diverse communities and plural societies—and how educational administrators, managers and leaders should play an appropriate role in the politics of governance and management processes. Leaders will search in vain for any reference in *Education and Power* to their political responsibilities and powers without any justification being made for their marginalization. Instead, on the grounds that nation states support capital accumulation and use schools to legitimate this process through reproducing and producing agents, knowledge and ideologies, an anti-leadership position is advanced when it is argued that contradictions arise and offer opportunities for resistance. Hence:

> I have suggested strategies and action on a variety of fronts: within schools and universities involving curriculum, democratizing technical knowledge, using and politicizing the lived culture of students and teachers, etc.; and outside school involving both educational practices in progressive labour unions, political and feminist groups, and so on, and in political action to build a mass socialist and democratic movement in the United States. (Apple, 2012, p. 151)

In the absence of any consideration of the relativity of the ideology of democratic socialism in schooling, this position appears to be a naïve sociopolitical movement posing as scholarship that intends to implement its ideology in education and resist any educational administration, management and leadership to the contrary.

Sadly, in tactical terms, the near-absolutism of this approach invited the unthinking acceptance or rejection of its proposals on similarly personal ideological grounds. Hence, visceral responses are more likely than rational. In strategic terms, it might have been more effective in a professional setting to offer practitioners a supportive philosophy and practical context of educational administration that gives equal respect to evidence-based priorities refined by democratic practices in the local and wider contexts, rather than presenting the coercive demands of an ideology.

If working in a context long imbued with American pragmatism, it might also have been more plausible and effective if justifications had backed up simultaneously into empirical accounts of successful applications, reports of blended solutions serving unique mixes of values and priorities in diverse settings, and studies that reported attempts to achieve some of many forms of desirable justice. The justice "bucket list" might also plausibly include economic justice, gender justice, intercultural justice, environmental justice, educational justice, etc.

As I reiterate in a later chapter, absolutism appears to provide relatively short pathways to irrelevance and obsolescence in the growth of knowledge. Leaders who would be philosophers-in-action also need to know that political philosophy, as with all scholarly subdisciplines, is constantly being transformed and that its conflation with any one ideology will simply lead it into a fundamentalist cul de sac. To illustrate, a recent review of leadership and management development in England came to the view that:

> Writing from the critical perspective has been dominated by . . . post-structural approaches that emphasize the power of discourse and processes of identity construction. Nevertheless, there has been little evidence in the journals reviewed here of socially critical approaches to leadership development which address either general issues of social justice or more specific questions concerning, for example, gender or identity. There is nothing to compare, for example, with some U.S. studies that explore in a grounded way how such perspectives might be effectively embedded in leadership development activities, the kinds of leadership identities that this might imply and the barriers to such developments. (Simpkins, 2012, p. 632)

It might also be the case that the field of educational administration is lagging so far behind that it is yet to experience six evolutionary trends in political philosophy that Miller (1998) noted over a decade ago. It has been revitalized in Western societies in recent decades by the impact of Rawls's liberalism. All forms of Marxism are in steady decline. Both conservatism and socialism have incorporated large portions of liberalism in attempts to remain relevant. Communitarianism may yet prove a rival to liberalism. It is not clear if liberalism will claim universal validity or present itself more modestly as an interpretation of the general political culture of the Western liberal democracies.

Returning to the field of educational administration, it seems entirely reasonable to acknowledge that Richard Bates (2006) has led the field in incorporating political philosophy into his research program—more recently claiming, for instance, that "It is this idea of the common good that sets out the foundation for approaches to social justice" (p. 145). It is, however, not yet clear why his common good justification for communicative rationalism should entirely preempt communitarian attempts to refine schools so that they serve the community and the public good and promote cooperative practices and values such as reciprocity, trust and solidarity. The indirect evidence reviewed in the chapter above, concerning Bill Foster's contributions, suggests that communitarianism and communicative rationalism tend to be integrated to substantial degrees in many Western liberal democratic settings.

Similarly, is it wise that a common good justification for communicative rationalism entirely preempt egalitarian liberalism, which stresses justice as fairness, equal liberty and equal opportunity, with inequalities only justified if they benefit the worst off? The evidence below is, again, that they are not mutually exclusive in practical circumstances and tend to be integrated to match ideals, policy, circumstances and opportunities. Indeed, there is a rich research agenda indicated here into leadership practice as an alternative to yet more purely idealistic and ideological projections. The practical potency of a nonfoundational epistemology is also highlighted.

And could there be a helpful role for a social contract that binds peoples to various forms of government in education, specifically the governance of classrooms, schools, institutions, systems and other knowledge organizations? The problem here is that the field is light on the comparative analysis and evaluation of governance arrangements and their justifications from group to global levels in educational administration. I return to this issue in the chapters that follow, which examine controversial cases of governance internationally.

This leads me to the point that it would be particularly helpful for politically critical research to locate descriptions and prescriptions in specific contexts. For example, the repeated claim that educational administration can become a substitute for politics (Bates, 1983, 2006) needs to be established with enough empirical certainty in context to permit generalization for theory building. It may be derived, quite reasonably, from Bates's personal experience as a senior educational administrator; although unlike Greenfield and Griffiths, he does not yet appear to have reflected critically in writing on this aspect of his auspicious career in academe. This issue will be raised again below in the context of a governance crisis in higher education in Hong Kong. The interim point here is that political philosophy in educational administration is likely to be more effective when claims are substantially grounded using methodological naturalism (as opposed to metaphysical naturalism). Methodological naturalism is a working assumption; that reality exists independent of our subjective experience, and it is a primary source of our experience of the world and science intended to make better sense of it. Metaphysical naturalism, however, is a belief that the patterns of causality investigated by science are the only genre of causality that exist or can exist. The former remains open to correction, whereas the latter is ideologically closed and unacceptably limited in its access to success that can advance the growth of knowledge.

Another related issue is the comparative capacity of educational administration, and even education more broadly, to actually deliver the many forms of justice noted above. This could mean looking outside of the modest efforts in our field to those with more highly developed theories and evidence-based practice regarding the management of development on a global scale.

One illustration was provided via new forms of information and communication technology. Intergenerational data from the United Nations concerning the dimensions of development were reprocessed using interactive tools of analysis and presentation (Rosling, 2007) to debunk many common myths about the so-called developing world. It was shown that most of the Third World is on the same trajectory toward health and prosperity as the West in intergenerational terms, and indeed, that many countries are moving twice as fast as the countries in the West did. Table 4.1 was derived from the analysis and indicates that education has been playing a comparatively important role as a means toward global developmental justice, yet far less so as an end in itself, with broadly the same potency in both realms as good governance.

It is too early to be sure, but Rosling's innovative analysis and interim conclusions imply that many forms of justice may be more effectively achieved locally and simultaneously by adopting a broad communitarian political ideology that incorporates degrees of communicative rationalism and egalitarian liberalism in a way not dissimilar to that suggested above by Hanne Mawhinney (2004). Rosling's interim findings also imply that educational leadership for developing countries may need to be reconceptualized as the facilitation of neighbor-based and interagency collaborations that focus on the struggle for learning in families and communities, align support services, boost access, personalize services and provide external links to further opportunities (Capper, 1994). The case study below from Timor Leste speaks to these issues.

In sum to this point, Bates and his colleagues' pioneering work in communicative rationalism appears to be indicating that educational administration may need

Table 4.1 Key dimensions of intergenerational development in developing third-world countries (Rosling, 2007)

Dimensions	Rated as means	Rated as goals
Human Rights	+	+++
Environment	+	++
Governance	++	+
Economic Growth	+++	–
Education	++	+
Health	+	++
Culture	+	+++

to promote a scholarship of integration to refine blends of political ideologies specific to purposes and to incorporate knowledge from sister fields in a global context, rather than be limited to localist interpretations of socialism. With these possibilities in mind, I now turn to intimations of egalitarian liberalism in educational administration.

As Table 1.1 indicated, John Rawls's highly influential version of egalitarian liberalism requires an analysis of the extent to which a hypothetical social contract between the governed and governors is being delivered by current arrangements. Rawls proposed that this abstract social contract be developed by adopting an imaginary original position of not knowing one's social status and not knowing what a good life is in a current context. He proposed this veil of ignorance as a way of guaranteeing that (a) neither self-interest nor group-interest would be deployed, (b) considered judgments would be made in a state of reflective equilibrium and (c) the resultant contract would reflect an equal concern for everyone and distributive justice. Evaluation with a view to improvement, he argued, should thereafter focus on the development of justice as fairness, with equal liberty and equal opportunity and inequalities only regarded as justified if they benefit everyone, especially the worst off.

There are limitations to Rawl's egalitarian liberalism apart from the heroic degree of selflessness implied. It was proposed as an alternative to utilitarianism (the *goodness* of greatest happiness and best consequences) and was driven instead by a concern for principled *rightness*. He developed his theory of justice on the grounds that each person has inviolable rights to justice that should never be displaced, even by community welfare rights. This approach privileges individual rights over collective and societal rights.

In order to reconcile the good with the right, when allocating scarce social primary goods in a just way, Rawls relied heavily on the concept of fairness. To the traditional distribution criteria of merit, needs, or rights, he added three principles that he argued must each be fully satisfied before the next is to be employed; having equal liberty, having fair equality of opportunity, and finally, taking account of differences and disadvantages. One problem here is the ranking of principles; why is liberty ranked above all others as a social primary good? Another is that the procedures automatically create a justification that backs up first into liberalism, then egalitarianism and finally either social democracy or welfare liberalism. This approach leads to two questions; are the current structures in society just, and is a minimum level of support guaranteed to the worst off?

There are also the issues of plausibility, human nature and universal morality. Developing a social contract from an original position behind a veil of ignorance has the appeal of procedural fairness, but it also assumes that envy, bargaining, gaming, caution and greed will be suspended, and that contracting parties will consistently use strategic analysis instead of tactical thinking about immediate utility.

Rawls also appears to assume that liberalism is the universal morality of rational individuals and that the good life should be decided by them to the limits of public harmony. Brown (1986, p. 78) responded to this pungently; that "without the grounding provided by Aristotle or Kant (and Rawls offers none such), reflective equilibrium as the systemization of ordinary moral thought can claim to be nothing more than a reshuffled pack of moral prejudices." A more generous interpretation is that Rawls's approach uses internal and external coherence tests to reconcile knowledge claims using principles of rightness. But what criteria of rightness and why?

In sum, Rawls proposed principles of rightness by regarding fairness in distributive justice that were based on a view of individuals having inalienable rights to "a fully adequate scheme of equal basic rights and liberties" (2005, p. 5), and that "social and economic inequalities are to be arranged so that they are both (a) to the greatest benefit of the least advantaged, consistent with the just savings principle [to provide intergenerational justice] and (b) attached to offices and positions open to all under conditions of fair equality of opportunity" (1999, p. 266)

Such egalitarian liberalism nearly surfaced in educational administration when political economy was introduced to the field by Bill Boyd (1982). By focusing initially on the differences between the goals of individuals and the professed goals of their organization, he was able to interpret them as rational choices made by individuals acting collectively to maximize their benefits with reference to the reward structures of their organization. This led to fresh means of understanding the political reconciliations of three values in public schooling; efficiency, equity and responsiveness to consumer choice. Although never quite describing such reconciliations as relying on social contracts, Boyd's (1992) reconceptualization of practice in educational policy making and administration a decade later focused on how well specific public choice theories explain and predict behaviors in specific settings in human service organizations. One example was how well reciprocal choices between teachers and students create schools as communities of shared values. In effect, this introduction of political economy to the field gave carriage to an unstated political ideology of egalitarian liberalism, along with elements of pragmatism and communitarianism.

Follow-up studies in educational administration that used political science as a methodology exhibited a similar range of undeclared political ideologies. For example, a study of how principals made sense of their internal and external environments using public choice theory (Johnson & Fauske, 2000) indicated that they were primarily and personally concerned with potential benefits and losses of legitimacy capital, and overall tended to express views not inconsistent with egalitarian liberalism.

The editors of a special edition of the *Educational Administration Quarterly* (Lindle & Mawhinney, 2003, p. 4) then aimed to "illustrate the dialectic necessary to further the development of thought in scholarship about the politics of education," confirming that educational leaders were tending to frame their practice as political in three major senses; as dealing with conflict, as managing the power environment and as finding the common ground as soon as possible. Although these norms of political practice were not inconsistent with an egalitarian liberalist's inclination to build social contracts, it was hinted that they may also have been suppressing issues related to diversity and undermining the legitimacy of schooling in a democratic society. Accordingly, the editors advised school leaders to "confront the difficult issues of diversity in schooling . . . [in their belief that] . . . the process opens up opportunities to succeed in schooling" (Lindle & Mawhinney, 2003, p. 5).

This advice did not include a justification for the proposed blend of democratic utopianism and social justice. It might, however, have recommended the use of political philosophy to identify and evaluate (a) the current political arrangements in public schooling, (b) the arrangements that determine winning and losing through education, or alternatively, (c) the methods of determining fairer outcomes in conditions of diversity.

It is interesting to note that a review of the growth of knowledge in the field of politics of education (Scribner, Aleman, & Maxcy, 2003) then helpfully identified three disparate and distinct theoretical streams in postbehavioralist times: micropolitics; political culture; and neoinstitutionalism (a sociological appreciation of how institutions interact, affect host societies, develop their structures and affect members), along with a blend of all three referred to as a *messy center*. The review also found that the theory of the field lacked a unitary paradigm and required a scholarship of integration and aggregation driven by complementary and competitive processes. Hence, although this thinking about thinking in the politics of education touched on the role of school governance, rationalism and structuralism, it could have reached further to suggesting criteria and processes from political philosophy that might have been used to examine how well current mechanisms, concepts and structures were justified.

Preliminary steps were taken in this direction. When their description of the messy center was elaborated by a review of the knowledge base, developmental needs and the level of theoretical maturity of the field (Johnson, 2003), *nagging headaches* were traced to four additional sources. First were issues associated with defining and focusing the field, which indicated an immediate role for political philosophy. Second were problems with theoretical hegemony and group-think, implying the need for an epistemological makeover. Third was the need to address and bridge the divide between macropolitics and micropolitics, implying the need for a scholarship of integration. Fourth were the challenges of sustaining conceptual and theoretical rigor, again implying the need for epistemological reform. The conclusion drawn, that the field was still seeking its identity and epistemological integrity, begged the question about the descriptive and ethical means by which it would develop a critical account of itself.

Various means were suggested in the special edition, although the justifications for them suggested a limited understanding of the potential roles of political philosophy. The reported inattention to racism in schooling was the basis for a call for socially critical analyses in the politics of education (López, 2003). Similarly, a call for a new politics of education in the areas of gender and sexual orientation drew on history and law using an explicitly neo-Marxist political ideology (Lugg, 2003). In both cases, it would have been a short step to evaluate the justifications for current political arrangements using political philosophy to develop a comprehensive case for reform in context.

One of the most interesting developments in recent policy research in British education has immediate implications for understanding educational administration, management leadership in institutions and systems in the nation state, as currently and variously conceived. From the declared perspective of critical sociology, and using social network analysis, Stephen Ball (2012) reported a study of the extent to which the global reach of market solutions in education is being driven through new policy networks by a neoliberal ideology. Leadership in schools, he asserted in passing, had been reduced to "performativity and governing by numbers . . . organized and facilitated by other techniques of organizational redesign . . . [and by] . . . reworking and narrowing the responsibilities of the practitioner by excluding 'extraneous' issues that are not directly connected to performance outcomes" (p. 34).

Although analysis and interpretation in Ball's (2012) study are commendably cautious, to a point, they give carriage to some problems. The main difficulty from the outset is that neoliberalism, the key construct in the study, is both vaguely defined (pp. 3–4), and yet serves as a pejorative catch-all term for practices leading to the globalization of market-based social relations that are characterized by commodification, profit making, capital accumulation and the blending of capital interests with the state. I felt the need to step back from this a priori position denunciating capitalism in any form in education, search for the unspecified ideology from critical sociology [it turned out to be communicative rationalism], and then ask about how the analysis of neoliberalist tendencies had been enhanced and limited by the perspective used. Political philosophy works at the level of meta-analysis to test the quality of knowledge claims.

We need some definitions here to avoid confusion. The political ideology of liberalism was originally shaped by the Enlightenment to advance liberty, equality, fraternity, pluralism and toleration in a just society in the face of the brutalities of aristocracy (rule by an elite) and laissez faire capitalism. It was elaborated into many variants, including classical liberalism and social liberalism. When classical liberalism was revitalized last century by Friedrich Hayek and Milton Friedman, it led to further variants including neoclassical liberalism, which called for less government to enhance individual freedoms and is sometimes confused with a more extreme version in the United States, libertarianism. In contrast, social liberalism holds that the state continues to have a legitimate responsibility to manage both the mixed economy and society through property, trading and civil rights, health, welfare and education, and to reconcile individual freedoms with societal interests.

Although neoliberalism emerged in recent decades as a reaction against social liberalism, and resulted in drier monetarist policies and some cuts to government structure during economic depressions, Western governments continued to provide social, welfare and educational services and manage their economies. Nonetheless, a key belief advanced by neoliberalism is that the control of the mixed economy should be shared more with the private sector to lift the efficiency of government and improve the prosperity of all.

A particularly influential example of neoliberalism gaining ground as a political ideology was the intervention strategy used by the International Monetary Fund, the World Bank and the U.S. Treasury—referred to as the Washington Consensus (Williamson, 1990). It advocated 11 mechanisms, particularly for the developing economies then in crisis in Central and South America: fiscal responsibility; investment in growth, health, education and infrastructure; tax reform; market-determined interest rates; floating exchange rates; trade liberalization; international capital investment; privatization of state enterprises to promote choice and competition; deregulation of market entry and competition except for oversight of safety, environmental, consumer protection and financial institutions; legal security of property rights; and the *financialization* of capital. It is interesting that the countries targeted mostly had left-leaning governments who retained most features of the Consensus (with the marked exception of enabling financialization by deregulating banking), but that they often supplemented the Consensus with up to five of their own interventions: state investment to raise productivity; contesting poverty and ethnic disadvantage; encouraging business start-ups; improving the quality of justice and primary and secondary education; and developing and absorbing new technologies. This process of blending dry economic and social reform agendas suggests the presence of a political ideology that deliberately extracts theory from the language of political practice whereby pragmatic *rules for success* are created on the common ground between capitalist and socialist impulses, and progressively embeds them as trustworthy knowledge in each individual's web of belief and in collective understandings in politics. It points to the presence of an inclusionary, poststructural and postmodern form of pragmatism—neopragmatism. How does this relate to political philosophy in educational administration?

Returning to Stephen Ball's data, we see a great deal of evidence supporting his claim that neoliberalism has been central to the development of many international entrepreneurial networks in recent decades—transnational policy advocacy and mobility that increasingly bypasses traditional government structures and an expansion of the policy space to include educational businesses, voluntary and charity organizations, and public-private partnerships. We also see substantial evidence of how such networks became *epistemic communities* with their own rules for arbitrating knowledge claims about issues mutually recognized as significant, and for legitimating priorities and interventions.

However, in all fairness, we must concede in passing that schools of thought in academe exhibit many of the same features. The processes systematically overvalue internal coherence and are seen in all effective sociopolitical movements, especially those in recent decades enabled by advances in interconnectivity provided by information and communication technology such as in the Arab Spring.

One advantage of political philosophy is thereby demonstrated. By identifying the political ideologies involved, we can distinguish between purposes (ends), and question their justifications and the sociology of process (means). In my experience, the means turn out to be remarkably similar whatever the sociopolitical movement, so interest should focus on the ideological ends evident in the language of the politics of education.

This means that we need to consider and explain the substantial presence of political ideologies other than neoliberalism in Ball's evidence. First is the saliency of philanthropism and altruism, variants of humanitarianism, in educational partnerships that are clearly intended to improve the human condition. Philanthropism is profoundly educational in that it would help people become more fully humane through self-development. Altruism is primarily concerned with the welfare of others.

One of the most interesting cases that Stephen Ball provided, the Clinton Global Initiative, is clearly based on philanthropism and altruism with educational intent and is derived from a deliberately centrist Third Way political ideology. Other cases, such as the Bridge International Academies in Africa and Gyan Shala, Omega and Enterprising Schools, in India, all exhibit facets of neoliberalism but simultaneously reflect the so-called triple bottom line promoted by the United Nations since 1992 for measuring organizational and societal success: economic, ecological and social (otherwise known as People, Planet and Profit; United Nations Environment Programme, 2012).

The most common feature in Ball's data, to my reading, is that all of these businesses use a blend of political ideologies to try to make a real difference by creating educational opportunities for people living in truly wretched social and economic circumstances. Having once visited the largest slum in the world, in Mumbai, and leaving feeling utterly incapable of developing a possibly viable intervention, the accounts gave me glimmerings of hope. I was therefore puzzled when Ball collated critical opinions of such partnerships from blogs and web sites that appeared to be fundamentally uncomfortable with social liberalism and social capitalism on two grounds; the pragmatic reconciliation of historically hostile political ideologies and the blurring of familiar structures and meanings in the language of leaders. His judgment was that:

> These new sensibilities of giving have led to increasing use of commercial and enterprise models of practice as a new generic form of philanthropic organization, practice, and language—venture philanthropy, philanthropic portfolios, due diligence, entrepreneurial solutions, and so on . . . Traditional lines and demarcations, public and private, market and state, are being breached and blended in all of this and are no longer useful analytically as free-standing descriptors. (Ball, 2012, pp. 70–71)

Once again, this argument confuses means with ends and seeks to reinstate foundational truths preferred by socially critical theorists who remain implacably anticapitalist. Instead, it seems to me, the evidence calls for political philosophy in theory building that accepts the meanings in the language used to explain purposes and experience and establishes their epistemic relativity, rather than impose an interpretation that appears to back up into a privileged ideology. It appears to call for linguistic pragmatism rather than making heroic and ad hominem generalizations; for example, that:

> Neoliberalism is producing . . . new kinds of social actors, hybrid social subjects who are spatially mobile, ethically malleable, and able to speak the languages of public, private, and philanthropic value. . . . Together, these people, their relationships and interactions, and morality, and money and ideas and influence are transforming social, economic, and political relations and enacting

the neoliberal imaginary in very real and practical ways in education and education policy. (Ball, 2012, pp. 144–145)

This conclusion reaches beyond the limits of the methodology and data to declare that the processes and outcomes examined fail to meet the criteria of a private ideology. It sets aside the presence of other ideologies, such as variants of humanitarianism, communitarianism and environmentalism, offers no comparative evidence about the nature and quality of current policy processes and outcomes, and yet concludes with the iconoclastic warning:

> I have tried to make my points through cases and exemplars. I have tried to open things up, point to possibilities, or things needing to be done, to tools that might be used, to ways of thinking about what is going on, about what is happening to us . . . before it is too late and other imaginaries are cast into the "field of memory" or excluded from rational possibility. (Ball, 2012, p. 145)

Helen Gunter (2012) presents a very similar analysis and conclusion using the metaphor of gaming to explain policy processes in Britain in recent decades. Her starting and startling assumption is that "The leadership of schools *game* [original emphasis] can only be understood and explained through examining the underlying thinking about the borders between the state, markets and civil society, and how this is manifest in debates about the purposes of schooling" (p. 9).

Game? Only? Surely there is a place for thinking about how we think about borders and purposes, and other a prior constructs of such socially critical critique, in her case of supposedly rampant neoliberalism. To continue, she labeled the dominant policy team of players during the New Labor period in office, 1997–2010, as the New Labor Policy Regime (NLPR) and as comprising "ministers, civil servants, advisers, private consultants, researchers and some headteachers." The NLPR was contrasted with the Policy Research Regime (PRR) that "was (and is) a preferred location for social science researchers and some headteachers with a focus on scholarly critical analysis of policy and the identification of alternative approaches to reform" (Gunter, 2012, p. 3). This dualistic analysis found that the NLPR and its soon-orphaned institution, the National College of School Leadership, had in effect "white-washed out" all previous, diverse and research-linked higher education in leadership, including the possibility of "Master's degrees becoming de facto accreditation for promotion" (Gunter, 2012, p. 63).

This conclusion is fine as far as this approach to policy analysis permits. It appears that a fuller appreciation of the production of knowledge involved using political philosophy might have reflected critically on the market and other interests of the members of the PRR, that is, applying the sauce used for the goose on the gander. More serious, further limits to the unreflective social democratic ideology in play were also revealed:

> PRR engages in *symbolic exchange* [original emphasis] regarding the interplay between theory, research, and professional practice, with activism around

social justice . . . with independently funded research and contributions to debates that are congenial to the Labour Party's reimagining of the comprehensive school; and academia is not passive, with opportunities being taken by a range of educational researchers to fire back at current reforms . . . with resources and networks to connect with those committed to democratic renewal. (Gunter, 2012, p. 146)

Gunter concluded by confirming, citing Richardson (1997, p. 4), that "I am well aware that I play and I am a player in this research *game* [original emphasis] and like all researchers I am deeply engaged in the politics of knowledge production; 'the "field" is also a battleground, a minefield, a war zone, as well as an open, inviting expanse.' I look forward to the debate and further research" (Gunter, 2012, p. 150). Perhaps this slippage from gaming into military metaphors will give pause for thought about the urgent need for political philosophy in British educational policy studies.

Finally, we can turn to fresh and provisional evidence of how network organizations are reconstructing governance through *heterarchies* (multiple structures and asymmetric relations giving carriage to decision making and policy processes) to help extend the case for political philosophy to help advance understandings of how power is exercised in education. Stephen Ball and Carolina Junemann (2012) interviewed 25 leaders from philanthropic network organizations providing educational services and related their perceptions to material culled from web sites. Because this methodology did not create a comprehensive description of a culture, it falls well short of being an ethnography as claimed (Ball & Junemann, 2012, pp. 12–17). Nevertheless, on the basis of qualitative data from two sources, they presented provisional findings around three themes (with ideologies implicit); enterprise in philanthropy (commercialism and humanitarianism), philanthropy and the enterprise curriculum (humanitarianism and entrepreneurialism) and the philanthropy and social enterprise (humanitarianism and social liberalism). Despite this rich blend of ideologies, they concluded that the discourse of enterprise (capitalism) was dominant in all areas, "both as a reforming narrative and an effective infrastructure, of network governance." They went even further to claim that this discourse reflected the relationships "between philanthropy, the Third Way and the Big Society indicated in the previous chapter" (Ball & Junemann, 2012, p. 47). I am not so sure.

To me, this study suggested a role for political philosophy in disentangling political ideologies embedded in research perspectives and in the structuration of knowledge claims. Indeed, this potential function of political philosophy was demonstrated when they went on to hedge their position, again without identifying and discounting their ideological commitments.

Three and interrelated discourses appeared repeatedly in the research interviews and in the educational programmes and activities of corporate philanthropies. One articulates a concern with issues of *social disadvantage* [original emphasis], another is *meritocracy* [original emphasis] and the third is *enterprise* or *entrepreneurship* [original emphasis], but the three discourses can be seen to have a relationship and constitute a loose but coherent "discursive ensemble" that articulates a particular vision and purpose for education. In the simplest sense, educational philanthropy can provide opportunities to students and families with talent and ability whose education is inhibited by disadvantage. . . . In a number of cases, this kind of commitment reflects the personal experience of individual philanthropists and gives rise to a hybrid of individualism and communitarianism that is focused on the issue and problem of social mobility. (Ball & Junemann, 2012, p. 58)

This preliminary evidence from recent policy research also provides good grounds for considering the neopragmatism or linguistic pragmatism developed by Richard Rorty (1989). He argued that only the language of experience is actually available as the material for political philosophy and that we should set aside our beliefs in the possibility of universal truths, epistemological foundations, being able to reconstruct or fully represent social and economic relations, or to achieve epistemic objectivity. This should ring bells in educational administration. Recall one of Gronn's (1983) finest papers, *Talk as the Work: The Accomplishment of School Administration*, and Hodgkinson's (1996, p. 85) axiomatic reiteration that "Language cloaks and has power. Language is the basic administrative tool."

Language, Rorty suggested, is to be regarded as vocabularies contingent on usefulness and social conventions, leading to a way of thinking he referred to as *ironism* in which political philosophers are aware of where and why they are placed in history and the relativity of their vocabulary. He held a *social hope* that doing without accounts that relied on representation and metaphors between the mind and the world would lead to a more peaceful human society, a prospect I find congenial. With help, to this end, Clive Beck (1999) argued that:

> A common view is that broad principles of right and wrong should be established by experts such as philosophers and theologians, leaving ordinary people to work out the practical details. However, I accept Richard Rorty's claim that the production of knowledge (including moral knowledge) is everyone's business even at the most fundamental level. We must reject the "trickle down" view of value inquiry and see everyone—academics and ordinary people alike—grappling with both general principles and practical questions.

The only exposés of neopragmatism I have encountered in the theory of educational administration are those provided by Trevor Maddock. He pointed out that "the kind of pragmatism being considered here is associated with the contemporary *neopragmatism* [original emphasis] orientation in philosophy, perhaps the dominant academic approach over the last decades of the twentieth century in the USA" (Maddock, 1996, p. 219) Evers and Lakomski (1996, p. 238) accepted and endorsed this characterization of their political ideology. What they found less congenial was Maddock also pointing out (1996, p. 217) that their materialist pragmatism embodied "three dogmas" comprising (a) a belief that coherentism should serve as an alternative to foundationalism, (b) a belief that naturalism provides a bridge between philosophy and the natural sciences and (c) a belief that weak realism is preferable to instrumentalism or idealism with regard to the nature of knowledge. The general problem here is that dogmas have foundational characteristics.

To go back briefly, because epistemology is not the central concern of this book, Maddock had earlier pointed out that the materialist pragmatism proposed by Jim Walker (1985), and elaborated in Evers and Lakomski's epistemology (1991), had been derived from Quine's version of neopragmatism, rather than his preference, Adorno's version.

> The non-foundationalism of the materialist pragmatists is based in the claim that they have developed a theory which is without foundations. The non-foundationalism of Adorno turns on the acknowledgement that all theories have foundations. If this is the case, the only way for philosophy to proceed which avoids the pitfalls of foundationalism is through the critique of all foundations. Arguably, the non-foundationalism of the materialist pragmatists is simply a lack of self-consciousness about foundations. Their theory is simply blind to its foundations. Their non-foundationalism is based on the conception of a theory as an interconnected web in which each component justifies the others. However, the assumption of the success and coherence of science and the role it has played in human society has not been justified, and particularly not in the abstract terms of materialist pragmatism." (Maddock, 1994, pp. 53–54)

Nevertheless, Evers and Lakomski's rejoinder, of direct relevance to political analysis, did not deny these beliefs and proceeded to advance justifications for them:

> Because some theories plainly help us to get around in the world much more successfully than other theories, and because these theories may not be distinguishable from the others on the grounds of empirical adequacy, we conclude that additional, or *superempirical* [original emphasis] criteria of theory choice are doing valuable epistemological work. These additional criteria include consistency, comprehensiveness, simplicity, and explanatory unity, and, when taken together with empirical adequacy, are known as *coherence criteria*. . . . Our argument for naturalism in epistemology follows from the fact that theories of knowledge make all sorts of assumptions about the cognitive powers of humans: how we learn and process information. . . . This is why we follow Quine in freely using our best natural science to help determine how knowledge is acquired. For us, philosophy (or epistemology) does not come before scientific knowledge; rather, it is continuous with science. (Evers & Lakomski, 1996, p. 242)

Although this all seems reasonable, so far as it goes, the discomforting possibility remains that their three dogmas, a web of belief about epistemology to be sure, may actually be based on a coherent yet foundational ideology of liberalist neopragmatism. Plainly stung by Maddock's critique, Evers and Lakomski went on to reveal that they do hold to a particular political ideology in a discussion of structuration:

> Our view of ethics (and politics) is in the Deweyan/liberal tradition. We argue that knowledge has touchstone advantages over ignorance, but that all knowledge is fallible. Maintaining conditions for the growth of knowledge would therefore cohere well, as a heuristic, with a range of other substantive theoretical claims, comprising a global theory. But the contingent material conditions for knowledge growth require some ethical infrastructure to prescribe the relevant distribution of resources and the social relations of inquiry. Our arguments in defence of values of tolerance, freedom, and respect for the welfare of others owe much to Popper's defence of the Open Society against Plato and Marx. . . . In administrative theory this ethical perspective coheres best with the organizational learning tradition of administration, a view of leadership as educative, that is, as conducive to promoting individual and organizational learning, and a democratic, participatory vision of society.
> (Evers & Lakomski, 1996, p. 245)

The question I must now leave in the air is the extent to which their political ideology (which is a liberal democratic version of neopragmatism, weakly communitarian and largely deficient of communicative-rationalism and egalitarianism) plays a foundational role in their theory building about theory building. Space now insists that I leave epistemology to the epistemologists and come back to neopragmatism in the practical politics of educational administration below.

A summary to this point is warranted. The intimations of communitarianism, communicative rationalism and egalitarian liberalism in educational administration reviewed in this, and in the previous chapter, signal three important and largely potential roles for political philosophy.

First are the technical methods of meta-analysis that can contribute to the growth of knowledge about the wisdom of political arrangements. Political philosophy offers a rigorous process of articulating the nature and blend of personal ideologies in use in particular situations. It can be used to distinguish the part that personal ideologies play in justifications for current arrangements. It provides means for identifying the relativism in any absolutist ideology that is creating an impasse in theory building. It enables a scholarship of integration that might reconcile justifications for arrangements that back up into blended positions. It encourages respectful tolerance of seemingly incommensurable components, whereas policy research is mounted to evaluate the alternatives and create common ground. It promotes the development of modest and tentative, rather than definitive, knowledge claims—principally because of the technical challenges of determining the extent to which principles are universal and reflect the assumptions and values of a particular political community or the nature of human beings, their needs, capacities and limitations.

Second is the form of understanding and type of critique that political philosophy can add to the rationally critical account of educational administration. Given the powerful role that educational administrators have in creating, managing and transforming the power structures in education, as well as perceptions of them, politically critical analysis and evaluation are essential components of educative reflection on practice. It is inconceivable that a comprehensive philosophy of educational administration would not employ political philosophy to explicate the substantive components relating to power.

Third is the capacity of political philosophy to review pragmatism and its potential to capture theory when embedded in the language of professional standards of public school leadership. One respectful approach might be to investigate the ethnocentricity of prevailing orthodoxy. Another will be to investigate the extent to which American pragmatism represents the full scope of American philosophy. It has been viewed disapprovingly by various continental philosophers as an "expression of characteristically American social attitudes; crude materialism and naïve democratic populism . . . reflecting a quintessentially crass American tenor of thought—a philosophical expression of the American go-getter spirit with its success-orientated ideology, and a manifestation of a populist reaction against the chronic ideological controversies of European philosophizing" (Rescher, 2005, p. 23.)

Another and potentially even more fruitful avenue might be to investigate pragmatism's suggested incapacity to reflect critically on its own assumptions or to develop the intellectual flexibility and modesty to search for advantages in communitarianism, communicative rationalism and egalitarian liberalism. It has been suggested that the continued strength of pragmatism in educational administration may be based on two mistaken assumptions about professional morality derived from another tradition in American thought:

> One that divides the terrain of ethics into public and private spheres. On one side of this divide are public values such as equality, liberty, and democracy to which all citizens subscribe; on the other side are matters of personal conscience such a religious beliefs, life style, and political ideology. This approach to the moral world is practically and politically important because it represents the way in which Americans realize *e pluribus unum*, or unity in diversity. Public values are not only what unite Americans into a single people but also, because they include commitments to toleration and equality before the law, what makes it possible for them to be diverse. Within the sphere of private values, Americans are free to determine and live out their diversity in meaningful ways. (Bull & McCarthy, 1995, pp. 623–626)

Such a pragmatic accommodation of diversity may lead an educational administrator to assume that public values are quite separate from private values; the former are to do with moral relations between citizens, and therefore quite properly the concern of professionals, with the latter a private matter between individuals and thus not the business of professionals. It may also lead to another assumption that public values are based more on reason, whereas private values are based more on intuition, feelings and cultural norms.

These distinctions collapsed for many when John Rawls's (1987) egalitarian liberalism portrayed the public and private spheres as having an overlapping consensus of alternative comprehensive moral doctrines. In his account, citizens and professionals were seen as having public commitments that are continuous with their private commitments. Individuals' commitments to public values could therefore be justified with both public and private reasons, such as maintaining a stable and just political order that coheres with the other conditions for a good life. Reasonable disagreements on public values can be tolerated while also sustaining a shared commitment to them.

On these subtle grounds, Bull and McCarthy (pp. 625–626) recommended that school leaders should be educated to expect and respect private ideologies and for religious beliefs to form part of parents' criticisms, as part of legitimate public deliberation over policy and practice in public schools. Parallel logic would suggest that practitioners, researchers and theorists in educational administration should expect and respect private ideologies and diverse beliefs to form part of legitimate public "thinking about thinking" concerning policy making and implementation and for administrative action to increasingly incorporate philosophy-in-action. This brings us back to the fundamental purposes and methods of political philosophy and their relevance to educational administration.

Probably the most sophisticated attempt to date to bring political philosophy to the attention of the field of educational administration is the collection edited by Eugénie Samier with Adam Stanley (Samier & Stanley, 2008). Although I indicate a limitation below, it is strongly recommended. It conceptualized politics on three levels: "the political philosophy and theory that provide conceptions and values, the political structures that shape formal institutions and informal constructions, and the political processes that characterize everyday political life" (Samier, 2008b, p. 3).

At the first level, the text provided innovative and elegant philosophical resources that may prove helpful in deepening political philosophy projects in educational administration. Let me illustrate with condensed summaries. There is an investigation of how cooperative and scholarly leadership in universities might reconcile Machiavellian realpolitik with Republican virtues (Migone, 2008). There is a humanistic case made using Kant's and Hegel's ideals about liberal democracy to require educational institutions to prepare students for citizenship, with reflective and critical abilities, and require states to provide for educational freedom (Samier, 2008a). There is an exploration of how Habermas related human interests to the politics of knowledge, advanced communicative and strategic action as methods of shaping organizational culture and suggested how power can be used in private lives and in civil society, and by the state to reach toward greater equality, justice and freedom (Milley, 2008). There is a description of how Hayek argued for deliberately light-handed leadership based on 19th-century Gladstonian liberalism, as an alternative to the state perverting the natural or spontaneous forms of social and civic order (Gronn, 2008). There is an analysis of how Bourdieu's political theories compare with those from critical theory and Foucault's conceptions of social structures, especially as regards discourse, taste, skills and other forms of capital, with implications on how to blend local traditions with skills to empower communities and extend literacy (Harris, 2008). There is study of how Arendt's hermeneutic theories of thinking, intelligence and meaning, as an alternative to the *thoughtlessness* of bureaucracy, lead on to forms of action, thinking and educational administration practices that focus primarily on the interpretative process of making sense (Mackler, 2008). There is an analysis using Foucault's ideas about ethics and societal structures to suggest that American public education is overly conditioned by structuralism, to the point where it is argued that the reform of schooling and technologies needs to be consistent with the U.S. Supreme Court's interpretation of the free speech clause of the First Amendment; as *freedom of thought* rather than merely as *freedom of expression* (Fazzaro, 2008).

At the second level, the text provides diverse examples of forms of political analysis in education. More brief, the examples include a postmodernist study of the negative consequences of high-stakes accountability on school leaders (Schmidt, 2008); the potential of alternative theoretical frameworks such as critical race theory, feminist poststructural theory and queer theory (Young & López, 2008); the speculated capacity of voluntary associations in civil society and educational leadership to bridge the state and the market globally in support of ideas of the public good (Bates, 2008); the possibility of German existentialism (after Husserl and Heidegger) informing the development of constructivism in adult education, specifically in museums (Diket, 2008); and finally, how politics of community can question imposed solutions to *underachievement,* managed participation and explore conditions of educational disadvantage from within the communities in which they are experienced (Angus, 2008). Although the substantive content analyzed was diverse, and each chapter made a significant contribution to the field, there were only two forms of political ideology used for analysis, communitarianism and communicative rationalism, without reference to their ideological relativity. They suggest a new orthodoxy of scholarly critique in the politics of educational administration.

This limitation became even more explicit at the third level where chapters explored current political issues and processes in education. Included here were critiques of neoliberalism in three Canadian provinces (Wallace, 2008); the role of neoliberalism evident in students' voices in undermining the trust and respect between teachers, students and communities needed for creative and productive learning in knowledge economies (Smyth, 2008); the *New McCarthyism* embodying a typology of right-wing perspectives being used to assault academic thought in American colleges and universities (English, 2008); and how supranational organizations are using their power to influence the education systems of nation states, most notably to achieve the economic and managerialist purposes favored by the International Monetary Fund (Bottery, 2008). Again there is a new orthodoxy favoring communitarianism and communicative rationalism over egalitarian liberalism and neopragmatism without justification, a hidden imbalance that this text sets out to challenge.

These first four chapters have revealed the latent, developing and increasingly critical role of political philosophy in the growth of knowledge in the field of educational administration. They defined the key concepts and tools of analysis offered by political philosophy to assist with the development of politically critical meta-analysis and evaluation in the field. A key point made was that given the concentration of power in the hands of educational administrators, and their command of structuration (Giddens, 1984, pp. 281–373) in educational organizations, political philosophy should be regarded as essential to reflective practice, to research into the politics of education and administration, and to theory building intended to elaborate the rationally critical account of educational administration. The brief examination of the history of educational administration showed that, although variants of the political ideology of pragmatism have been dominant for many decades, there is growing evidence that communitarianism, communicative rationalism and egalitarian liberalism are becoming increasingly influential in advancing the growth of knowledge in the field. There is a recent possibility of a new orthodoxy in political philosophy emerging in educational administration that would favor a blend of communitarianism and communicative rationalism.

Two interim recommendations are offered prior to illustrating the central propositions of this book with a series of case studies. The first is that the technical capacity of political philosophy be openly employed in the field to question, deconstruct, reconstruct and reconcile ideologies during theory building. Reasonable disagreement on ideological grounds can be tolerated while maintaining a shared commitment to advancing a rationally critical account of the field using political philosophy. This approach will be enabled by adopting a nonfoundational epistemology.

The second is to boost the development of politically critical practice, research and theory in the field to better understand and develop current concepts, political arrangements and their justifications during policy making and educational leadership.

In sum, to this point, if power is the first term in the administrative lexicon, and moral dilemmas are at the heart of powerful administrative practices, then political philosophy should be used to provide a provisional *last word* evaluation of the structuring and use of power by leaders. The coming chapters are case studies of educational administration in controversial circumstances and are offered to further illustrate the fecundity of political philosophy, before considering its limitations.

Part II

Case studies of becoming an educational leader

5 Becoming a primary school principal in New Zealand

This chapter, originally developed in collaboration with Rangimaria (a pseudonym), uses political philosophy to question the quality of the professionalization policy and provisions for newly appointed primary (elementary) school principals in New Zealand/Aotearoa. It also questions how wisely the Ministry of Education is using its power in a liberal democracy to determine such professional development structure. It does this by describing a typical setting for novice leadership, giving voice to a newly appointed female and Maori principal, evaluating the purposes and scale of funded professionalization and then pointing to aberrant outcomes enabled by the ambiguous distribution and misuse of power in the school system.

When the case study basis for this chapter was first drafted in the mid 2000s, Rangimaria was the principal of near 60-pupil, three-teacher, coeducational, rural and decile 7 state primary school.[1] Our primary purpose was to raise policy issues concerned with improving the preparation of primary school principals. We shared four assumptions: good leadership can be taught and nurtured; the primary purpose of leadership in schools is to facilitate high quality teaching and learning; principals' learning needs vary as they progress through their careers; and intercultural leadership perspectives can inform theory and practice in a multicultural society. This chapter condenses the original account and adds political philosophy to the analysis.

A brief description of the school, its facilities and its geographic and socioeconomic setting follows. It is accompanied by Rangimaria's *verbatim* account of her preparation, induction, experiences and development as a primary school principal. A review of leadership professionalization policies and practices of the state education system then leads to a tentative summary of key policy issues and implications related to the structures of power in primary education.

Rangimaria's school is on a quiet, tar-sealed rural road. It is typical of small rural schools in New Zealand. A notice board decorated with Maori carving welcomes visitors. A wheelchair ramp takes visitors into an airy reception area tastefully decorated with children's art. This area provides access to the school secretary's office, the principal's office, a resource room, the staffroom and three classrooms—all carpeted. The internal decoration of the school is fresh and bright, predominantly in green pastel colors. Large pin boards display children's work.

The open architecture of the school features a functional assembly of prefabricated units with gently sloping, green corrugated iron roofs. The outdoor areas include asphalted playing areas, grassed sports areas and large shade trees on more than a hectare of flat land. The school has other stand-alone buildings: a library, a hall, a meeting room and a teacher's residence. The school also has a vegetable garden, a climbing frame area and a sandpit for junior students and a "confidence course" for the senior children.

Beyond the school are rolling grasslands and blocks of pine trees. Dairy farming in the area is doing well, primarily due to Fonterra's successful marketing of milk solids into China. The economics of forestry are steadily recovering from the international recession with demand growing from China and India. A short distance from the school and along the main road is a small town built around a junction, a transport business and a dormitory suburb of a nearby regional city.

Compensation settlements in recent years at the Waitangi Tribunal have seen substantial transfers of land ownership from the government to iwi (tribal federations) trusts in the region and early revitalization of the Maori economy and long-term investment, such as education scholarships. More than 50% of the school's children self-nominate as Maori with nearly 70% boys. They present themselves as smartly dressed, active, confident and bright-eyed learners.

The principal, Rangimaria, identifies herself as Maori. She is a woman in her late forties, married and the mother of children that have left home. Her husband, who also self-defines as Maori, is a middle manager in a company located in the nearby city. They are comfortably well-off and middle-class professionals.

Rangimaria's office is unpretentious. She has two desks linked to form an L-shaped work surface. She has a modern computer that enables her to communicate online with her secretary and teachers through an intranet. She also has links to the ministry and its databases via a high-speed network, regularly submitting information and receiving directions. She has filing cabinets under two other work surfaces and bookshelves. From her office, she can see along the verandahs outside each classroom and across the asphalted and grassed playing areas.

Rangimaria came to this three-teacher school as a senior teacher at the beginning of a school year in the late 2000s and was promoted to principal in early February the year following. Her career trajectory has been meteoric. She taught for seven years after teacher training, served one year as a teaching principal in a sole-charge (one-teacher) school, one term as a senior teacher and two terms as an acting principal before being given permanency as principal of her current school.

Her professionalization centered almost exclusively on becoming a teacher with negligible preparation to become a leader. She did not receive preparatory training or higher education prior to taking up any of the four leadership roles she has experienced: team leader, senior teacher, deputy principal and principal. The learning of leadership in each case was done on the job and through short training courses after appointment, with some mentoring and networking.

As a school principal, Rangimaria is responsible for the management of three teachers, a school secretary/teacher aide and a part time cleaner. Her school is governed by a local board of trustees that comprises six elected parents, an elected staff representative and herself, *ex officio*. She also reports electronically to the Ministry of Education against national priorities and regularly to its regional officials about implementation. Her story follows, lightly edited.

My legal name is Rangimaria. When I was young, people used to pronounce it wrong, even Maori, although it is not so bad these days. I disliked it intensely when people got it wrong.

My parents are both from the [coastal area]. I have maintained my connections with my iwi. Many family members still live on the coast. My whakapapa [genealogy] means that I know where I come from. The whenua [land or placenta] holds great significance for Maori.

My whakapapa gives me a greater depth of understanding of Maori children and how they think. I love teaching and came to this school because over 50% of the roll are Maori children. My last school was a sole-charge principal school with 98% rural Pakeha [non-Maori] children. I tried it for a year, and it was totally different. Before that I had been at a city school with over 70% Maori kids. When a senior teacher position came up in this school, the Maori roll appealed. I had to decide between staying in a European school as a principal or stepping down to senior teacher to be in a school with over 50% Maori students.

I started in this school last year and was here two weeks when the principal offered me the deputy principal position. She said that my pay level would have to go up, so I said that was OK.

In the second term, she called me into her office and said she had been thinking about a six-month secondment into the ministry. She wanted me to act as principal. I accepted the acting position, with reservations. At the end of the six months, she resigned as principal and took another position in the ministry. The principal's position here was advertised. I was appointed permanent principal by the school's board of trustees about a month ago.

Looking back, I did seven years as a teacher, then one year as principal of a sole-charge school and then less than a year here as a senior teacher before being appointed permanent principal.

Everyone said "Don't go to a sole charge school. That's a lot of work." The challenge for me was the professional and cultural isolation. I had gone from a city school with over 300 children to a school with 10 kids. I absolutely loved the teaching. It was also my first time at teaching senior level. You could see every student every day, spend quality time with them, and when you set work, it was always finished. The senior kids were of similar ability and so were the juniors, so they were grouped for learning.

While I loved the teaching, the professional isolation was difficult. There was no one to bounce your ideas off. The nearest school was 20 minutes away. The community was very different. In term three, my board resigned, so in term four, I worked with a commissioner.

At the end of the year, it seemed to me that the board had not looked after me. I had done my job, but the board had not done theirs. From the beginning, the board gave me the impression that I was an outsider coming in. I didn't live in the community; I stayed in the school house for two terms, but it didn't work for me, so I moved back home and commuted. It was a 45-minute drive each way.

Most of the Maori children in the area went to a nearby bilingual [Maori and English] school. When I started the sole-charge position, there were two Maori children in the school, but they moved when their parents got a farming contract in another area. The sole-charge school had an all-Pakeha community, and I was able to make some very positive connections with many of them. The key issue I had at this school was having to work with a very small board who wanted to have "more say" in management than I thought was appropriate.

The school community here is lovely, much more open. They were ready for a change in principal. The communication here seems to be good, and getting even better after two terms. It is partly because they have got used to me and how I do things. Also they have seen that I am an effective teacher.

In hindsight, I always go back to the fact that the board at the sole-charge school was all women, MWFs, middle-aged white females, who loved to tell me how to do my job. We had trouble with communication, so I brought it up as an issue with the chairperson. As with any issue I raised, it was very different when it was discussed later at a board meeting. After some discussion amongst themselves, the board chair and the treasurer said that I had the communication problem. They did not want to work on our communication and resigned.

A commissioner was appointed by the ministry and that worked out very well, a really nice guy. At the end of the year, it was obvious that the board members who had resigned were going to move their children to other schools. In discussions with the commissioner, he advised me that my own future should be my priority. He explained that if I found another position, the children who were left, and the community, would get over it.

There was a teacher in the community that had applied when I applied for the principal's position. She did not have what they wanted, that is, junior school experience. She did live in the community and had been commuting to a city school. The commissioner put her in as an acting principal when I resigned, and it turned out to be a good solution. Fifteen months down the track, I believe the school still does not have a board, and the Commissioner is still in place.

My attitude to the whole experience at the sole-charge school was always "What have I learned from this?" Coming here and stepping up into the acting principal's position meant making sure that my communication was effective, so that the same thing didn't happen again. Before I went to the sole-charge school, I thought my communication was pretty good. At the end of that year, I had to say to myself "Was it as good as you thought?" "Could you have done things differently?" The experience created doubts, and I carried those doubts through to my current job and worked really hard at building networks. Maybe they were right. There were a couple of things that I would now do differently. But overall, I always put children's learning first in my decisions.

Looking back, there were many signs of successful communication at the sole-charge school. The board was only three people. Initially it was four, but when the Maori family left, the Maori trustee left. When it came to decisions, it was always two versus one. My communication issues were with the board chair, but the treasurer always chose to follow her. They would always back each other, even if one of them was wrong.

I learned that communication and trust between a board chair and a principal must be highly effective. They have to be open with each other. The chair of the board at this school walks in and always asks if I have any issues. Sometimes I ask him if he has any issues. The communication is always open. We always go back to the line between governance and management.

In my interview, they asked me where the line is, and I said "It changes." You always have to go back to agreeing where the line is on each issue, so there is no misunderstanding. It's helpful that half of the board at this school are men. They seem to be more focused on their own individual roles and on getting things done. They don't meddle in others' responsibilities.

I always wanted to be a teacher. When I was 17, I promised my father that I would be a teacher. I assumed that all parents in the 1970s wanted their kids to become teachers because that was looked upon as being quite a good career. I had got my university entrance by then and promised my Dad that I would become a teacher. But I didn't. I did some of this and some of that, everything except teaching.

My Mum and Dad were farming people. My father was also very clever, a justice of the peace, a toastmaster, an articulate man of the land. He was a kaumatua [elder] and chairman of the marae in the days when everything was based around the marae. He was comfortable dealing with all types of people, even politicians. So the promise was always with me, and after "mucking about" for a number of years, I finally said to my husband when I was in my thirties, "I want to go and do my teacher training. If I don't do it before I am 40, I will never do it."

The decision was also triggered by a sense of security. Our children were older, and the oldest had left home. We were more secure. Our relationship was good. Our family relationships and finances were good. We were comfortable. Then I remembered that I had made a promise to Dad.

I always thought I would make a good teacher. My sister had trained several years earlier as a secondary teacher, and I could see how much she enjoyed teaching. It was a significant shift because I gave up a full-time job with [a government department]. When I told the other staff in the department that I was leaving to do teacher training, many of them said that they had dreamed about having other careers. They had all these things that they really wanted to do in their heads that they did not follow through on. Some of them are still there!

I gradually realized that I wanted to offer leadership as I went through the steps of accepting more and more responsibility. I went to my first school as a beginning teacher and stayed there for seven years. I worked my way up. I became a team leader, a senior teacher, and it got to the stage when I felt that I had to get out of my little comfort zone, where I knew all the procedures, processes and the kids.

When I had been in my first school for about three years, the chairperson of the board encouraged me to stand as the staff representative. I did that for four years and loved it. I realized that I was learning more and more about how a school runs. If that woman had not told me to go on the board, I probably would not have considered principalship.

After seven years I felt the need to get out, spread my wings, make my own mistakes and learn from it. I realized that in a big school one of the rewards you get for working well is more work. I was doing all this extra work, and the benefits were going somewhere else. I used to think that the one who is getting the pats on the back is not me! It is the one at the top! I love teaching, and I'm not afraid of hard work, so I decided that I would give the principal role a try.

I expected leadership to be scary. Initially I thought that you had to know everything. I thought I could not be a principal because you have to know everything, and all I know is how to teach. That is why I chose a small school to start. I thought "I can't do much damage if it is such a small school!" I knew it would mean hard work, but I was used to that.

I didn't really prepare for my sole-charge principalship. I just went in and started teaching. There was no systematic induction. I organized a visit of my class to the school in December 2007 before I came in the New Year as principal. I visited the school in January. No meeting with the board. It was "turn up on the first day and start." I turned up a week early, organized teaching resources and tidied up the staffroom and moved the library. My induction was tidying up the school and putting resources back to where they were supposed to be.

It was great in term one. I was focused on setting up learning programs and getting to know the kids. In term two, I had these little niggling doubts that things weren't right. By term three, I knew that the state of communication between the chair of the board and me was not right. I had two options: to let things carry on as they were or insist on change. That is when I decided to express my concerns to the board chair. The governance relationship was not working, and it needed to work well so that I could do my job well. Honest communication was missing in the school culture. When decisions were made and agreements reached, what happened in reality was different. We never seemed to discuss the mismatch. I was looking for honesty in communication, agreements and implementation.

For example, we had a Parents and Teachers Association. It was run by the parents to raise funds for school projects and resources. My husband and I supported these fundraising events, sometimes standing out in the cold all day. After the event, the funds raised were put into a separate bank account controlled by the parent group. They would not release money to help with learning resources and programs. We were scrimping to buy teaching materials while they sat on $20,000, doing nothing. When I asked for minutes of their meetings and bank statements, they did not have any. I went to the board chair, but she refused to intervene.

One board member, a forceful lady, would come into school on "board business." Her daily presence on site was unnecessary, and during these periods, she took to giving advice on teaching and other events. I felt that she was not doing her job but telling me how to do mine. She kept interfering in my management decisions. She had crossed the line from governance to become a school manager. I asked her not to do this. I also asked the chair to speak to her about her role. The chair said "I can't. She is my friend."

When I first arrived at my current school, my impression was that the boundary between governance and management was very strict, very formal. I learned the word "territory." The previous principal and I had a good relationship, but there was always an underlying feeling that things would always be done "her way." At the time, it seemed to me to be a power thing.

I am now much more informal as principal, more flexible. If anything, this has improved the relationships between myself, the community and the board. Honesty is more evident. For example, even when I was acting principal, I mentioned to the principal that "the board would be silly to let her go on another temporary secondment because it was about improving her career, not student's learning." However, it became clear that they were happy for her to go and to give her leave for a second secondment. In the end, she decided to resign. These discussions showed me that there was a high level of trust and openness between us, as leaders. If there is respectful and honest communication, then it takes you through any misunderstandings that arise.

Professional development helped me but always came after my appointments. When I was appointed the school literacy leader at my first school, I went on several day-long workshops that helped a lot. Once I had started at my sole-charge school, I joined the First Time Principals (FTP) Programme. It was very interesting. You received support from the School Support Services, access to a mentor and attended two three-day workshops in Auckland with other first-time principals. The groups at the workshops were based on the size of your school, so we could discuss common issues. The keynote speakers presented research findings, and we followed up with group discussions. I was given a great mentor, and the networking was very helpful. Some of these friendships are still going. One of principals in my group brought her sole-charge school to visit us here last year when I was acting principal. It was awesome. The kids loved it.

The aspects of the FTP that really worked well were the workshops, the mentoring and the networking. The aspect that was not effective was school support. I saw my school support person twice in the whole year, but I had to go to her. She never visited my school. She was always busy, probably with too much to do. If I wanted to discuss anything, because we lived in the same city, it was easier for me to drop in to her office. But she was often "tied up" and "booked out" for weeks. One barrier at my last school was that it was often difficult to get relievers to come into the sole-charge school. It meant that I missed out on some professional development that would have been really useful.

After I had been appointed here as a senior teacher, I did the National Aspiring Principals Programme (NAPP) run by experienced principals for the local Principals Association. The course has four one-day workshops spread over a year. They cover basic management and leadership issues. I enjoyed reinforcing what I already learned from the FTP workshops and picking up tips from other leaders who had been through visioning processes and strategic planning. The networking was very helpful.

Being "the boss" leads me to think a lot about what sort of a boss I am. Above all, I try to be fair. Fairness means teachers knowing what I expect and why, and, at the end of the day, being able to relate expectations back to student achievement, student learning, safety and welfare. If teachers come to me and say "Rangimaria, this is what I want to do, this is why I want to do it and they can show me how students will benefit," then I usually say "Go for it!" At the end of the learning experience, I expect them to come back to me and explain what worked and what didn't.

The teachers tell me that the change from strict to interactive professionalism means them having greater freedom to "think outside the square" and to try approaches that they would not have tried before. I often say "I don't know if it's going to work, but we are going to give it a go." Teachers change slowly. We are getting there. There is still some territorialism over resources but more thinking about using resources to help learning. There is only one teacher left from two years ago, so the old strict culture is going. The new teachers collaborate easily in the new culture.

Parents have responded to the changes by saying that "There is a different atmosphere around the school. The kids are happier." It used to be "Sit up straight" and "Don't move," and the parents felt that that was unnecessary. We have an Ag Day [Agriculture Day] here. After my first Ag Day, the board chair said, "I am sick and tired of hearing all about you. All I have had is parents telling me how wonderful you are."

The cultural change has also freed up the communication of complaints. I had two parents come in separately to provide feedback on a young teacher. They took their issues to the board chair who sent them to me. I listened, along with a board member who was there with the permission of the parents. The issue was about a very good beginning teacher who did not yet have all the strategies, knowledge and behavior management skills she needed to teach efficiently.

When I provided a summary for the teacher, she asked "how can they say that when they have not been in my room?" We assumed that a teacher's aide was passing on criticisms to other parents. Comments made by the parents included "the kids have too much fun!" The teacher and I discussed some simple strategies to fill in some of the gaps in her experience. I have got better at carrying criticism back to colleagues. When dealing with parents and teachers, it's best to let them have their say, so they "get it off their chest," and then collaborate with them to make improvements.

When I arrived here, I was the stranger. I was soon a deputy boss, but my authority was ambiguous. The longest serving staff member had the greatest difficulty with this, claiming not to know who was in charge. The secondment was only 0.8, so "the boss" came in on Fridays. The boss and I had distributed portfolios, so we were clear on responsibilities, and all the staff were in the loop, but this teacher saved up her questions for the boss on Fridays. The principal asked her why she had not raised them with me during the week, and she claimed to be confused. She was pleading ignorance, but it might have been game playing.

The biggest policy issue we hear about at the moment is national standards. The government and the ministry want us to match student learning against benchmarks and report on this at specific times each year. The purpose of this is to enforce evidence-based teaching and reporting. Part of the problem with this is that students in a year group have a wide range of abilities, needs and outcomes, and teachers need to learn how to make appropriate professional judgments. Another part of the problem is that teachers have doubts because there have been no trials nationally that have *shown evidence of success in using national standards. A third concern is that the emphasis on standards distracts the government and the ministry from the need to provide appropriate learning resources. It also distracts attention from the need to improve the quality of teaching—investment in professional development is needed to respond to the outcomes of reporting. For me, it means helping my teachers come to grips with reporting against national standards while they are still learning about the "new" national curriculum that came out in 2007.*

My big successes as a principal in this school have been in identifying the children's needs and the gaps in learning, by testing and visiting classrooms and using my experience. This has led to a much more exciting curriculum and improvements to teaching, such as Education Outside the Classroom, to visit "the world out there." The two new teachers will help speed up this process. When I got here, the evaluation data stayed in a bag. It was not used to identify needs, gaps and students' next learning steps. I have introduced an "evidence book," so that we log test data and keep running records on each child's progress.

The biggest challenge I have is that my teachers are just getting their heads around the New Zealand curriculum launched three years ago, while the government is insisting that we also report learning progress against new national standards. We will get there, but it will take time. In all this, my greatest hope is that the kids will get to where they should be. As long as I can say I have done my best, then it will have to do. I benchmark everything using evidence of student achievement.

Given the purposes of this chapter, it focuses first on how Rangimaria came to understand power as a dimension of school leadership. Basic to her understanding of her political and professional self is her ethnic identity. Her pathway to leadership was indicated by her promise to her father, a revered tribal leader, indicating traditional notions of inherited leadership traits. It was paved by a period as an elected staff representative on a school board of trustees and then initiated with an appointment as a sole-charge or teaching principal, suggesting an attitudinal change about leadership related to familiarity and confidence.

Her greatest challenge was learning to share power across two divides: governance and management, and Maori and Pakeha. When the legitimacy of her leadership was undermined by the mass resignation of her board of trustees, a ministry agent, the commissioner, helped her to deselect herself from this culturally uncomfortable setting and its norms of accountability, and to select another school community where the cultural affiliations with children, parents and colleagues were immediately more congenial and allowed her to assert her professionalism relatively unhindered as a master teacher.

In the new setting, Rangimaria acquired the power to define the line between governance and management in her school, issue by issue. The formal power of the board of trustees to govern school policy was reduced to a list of functions that she deemed to be supportive of her professionalism. Moral legitimation of her leadership was therefore based neither on (a) specific principles embedded as structures and formal duties, (b) a strategic consideration of consequences, nor (c) determined by consensus among appropriate stakeholders, but on her current and pragmatic professional judgment about the best interests of children within the perceived limits of ministry policy. This approach to legitimation usurps the formal powers of the board of trustees to govern school policy and marginalizes local stakeholders represented on the board of trustees. It restricts the legitimation of her leadership to the vagaries of public perceptions of her professional standing, that is, makes her vulnerable to local opinion leaders.

The aspects of professional development considered least helpful by her, such as the implementation of evidence-based national standards overtaking a previous government's national curriculum, offend Rangimaria's sense of righteous and self-managed professionalism. The aspects of professional development considered most helpful are those that support and extend her unique and culturally specific view of her professionalism. The common denominator here is a professional ego driving leadership services in a way that is relatively unmediated by educative governance. This is not appropriate in a school that, by definition and national policy, must be a learning organization. Rather than attribute blame to the individual, the policy issue here is how such a situation came to be through the processes of professionalization, and who controls these processes and to what ends.

The wider policy context is now reviewed to identify how the use of power impacts on the professionalization of principals. The power to determine leadership professionalization policy is vested in the Ministry of Education. In 2009 it announced a new *Professional Leadership Plan 2009–2012* (PLP; 2009d). Curiously, the PLP was clear on priorities, very weak on justification, and vague and scarce on opportunities. The detail of the PLP program actually had to be collated from three other sources: the Collective Agreements (Ministry of Education, 2009a), Professional Development provisions (Ministry of Education, 2009c) and Information for Experienced Principals (Ministry of Education, 2009b). The objectives of the PLP and the scale of opportunities it offers to leaders in primary and secondary schools, are summarized in Table 5.1 and suggest a professionalization policy and program in need of strategic review and refurbishment.

Because these provisions were to meet the needs of over 15,000 teachers designated as being in leadership positions (Ministry of Education, 2008) in a workforce of about 50,000, they can be regarded as being inadequate in scale. Worse, this parsimonious level of investment in leadership preparation was overtaken by crises in supply and quality triggered by the bulge of Baby Boomer retirements.

To clarify, the bulge is resulting in accelerated career advancement and leader turnover and growing concerns over leadership quality. As Rangimaria's case illustrates, accelerated promotion without preparatory training or higher education prior to leadership appointments, especially by Maori and Pacifika leaders, had become the norm in New Zealand primary schools. Table 5.1 shows that the ministry's leadership professionalization policy favors low cost and minimal leadership training after appointment over prior and systematic higher education and training in leadership.

This was not fresh news. The crises in the supply and quality of educational leaders had been developing steadily for many years. In the year ending May 2008, leader turnover rose to over 1,200 educators leaving the middle management, senior management, and principal positions in primary, area, secondary and special schools (Ministry of Education, 2008). The key policy issue at that time was deemed to be the sexism and racism evident in local boards of trustees' selection practices that were occasionally impeding the appointment of the best person available (Brooking, 2005, 2008a, 2008b, 2008c). It led to the development of

Table 5.1 The objectives and scale of opportunities offered by the *professional leadership plan 2009–2012*

Level	Objectives	Scale of opportunities
Middle and senior leaders	Middle and senior leaders are to: 1 Implement national standards in literacy and numeracy. 2 Improve the achievement of every student with a particular focus on Maori, Pasifika and students with special education needs. 3 Embed teaching practices that are culturally responsive and based upon the evidence of what improves outcomes for diverse students.	The funded opportunities include: • Access to 75 one-year study leave awards. • Access to 40 (from 2009)/50 (from 2010) 10-week awards of paid sabbatical leave. • Access to one Konica Minolta Dame Jean Herbison NZEALS Scholarship per annum. • Access to within-school professional development in literacy, numeracy and curriculum. • Access to management units, allowances and release time. • Access to leadership and management advisers. • Access to specialist classroom teachers. • Access to online tools and resources through the Educational Leaders web site. • Access to professional networks.
Aspiring principals	Aspiring principals are: 1 To be identified and developed for principal positions in hard-to-staff schools, with a focus on developing Maori and Pasifika teachers as principals. 2 To ensure a pool of quality applicants.	The funded opportunities include: • Access to 75 one-year study leave awards. • Access to 40 (from 2009)/50 (from 2010) 10-week awards of paid sabbatical leave. • Access to 230 places per annum on the National Aspiring Principals Programme. • Access to one Konica Minolta Dame Jean Herbison NZEALS Scholarship per annum. • Access to within-school professional development in literacy, numeracy and curriculum. • Paid management units, allowances and release time. • Access to leadership and management advisers. • Access to specialist classroom teachers. • Access to online tools and resources through the Educational Leaders web site. • Access to professional networks.

First-time principals	FTPs are to be inducted in order to: 1 Manage school operations effectively and efficiently. 2 Lead change to create the conditions for effective teaching and learning for every student, with a particular focus on Maori, Pasifika and students with special education needs. 3 Engage with family and whanau to improve student outcomes.	The funded opportunities include: • Access to 200 places in the 18-month First-time Principals Programme. • Access to 75 one-year study leave awards. • Primary and area school FTPs in U1 and U2 schools—10 days professional development release time over 18 months. • Access to one Konica Minolta Dame Jean Herbison NZEALS Scholarship per annum. • Access to regional office induction program. • Access to leadership and management support. • Access to within-school professional development. • Access to schooling improvement. • Access to support for schools at risk. • Access to online tools and resources through the Educational Leaders web site. • Access to professional networks and management advice.
Experienced principals	Experienced principals (>5 years) are to have their knowledge and skills further developed to lead change in order to: 1 Create the conditions for effective teaching and learning, with a particular focus on: a Those who are leading initiatives to raise Maori achievement. b Achieving measurable gains for all student groups in participating schools. c Engaging with family and whanau to improve student outcomes.	The funded opportunities include: • Primary school principals—Access to 80 (from 2009)/100 (from 2010) 10-week awards of paid sabbatical leave. • Area school principals—Access to three 10-week awards of paid sabbatical leave. • Secondary school principals—Access to 50 10-week awards of paid sabbatical leave. • Access to one Konica Minolta Dame Jean Herbison NZEALS Scholarship per annum. • Access to 75 one-year study leave awards per annum. • Access to within-school professional development. • Access to schooling improvement. • Access to support for schools at risk. • Access to professional learning groups. • Access to online tools and resources through the Educational Leaders web site. • Access to professional networks and management advice. • Access to 300 places in the pilot 18-month Experienced Principals Programme.

workshops encouraging Maori and Pacifika women to apply for leadership positions and workshops for school trustees on selection criteria, the former intended to boost communicative rationality, the latter communitarianism.

Although these initiatives helped, they also masked the deeper workforce dynamics driven by leader retirement demographics, accelerating churn in leadership roles and the legacy of a leadership professionalization policy characterized by low cost, minimal preparation and learning on the job that appeared to celebrate heroic amateurism.

Early concerns over leadership quality and quantity were expressed in the Early Childhood Education sector where negligible preparatory provisions and an aging leadership cohort were swamped by a major expansion in funded student places (Grey, 2004). In the primary and secondary education sectors, the quality of applicants, the performance and the career patterns of principals were increasingly identified as problematic (Brooking, 2008a; Collins, 2006). This occurred about the same time as school roll projections (Daniel, 2006) and workforce analyses (Galvin, 2006) were pointing to a coming crisis in the demand and supply of leaders.

New Zealand lags behind the state education systems in Australia, which have long invested in helping educational leaders acquire specialist postgraduate qualifications in leadership, mostly prior to appointment. The twin aims of such investment have been to enable research-based learning about leadership and to achieve threshold competence on appointment. The result is that about 44% of school leaders in Victoria, 34% in NSW and 53% in Tasmania hold postgraduate qualifications in educational leadership (Gamage & Ueyama, 2004; Gurr, Drysdale, & Goode, 2007). The equivalent figure in New Zealand is about 9% to 12%, according to one study in 2006 (Robinson, Eddy, & Irving, 2006, p. 152) and another in 2008 (Robinson, Irving, Eddy, & Le-Fevre, 2008, p. 157). Together, these studies confirmed the comparative paucity of investment.

New Zealand's educational leadership professionalization policy also ran counter to some international trends and parallel to others. Traditionally, as noted above, the trend in England had been toward a Master's degree serving as de facto accreditation for promotion (Gunter, 2012, p. 63) until the Third Wave era when the Teacher Training Agency was set up in 1997. It offered instead mandatory skills training for aspiring headteachers; the National Professional Qualification for Headship. The National College of School Leadership was then established in 2000 with an annual budget of £100 million to deliver school leadership development and fund leadership research. Demand for research-based leadership Master's degrees provided by universities collapsed, and although a minister mooted making "teaching a Master's level profession" (Balls, 2008), nothing came of it. At about the same time, the New Zealand government cut costs by closing its Principals' Development Planning Centre (McGregor, 2008).

Educators in New Zealand are broadly aware and critical of the consequences of this limited investment, as revealed by a series of connected enquiries I mounted. The series was supported by a Konica Minolta Dame Jean Herbison Scholarship awarded by the New Zealand Educational Administration Society, so that I could conduct a national review of the preparation and succession of educational leaders in New Zealand or Aotearoa.

A pilot study of secondary school principals' perceptions of their preparation as leaders suggested that the approach in use was more likely to deliver amateurism through serial incompetence rather than systematic professionalization (Macpherson, 2009a). A study of neophyte leaders' views on leadership preparation and succession strategies reported accumulating evidence of serious supply and quality issues (Macpherson, 2010b). A survey of senior leaders found that they shared the view that it was time for a career-related professionalization policy and provisions (Macpherson, forthcoming). A national survey of educators confirmed that there was widespread support for a more comprehensive suite of leadership preparation and succession strategies commonly used overseas (Macpherson, 2010a). Finally, a policy review confirmed that there were substantial differences in leadership development between New Zealand and Australian education systems and best practice internationally (Macpherson, 2009b).

The key policy issue here is how current power structures are impacting the professionalization of school leaders in New Zealand and how improvements might be devised. The evidence suggests that the ministry's PLP has five fundamental flaws regarding the preparatory professionalization of leaders for New Zealand's primary schools.

First, the objectives of the middle and senior management program in the PLP focus on national standards, student achievement and pedagogical development with a view to management skills delivering fidelity in policy implementation. It is not about the development of professional leadership capacities and services needed in self-governing and self-managing schools. It confirms the need to rethink the formal distribution of power between the ministry and board of trustees and to clarify the services required of principals and others in leadership designations.

Second, with the exception of the NAPP in the PLP, access to provisions occurs after appointment to leadership positions, with the perceived result that leadership professionalization is more likely to be characterized by amateurism through serial incompetence rather than by systematic preparation to achieve threshold competency. This signals the need to revise the distribution of power to determine appropriate higher education and skills training between (a) the ministry, (b) the university research groups technically able to provide evidence-based postgraduate education in educative leadership and (c) other providers that are expert at delivering short-term and role-specific skills training.

Third, the NAPP focuses on expanding the pool of quality applicants for hard-to-staff schools, particularly Maori and Pasifika teachers, in a context where self-governing and self-managing schools educate students of varying ethnic blends reflecting the national profile (nearly 70% identify as New Zealand European, nearly 15% as indigenous Maori, just over 9% as Asian and nearly 7% as Pacific Islanders). A real danger here is that principal selection conducted in haste or by a commissioner is more likely to reflect ethnic matching between principal and community power brokers and reinforce societal divisions through schooling rather than advance intercultural leadership. This signals the need for the PLP to be replaced using a policy process in which the ministry is required to share power with legitimate national stakeholders. The challenge here will be to articulate how teachers might be professionalized to deliver intercultural leadership services appropriate for a healthy multicultural society (Rizvi et al., 1990).

Fourth, priority for study leave awards in the PLP is given to achieving an "All Graduate Profession." An unintended effect is that leadership professionalization is being retarded by comparative underinvestment in postgraduate education in leadership. This is unlikely to change unless the ministry's power to determine the levels of knowledge that can be accessed during the professionalization of leaders is shared with expert and politically disinterested researchers.

Fifth, most leadership training provisions aim to improve principals and implement policy. This is in a context of governance and management devolved to school communities and where leadership is increasingly being distributed within schools. Leadership education and training needs to aim at leadership capacity building in school communities. To ensure this happens, the ministry's power to control the focus of leadership professionalization needs to be distributed across professional associations representing the different leadership designations and other national stakeholders.

Clearly, this brief case study is an inadequate base for generalizing across a system. On the other hand, the accumulating evidence from limited prior research, the summary of current preparatory opportunities and the serious policy flaws found in the PLP policy and program triangulate closely with the experiences of one neophyte practitioner. This preliminary degree of triangulation provides grounds for tentative conclusions and implications concerning the professionalization of educational leaders, with special reference to the current deployment and structures of power.

The first implication concerns the narrow objectives of the preparatory program for middle and senior managers. It is far more likely to encourage appointees to adopt *Kiwi pragmatism* as a political ideology in their personal philosophy of educational leadership than consider and apply communitarianism and communicative rationalism required for professional team and executive leadership roles in self-governing and self-managing community schools.

Another related implication is that Kiwi pragmatism is likely to inoculate neophyte leaders against responsiveness to the national will. Although the election of a center-right coalition government in 2008, and its reelection in 2011, saw the emergence of more egalitarian liberalist priorities, the scale and purposes of the PLP remained unchanged. This suggests that the ministry's centralization of power, in this case the unshared authority to determine the professionalization of principals, acts to ensure that change, a precondition for improvement, is prevented. The strategy of dynamic conservatism in educational administration has been well understood since research reported the phenomenon in British Columbia, Alberta and Quebec (Martin, 1993).

The third implication, with the exception of the NAPP, concerns access to provisions occurring after appointment to leadership positions. Most neophyte leaders in primary education cut their teeth in small rural schools. This raises serious questions about sole-charge and small primary schools as sites for "trial and error learning" about leadership encouraging Kiwi pragmatism, rather than sites of community capacity building, democratic governance in a liberal democracy and the achievement of equity and social justice through fairness.

The fourth implication follows the NAPP's focus on expanding the pool of quality applicants for hard-to-staff schools, particularly Maori and Pasifika teachers. Such an approach is more likely to result in ethnic gaming between principals and communities, as represented by board of trustees, than advancing the quality of intercultural leadership as valued by communicative rationality. Although the political reconciliation of careerism and the ethnicity of local majorities can occur as a direct consequence of the ministry's pragmatic workforce management practices, it is unlikely to reflect an appreciation of the educational needs of New Zealand school students in a multicultural society.

The fifth implication follows from how the priority for study leave awards leading to an All Graduate Profession could be undermining New Zealand's chances of achieving an international benchmark; an All Master's profession of educational leaders (Lumby et al., 2008).

The sixth implication is the extent to which leadership capacity building in school communities is being limited by training that focuses on the principalship. It can limit the capacity of leaders to facilitate liberal democracy in school governance and may encourage them to generate a myth of omnipotent professionalism to legitimate even greater local autonomy, with the possibility of local tyrannies evolving in school management.

In sum, this chapter raises the possibility that neophyte leaders of primary schools are being systematically invited by the ministry's professionalization policy and provisions to adopt a political ideology of Kiwi pragmatism rather than implement national policies that have long promoted communitarianism and communicative rationalism, and more recently, egalitarian liberalism. The situation appears to violate the organizing principles of New Zealand's liberal democracy.

If so, then the ministry's leadership professionalization program could be part of a wider strategy of recentralizing power away from three other legitimate interest groups in the politics of primary education: school communities, a national parent advocacy entity and the team of responsible ministers—the Minister and the Associate Ministers of Education.

Note

1 A Decile 1 school has children from areas with the lowest 10% socioeconomic status in New Zealand. Decile 10 schools have children from the areas with the highest 10% of socioeconomic status. Decile rankings are used to adjust the distribution of resources to New Zealand schools as a form of positive discrimination.

6 Becoming a school director in Timor Leste

This chapter conveys what it is to become a primary school director in the youngest country in the world; Timor Leste (Portuguese for East Timor), which gained full independence in May 2002. The historical and policy context of school leadership is summarized with special reference to the distribution and use of power in the state's public education system.

The history of a remote village primary school is first provided verbatim by the chairman of its Parents and Teachers Association (PTA), a local advisory group of stakeholders.

The school director then explains what it was like to be born in 1976, the year after the Portuguese abandoned their colony and the Indonesians invaded the country to administer it for 24 years. He describes how he and his family survived the brutality of the Indonesian withdrawal in 1999 and how he committed himself to education as his personal contribution to national independence.

His account of becoming a school director is therefore embedded in a context of post-conflict reconstruction and emphasizes how primary school leadership in Timor Leste gives expression to national aspirations, reconciliation and development through independence. At the same time, an analysis of powers in the wider context suggests that these aspirations may be compromised in part by wider political structures and machinations.

Oddly, one of the most complex challenges for school leaders in Timor Leste is managing the language(s) to be used locally to enable learning while leading the development of their schools in a national education system. Most people, especially those is rural areas, speak their own ethnic language at home. These ethnic languages signal very early migration and settlement patterns. Mambae and Tokodede, for example, are related to modern Tetun and belong to the Austronesian language group of the Mesolithic hunter-gatherer-fishers that first arrived about 13,000 years ago (Wheeler, 2004, p. 20). Other languages, such as Bunak and Makasse, arrived with the Neolithic agriculturalists that migrated from Asia about 2000 BC.

Fortunately Tetun is spoken by most Timorese, in most districts, and is regarded as the country's working language. There are, however, exceptions, such as in Los Palos in the far east, and in Occussi, the East Timorese exclave in West Timor, where other local ethnic languages dominate local politics. The key point here is that a primary school director has to be verbally fluent and culturally adroit in the terms of local ethnicity, as well as in national aspirations expressed in Tetun, in order to navigate successfully through the intense and continuing rivalry over scarce resources.

Timor Leste has an estimated 10 years before the oil and gas reserves run out, and if there is no tax-paying middle class by then, the country could slide back into poverty and become what the United Nations refers to as a failed state. There is, nevertheless, reason to be hopeful.

By 2012, Timor Leste was 28th on the List of Countries by Failed States Index, five places better than it was in 2011.[1] The political factors used to measure failed state status include the criminalization and/or delegitimization of the state, the deterioration of public services, the suspension or arbitrary application of law and widespread human rights abuses, the security services operating as a "state within a state," the rise of factionalized elites and the intervention of external political agents.

Such phenomena are all part of Timor Leste's recent history and help account for residual effects faced by school directors, in addition to those that date from earlier conflicts over resources. A school director may have to provide leadership across the East-West political fault line in Timor Leste that was originally generated in intertribal historical times.

By about 1500 AD, the country was governed as many small kingdoms that engaged almost constantly in numerous boundary and resource conflicts. These disputes and their origins are commemorated today in highly colorful traditional dances with weapons at community events. The Dawan (Atoni) people were probably the largest ethnic grouping who gave their loyalty to the warrior elites that managed their many small kingdoms.

Nevertheless, when the Tetun (Belu) people settled into the fertile central areas in the 14th century, they pushed the Darwan kingdoms westward, expanded the boundaries of their own four kingdoms and then encroached further into Timor Leste. These dynamics in recent centuries created a deep East-West schism.

This may seem irrelevant to schooling until it is realized that the internal security of the country, and therefore safety in schools, was severely compromised in 2006 when soldiers from the western regions alleged unfair discrimination over promotions and discipline, and mutinied. Their claims evoked this ancient East-West fault line and destabilized the government and public education. People were killed, and schools were burned in the turbulence. Calm was gradually restored when the government asked the United Nations for peace-keeping troops and police (Rosser, 2009).

Two other deep divides in Timor Leste's society and education that school directors must navigate were created by the countervailing forces of colonization and resistance. The Portuguese and Dutch empires competed for control of the island of Timor from about 1568 for 300 years, largely by playing the local kingdoms off against each other, until they finally decided to subdivide Timor in 1916 and focus on their main interest—coffee extraction. Although the Portuguese built churches and token forts in what they called Timor Leste, they constructed only the roads and bridges they needed to link their coffee plantations to ports.

The Catholic Church gained a strong foothold in all areas and built many primary schools and a small number of relatively high quality regional secondary schools. This created a Catholic enclave in the midst of Indonesia, the most populous Islamic country in the world. The Church, however, remained very conservative, and its teachings today contribute to one of the highest national birth rates in the world—effectively neutralizing many national education, health, welfare and social development policies.

The authority of the Portuguese rulers, however, was relatively weak outside of regional centers. They reached accommodations with the *liurai*, the traditional Timorese rulers, and focused on extracting coffee. Traditional beliefs and local governance practices tended to be unchallenged by the Portuguese and many persist to this day, including a degree of tolerance for murder intended to curtail witchcraft (Wright, 2009). Although such norms and practices are increasingly contested (Herriman, 2009), they confront the view of the first president (Gusmao, 2005); that such traditional laws should somehow be integrated with modern justice.

The other effect of Portugal's soft and exploitative colonization was that it nurtured a societal capacity to resist imposed change, to the point where it became a celebrated national trait. To illustrate, the Portuguese introduced forced labor and taxes in 1910, to improve the productivity of their coffee estates, but were forced by resistance to abandon these coercive practices in 1916. When the Japanese occupying forces brutally insisted on cooperation from 1942 to 1945, the resistance of Timorese villagers became implacable. When resistance turned into active support for an Australian guerrilla force, the Timorese suffered terrible retribution. Sadly, this trait can be manipulated easily today by politicians wanting to impede change for partisan advantage.

Nevertheless, this capacity for resistance has been raised to the status of a national characteristic and is popularly held to be exemplified by Xanana Gusmao, guerrilla leader and first president (Niner, 2000). Although the Portuguese returned after World War II, they were not welcomed. Their benign neglect of Timor Leste ended in 1974 when economic and political crises in Portugal forced it to give up its colonies. The Indonesians took the opportunity to invade and annex what they regarded as a long alienated territory deep within its massive archipelago. They ruled from 1975 to 1999 but faced a gradually escalating insurgency.

Portuguese was, therefore, the first language of colonization in Timor Leste. For 400 years prior to Indonesian rule, Portuguese was the language of government, the Catholic Church and education. And to the consternation of many primary school directors, who are neither literate in the language nor inclined to be so, it has recently been reintroduced as the basic language of education, starting from the lower grades of primary schooling. Teachers' explanations and school directors' instructions may well commonly be in Tetun, yet many schools still hold on to their Indonesian textbooks and occasionally refer to the recent glossy textbooks and policies issued in Portuguese. Although discussions about teaching and learning may be in Tetun and Bahasa Indonesian, formal documentation in the ministry and minutes of executive meetings tend to be in Portuguese, effectively excluding many, especially women. The status differentials and inefficiencies created by the current language practices are widely evident in the ministry and appear to contradict wider public use and defy common sense, until the politics of resistance during the Indonesian occupation are taken into account (Macpherson, 2011).

Portuguese became the language of resistance during the Indonesian occupation. Many of the current political leaders, almost all men, were educated during the Portuguese colonial era and spent most of the Indonesian occupation in Portuguese possessions such as Mozambique. When they were returned to power in the post-1999 period, these men promoted a unique brand of nationalism that stressed Portuguese cultural values and the use of Portuguese language as a marker of a unique national identity. They embedded a language policy in the new constitution that recognized Tetun and Portuguese as official languages and Bahasa Indonesian and English as working languages.

Another challenge for primary school directors is that Bahasa Indonesian is the second language of colonization. It is also the language that most East Timorese leaders were educated in during the Indonesian occupation, the language of government and commerce for 24 years, and the language that most still prefer to write in. Although the crudity of the invasion in 1975, the oppressive rule, and the very nasty withdrawal by Indonesian troops in 1999, is part of the living memory of most East Timorese (Dunn, 2003), they also recall the extensive construction of roads, bridges and schools and the awarding of scholarships to Indonesian universities during the occupation (McGuinn, 1998).

There also appears to be a tolerant understanding of the three major political blunders that occurred in 1999. No one expected the Indonesians to offer the East Timorese a referendum. The Indonesians did not expect the massive rebuttal by the East Timorese. No one anticipated the viciousness of the resulting chaos (Greenlees & Garran, 2002). And although the behavior of some Indonesian regiments and the local militias they sponsored will never be forgotten nor forgiven, there is very little residual resentment in Timor Leste today toward Indonesians *per se* or their language. The land border is open and goods flow freely. One of the most popular annual Timorese cultural festivals is when Timor Leste plays West Timor at football, essentially for bragging rights.

The final language challenge for primary school directors is that English has played a major role in government since 1999. It was the language of the commission that managed the referendum in August 1999. The UN mission that managed East Timor's transition to full independence in May 2002 conducted all of its affairs in English. The UN mission that returned in 2006, when internal East-West factionalism undermined the government's capacity to maintain internal security, restored calm using English. English became the language of peace.

Educators are also acutely aware that, alongside Tetun, English appears to be emerging rapidly as the second language of choice of the young, by far the largest cohort in the population, especially so among those living in Dili who are ICT savvy. Primary school directors and teachers wishing to comply with the national policy of introducing Portuguese "bottom up" are understandably concerned when they and their students have limited access to formal language instruction and that mandatory professional development is almost exclusively devoted to Portuguese.

And how do they and their colleagues cope? They dead hand official policy with passive resistance and get on with helping students learn. Classroom video footage has also shown that they unconsciously switch codes extensively, including using local ethnic languages, to check that learning has occurred (Quinn, 2008).

Does this apply to wider education policy? The thin evidence suggests that the answer is probably yes, principally due to scarce resources. The limited system-wide research available shows clearly that language policy remains one of the most intractable problems in education since independence (Beck, 2008a, pp. 6–9), particularly the absence of a common language to teach teachers with and the lack of teaching resources in any language. The other major challenges are the poor quality of education in terms of teacher capability, teacher qualifications and the curricula at various levels of learning. There is also high absenteeism of teachers and students, high attrition rates, high repetition rates, high adult illiteracy, a gender imbalance with only 30% of teachers in primary schools being women, poor class-room facilities, teacher: student ratios typically about 1:40 and about one-third of the population being of school-age. The demands on scarce resources are immense.

To illustrate, it has been estimated that the education system will need 140–280 newly trained primary teachers per year, 100–170 newly trained pre-secondary teachers per year, and 90–240 newly trained secondary teachers per year, until 2020 (Romiszowski, 2005), with variances mainly due to uneven enrollments and retention. The actual numbers enrolling in the early years of the primary school teacher training course at Baucau has been about 50 (Beck, 2008b), and the country has had to rely on imported expertise (Connell, 2008).

Nationally, the struggle to develop the education system is a major concern for the leading political party, the National Council for Timorese Resistance (CNRT). The main challenge the CNRT has reported is to coordinate the contributions of international aid agencies, as well as "enforcing tight deadlines to coordinate school and warehouse rehabilitation; rebuild the ministry; provide furniture, textbooks and school supplies; recruit teachers, ministry and district office staff to reopen schools, [which] left no time for sector-wide planning and capacity building with Timorese colleagues" (Supit, 2008, p. 20). The inspectorate was established in 2008, with 65 school inspectors who were directed to sustain the quality and accountability of between 20 and 30 schools each. Some of these schools are so remote that they take all day to reach by motorbike and on foot from regional headquarters.

In this context of national independence and reconciliation across language and ethnic lines, primary schools were established and leaders selected. To illustrate the local context of appointing leaders, and the political ideologies involved, we can take the main road south from Dili, the capital of Timor Leste. It zigzags up the face of a steep and dense eucalyptus forest for about 30 kilometers, before it crosses a rugged mountain watershed. The bush thins out dramatically and becomes much like a steep, dry and red earth Australian landscape.

Another 17 kilometers of narrow, partially sealed and badly potholed road gradually drops a little into the fertile highland district of Aileu. The main town, also named Aileu, is only 47 kilometers from Dili, but it takes an hour and a half driving time to get there.

Aileu is a town of sharp contrasts. It is surrounded by intricately watered rice fields, vegetable market gardens and sparse Australian-like bush. It has a vigorous market and a disproportionate number of boisterous young people with ready smiles. They seem unaware that some of the main buildings in the town center are still burnt out husks.

Another seven kilometers into the mountains northeast from Aileu is the remote village of Aikua Rinkua. Getting there means driving very slowly up a wide and shallow river bed in the dry season and then walking the final two kilometers. Through interpreter Johnny Viegas, the then President of the PTA, Sr. Paulino de Jesus Araujo, took up the story of the village primary school and how its director was appointed.

We established the school in 2005. Our community realized that it was taking far too long for our children to walk to other remote schools and that our numbers were growing. At that time, I was the Suco Chief [Village Chief], and the current school director was a teacher at another school. I called the community and the current school director together to discuss the idea of having a new school. We decided that I should put a proposal to the Aileu District Education Office. They supported the proposal and sent it on to the Ministry of Education in Dili.

We waited two years for approval. In the third year, the district education office informed us that our proposal had been approved. They also sent staff to survey our families to identify the number of children that would probably be attending. The survey showed that our proposal met the ministry requirements. We were asked to indicate the land to build on. Things were getting urgent, so we decided to use the home of the current school director, who comes from our village. Fifty children attended, so we divided the house into three classrooms and organized four teachers.

The opening ceremony was held on July 25, 2007. It was organized by the district education office. It included a formal signing of the authorization from the Ministry of Education for Aikua Rinkua to run a public school. There were speeches by the Superintendent of the Aileu District and the Suco Chief. All school directors in the Aileu District attended, along with about 100 people from the community. The school director's wife organized the feast. It was a very important day in the life of the Aikua Rinkua community.

The school is located in the middle of the village. The parents have large gardens that primarily produce potatoes and hillside plantations that grow coffee bushes. Looking south you see large rice fields and the main road. The steep ground to the north provides us with water and coffee, and east and west are the gardens.

The community is very pleased that their school is nearby. The parents feel that the government has supported their remote suco, and they feel proud that they have been able to have their children learn so close to home. They feel that they have real independence: independence to learn from home; independence as East Timorese to have education in our own village; and independence for the parents to collaborate with our teachers to help direct and support our children's learning. Independence means everything to us East Timorese.

Our school has four grades. Grade 1 has 12 boys and 8 girls. Grade 2 has 9 boys and 4 girls. Grade 3 has 5 boys and 2 girls. Grade 4 has 4 boys and 6 girls. That totals 30 boys and 20 girls, 50 all together. We have one permanent teacher, the school director, a male, another contract male teacher, and two voluntary teachers, one male and one female. They are each paid $183 USD per month.

Our classrooms have sufficient tables and chairs for the students. They are organized in straight lines facing the blackboard. The classroom has a dirt floor; there is no ceiling, and in the rainy season, the roof leaks a little, but not enough to stop the teaching and learning. We have window frames but no glass. We have door frames but no doors. We can't lock up, but nothing ever gets stolen. The school has never been painted inside or out. One of the three classrooms is now used as the teachers' room, as the school director's office, and for community meetings.

The curriculum is based on the national curriculum; Portuguese, Tetun, mathematics, history and environmental science. The pedagogy is a little different by subject, but the teachers all use direct instruction, textbooks in Portuguese, the blackboard, questions and answers, and their own teaching aides and materials. Although the textbooks are mostly in Portuguese, the teachers explain things in Tetun. We also speak Mumbai at home, but it is not used at school, mostly Portuguese with Tetun. Even though the constitution determines that Portuguese will be learned, the parents are happy that the explanations are given in Tetun. We are also happy to retain Mumbai as a home language and to have Bahasa Indonesian and English used in the market and for international travel. The community down in Aileu has organized English classes out of school time, and some of our people walk the seven kilometers to those classes.

Our school is very special to us. We are interested in building relationships with primary schools in other parts of the world. The reason is that Timor Leste is now an independent part of the international community. Such relationships would help the teachers learn more about different countries and teaching methods. These relationships would also help students learn from each other. Letters are welcome and can be addressed to the School Director, Aikua Rinkua Primary School, Aileu, Timor Leste.

Our remote school makes us all feel very proud. It is not in a city or in a town. It is in our community. Education is available for our children in our remote village. We have independence in our new independent country.

The founding director appointed to lead the Aikua Rinkua Primary School was Sr. Paulino de Carralho. He is a short, slight man with an intense yet gentle disposition. I was introduced to him under a large shade tree outside the Aileu District Education Office in early 2009. He seemed ill at ease until our interpreter Johnny offered to bring chairs outside and conduct the interview under the tree. He then touched the tree, it seemed to be for assurance, sat and relaxed.

Paulino was dressed modestly, deferred readily to others who called by to greet him. He was obviously widely known and deeply respected. He gave carefully considered answers to my questions. His wide smile and generous wit were evoked whenever a joke was made about the remoteness of his village and school. His story was anything but funny.

I am 33, born in January 1976. Our country was at war at the time, although the conflict eased a little in 1980. I was told by my parents that the Portuguese were cruel, dictating how we lived. They also told me that it was the Carnation Revolution in 1975 in Portugal that led to the Portuguese finally leaving, and soon after that, the Indonesians invading. In between, they said we had a short sweet period of independence.

My first memories are of my mother's message being passed on through my father, after she died at the end of 1976, "You must go to school until you get your degree." I was brought up by my uncle and auntie who paid my school fees up to 1990 when I rejoined my father.

The situation was very bad in our family. We had no economic support, often short of food, so I had to leave again. A priest in Manututo took me in, and I stayed there for nine years, until 1999, when the Indonesians finally left. I was educated from pre-secondary up to secondary levels in the St. Antonio Catholic School in Manututo until 1995, and I then worked on in the school for four years as an administrative assistant.

When the Indonesians left in September 1999, it was traumatic. There was an East Timorese Militia Team linked to the Indonesian Army unit in Manututo who destroyed community homes, tortured a young man and stole community property. The situation became so critical that the priests and the community all ran away to safe areas in their home villages. I escaped from Manututo by myself, walking six hours through the night to Aileu. I was 18, frightened and very pleased to find my father. But another militia team in Aileu supported by the Indonesian Army burned our family house. So all of my family ran away to the mountains, and we lived off the land. We used to creep down at night to our crops to collect food, but it was very dangerous, and we had to return to our hiding places.

We still have mixed feelings about the Indonesians today. The education they provided, the roads, bridges and university places, we appreciate. But the behavior of their army and their militias was not like human beings, without any respect for people, killing freely. So when the Indonesian army and their militias left, and the UNTAET soldiers arrived, we returned to Aileu. We found everything destroyed. It was hard to find food. We survived through the garden and the rice field. We used palm trees to build houses. In 2000, the UNHR provided construction materials so we could build new houses.

In September and October 2000, we collaborated to identify a qualified team to rebuild education in Aileu's subdistricts. I started as a teacher teaching all subjects in a primary school in Besilau. I was not formally qualified to teach, but my education and experience as an administrator at Manututo helped me. The Ministry of Education screened us using a test in Portuguese, Tetun, mathematics, Indonesian, environmental science and history. I passed and taught at Besilau for seven years. I was paid $120 USD a month for those seven years.

I was married in 2003, here in Aileu, to a one-time classmate in Manututo, from Emera. We had three children, two boys and a girl. The eldest is now six. We hope they will all be teachers. While I have not yet achieved my mother's advice to me, I have got my Diploma 3 in education from the Chrystal Institute, Dili and will wait for opportunities to improve my qualifications.

I was invited by the Suco Chief to help build a new school in my home village. I could not say no to him and my people. I was also interested because of the high number of dropouts in my village from other schools. There was no real opportunity for our parents to escort their children long distances to other schools to ensure their safety. The memory of war is with everyone. And the other reason for agreeing was about local development. Our community will grow, and the local population will grow if we have local schooling. I have never thought of doing any job outside of education. It means that I can focus on service to my own community.

So when I knew that I was going to be the director of a new school in my home village, it was like a dream come true. The local community trusted me. I consulted other school directors to prepare for the role. I also recalled my experiences in Manututo and Besilau to identify what I would need to do. So, I started as a school director on the day the school opened, July 25, 2007.

I felt over awed by a heavy sense of responsibility. I was very nervous on the day, but all the local school directors came and offered me support. I was also supported strongly and carefully guided by Sr. Augusto Manuel, our district superintendent in Aileu. He told me "that is your village, your community, your people, and I trust you to carry the responsibility." My wife organized the feast, and she stood with me.

So the next day we started taking enrollments. It took two weeks to check all birth certificates and the other details needed and submit them to the district office. In the third week, we organized the students into age groups and started teaching. The district office had delivered enough tables and chairs for the students and the teachers. I rented a car to help transport the textbooks and teaching and learning materials to the end of the road. I invited three local boys to unload the supplies and carry them to the village. I invited three locals to help teach the children; they were unpaid volunteers who had finished secondary school. In 2008, the teacher recruitment process changed. I recommended that the three volunteers sit the Ministry test but one failed. Currently I have three teachers that have all passed the text.

The most surprising thing to me about starting up as a school director was that I could lead as a local person. Second was that the government recognized me as a competent leader. And third was that my community trusts me to lead education in our area.

So my approach to leadership is firstly about being a good example to the community. This means not being involved in cock fighting or gambling, always growing the respect of the community. Secondly it means communicating effectively about the school's activities such as explaining the curriculum. Thirdly it means delegating responsibilities to colleagues, so they share in community leadership and improve their own standing in the village. Fourthly it means always checking the teacher's punctuality, so that they check the student's punctuality. And yes, I copied the school director at Besilau, who always spoke to his staff nicely, with respect, and was always punctual, setting a good example. He always planned carefully for each day, each week, each trimester, and each year, and shared the planning and the plans with us. In these ways he developed excellent relationships with each of his teachers.

I also watch how my leadership affects my colleagues. When they make mistakes, it is important to speak with them quickly about the mistakes, but to speak softly so they are not embarrassed and my relationship with them is not affected. I have the same teachers I selected over two years ago, and they keep getting better.

There have been problems. The first difficulty I had as a leader is that some of my colleagues had a limited capacity to resolve their problems with students and referred all of these problems to me as school director. Now, if I resolve a problem, I always follow up with a meeting with my colleagues to discuss what happened, so that next time they can solve the problem without waiting for me to get involved.

Another type of leadership difficulty has been about organizing the School Feeding Programme. There are people in the community who seem to believe that I am corrupt and my family is eating more than we should. This tendency is countered by meeting with parents and children to explain how we manage the food, the cooking and the sharing of the food each day. We invite local and remote parents to come in to help with the School Feeding Programme, and this generates transparency and wider understanding.

My second year as school director was very different than the first. I discovered that my voice was invited at district meetings of school directors. The district superintendent asked me to explain to other school directors how I had made some improvements. My voice was respected. And then the school was provided with a new roof, which lifted our spirits. And then our school inspector was appointed, and he visited each month to talk over our problems. This helped me with encouragement. It motivated me to accept some of our poor conditions, to make a number of improvements with colleagues and community members, to change a number of administrative procedures and to consider how other remote schools were doing their planning.

My third year as a school director has been very different again. Some very remote communities have moved closer to our school so that their children can get access. We believe that it is partly a result of our school's reputation improving, partly a result of our school getting support from the government, the improving quality of our community's educational facilities as our all-weather roads and tracks improve, our school is becoming less remote.

On the other hand, the most difficult aspects of my job are to do with access to the village, its remoteness. It is seven kilometers from Aileu with the last two kilometers on foot. There is no electricity. It is difficult to deliver textbooks and impossible in the rainy season when the river floods and we are cut off, sometimes for months. We need a library, textbooks and graphics to counter the remoteness. We need high quality pictures that show our students what life is like in other places. We need mathematics textbooks with pictures and concrete learning materials rather than trying to teach applications on the blackboard. We need to be able to talk with other teachers to share out problems and solutions that work. It is all about overcoming remoteness.

I also worry at night about my colleagues using paraffin lights to do lesson preparation. The black smoke is not good for their respiration. And the cold at night makes it hard for them and students to study.

Is being a school director a lonely job? No. It should be always be a team leadership role. A community leadership role. There should be no reason for being lonely. The most satisfying aspects of my work are my relationships with my colleagues, our excellent performance evaluations and the support we get from our community.

Looking out five years, I want to have improved the professional development and training in my school, especially in curriculum, pedagogy and cultural activities. The big changes I want to see include the construction of a new school to shift the school out of my home, water and sanitation facilities, solar panels generating electricity, laptops for administration and teaching and learning, a library, filing cabinets and so on. I expect my job to change steadily as better resources arrive and as leadership training is provided.

In ten years, I imagine that I will still be a school director, providing politics don't come into play. I may well be at the same school, because it is my family, my community, in my country. It all depends on the Ministry of Education and on the politics of education. So, my advice to teachers in Timor Leste thinking of becoming a school director is to find a good mentor, build good relationships with colleagues and school directors and develop excellent relationships with your community. That is the best insurance against politics, but you can never be sure. So, I plan to refurbish my school buildings, the school gardens and the facilities for teaching and learning. Especially in mathematics, I need models and objects to help children learn.

The interview came to an end. It became clear in casual conversation that Director Paulino had walked the seven kilometers at the invitation of District Superintendent Augusto Manuel to tell his story, and that he was now ready to return the same way. He smiled widely to accept an offer of a lift. He stood and looked around Aileu with apparent satisfaction at what he saw.

We took the chairs back into the district education office while he waited. When we came out, he was still gazing silently at the local landscape. Through Johnny, I asked him why he so enjoyed the view, expecting him to explain his family's long connections with the land. Instead he explained that he did not like coming into the district education office because it had been built in Indonesian times and used to direct education and to "interrogate" local people, sometimes resulting in their deaths.

To ease the tension, I asked him what was different about this building and his remote school. He chuckled at the reference to remoteness and replied with a gentle smile,

"There are no bad spirits in our school. Our school is our independence."

It is evident from these two accounts that the chairman and director of Aikua Rinkua Primary School were both committed communitarians. They explained that their school is intrinsic to the nature and development of village society, much as Giddens (1984) described structuration, both the medium and outcome of educational processes. They saw their village school as reproducing the essence of East Timorese cultural identity and as creating fresh and integrated social and economic relationships between students, teachers, parents and other villagers.

As a political entity, they expect the school to function as a collective that delivers local policy settlements and bestows learning rights and obligations on all villagers. Central to this function was the integrity and value of traditional practices, such as the local approach to socially constructing meaning and arbitrating diverse demands. And when they evaluate their school, and account to wider professional groups, they stress the extent to which teaching and learning and leadership practices promote community; serve the public good; embed cooperative practices and values such as reciprocity, trust and solidarity in the village; and most important, deliver a collective independence. The director's greatest fear was that alternative and arbitrary political ideologies would disturb their communitarianism.

His fears were warranted. Returning the 47 kilometers to Dili, and to the Ministry of Education, very different combinations of political ideologies were evident. I was embedded by New Zealand Aid in the inspectorate of the ministry between January and June 2009 to assist with capacity building. During this period, I researched the establishment and administration of the Inspectorate in the Ministry of Education and conducted structural-functional and cultural analyses of the administration of two of the largest regions, Baucau and Maubisse, prior to helping develop the *School Inspector's Manual* and a draft strategic plan and budget for the inspectorate.

I reported that the inspectorate, led by an inspector general, had a symbiotic relationship with what I termed the "schools directorate" (because it did not yet have a formal organizational title) led by a director general (Macpherson, 2011). Although the inspectorate was required to improve the quality and accountability of all services provided by the schools directorate, the close symbiosis encouraged between the sister bureaucracies by the minister of education had resulted in serious goal displacement in both organizations, degrees of confusion and paralysis in implementation.

Four major reasons were identified. The minister comanaged the schools directorate and the inspectorate as a chief executive officer (CEO), which confused functions and lines of responsibility and triggered structural politics that diffused power rather than mobilized and focused it in support of educational ends. Formal communications in the ministry were conducted in Portuguese, although few were competent in this language, which initiated a politics of miscommunication.

Regional directorates and regional inspectorates were required to collaborate closely in review and development planning, whereas the activities of the latter were funded and administered by the former. This enabled game playing and other forms of resource micropolitics.

Finally, the cultural norms of avoiding overt conflict in a post-conflict context had become so pervasive that performance management in the ministry had been neutralized by a politics of political patronage, organizational ambiguity, scarce resources and petty corruption.

The findings implied the need for a review of the national language policy with a view to a more effective and efficient use of scarce resources and organizational science in the education system. There also needed to be a clearer distinction between policy making and policy implementation in the minister's office, and more systematic capacity building in strategic leadership, planning and budgeting in the schools directorate and in the inspectorate. Three critical issues were the need for a more practical and inclusionary language policy, a compensation policy that served as an incentive regime, and delegitimizing and confronting corruption from the highest levels.

Turning to the political ideologies evident in the ministry, there was little evidence encountered of power being used to systematically advance communitarian, communicative rationalist, or egalitarian liberalist purposes. Instead, the prevailing use of power and its diffused distribution in organizational structure strongly encouraged what might be termed *East Timorese pragmatism*, an understandable method of "gaming" the political ambiguities of working in dual and dueling bureaucracies.

East Timorese pragmatism was particularly evident in central and regional operations as a politics of structural and role conflict. To clarify, as at March 2008, the schools directorate comprised eight national directorates, each led by a national director: policy, planning and development; administration and finance; school curriculum, materials and assessment; school accreditation and operations; adult and non-formal education; professional training; technical and higher education; and culture. All boundaries were contested.

By January, 2009, in each of the five regions, the schools directorate comprised a regional director and six chefes (heads) of departments in the same functional areas as the central directorates, less adult and non-formal education. Each chefe had a head of section and between three and six staff to liaise with school directors. Again, all boundaries were contested.

The reporting lines had two serious flaws. The chefes had to report to their regional director as well as to their national director, providing ideal political conditions for structural and role conflict. Similarly, school directors had to report to all six chefes, through district coordinators, as well as to their district superintendent through their school inspector. Hence the vigorous politics of structure and endemic paralysis in the very structures and relationships intended to deliver policy implementation.

The Office of the Inspector General comprised the inspector general, the adjunct inspector general, two national inspectors (one financial and one pedagogic), a translator/ investigator/ joint office manager and secretarial support staff. In each region, the inspectorate was led by a regional inspector with up to three district superintendents and between 15 and 20 school inspectors, depending on the size of the region.

However, the way in which power was exercised by the minister acting as a CEO resulted in a cycle of organizational convulsions. He was constantly assailed by the expert advice and ruthless resource leverage by a plethora of aid agencies vying for influence. He released the political pressures created by calling his senior staff together for consultations every two weeks, sometimes announcing decisions on the spot or clarifying them later by formal written dispatch. This established a very short-term, highly politicized and centralized decision system.

Because those invited to these meetings include the director general, the national directors, the regional directors but not the regional chefes, there was rarely any systematic follow up implementation planning at the regional level, only attenuated symbolic action. Indeed, sophisticated planning proved impossible before the next meeting was called, and in any case, had to be promptly abandoned with each new set of decisions.

Relationships were also regularly disturbed when the functions of the schools directorate and the inspectorate were muddled. Together these internal political machinations undermined the development of the strategic management capacity of the senior executive team in the schools directorate.

Similarly, because those invited to these meetings also include the inspector general, the adjunct inspector general, the regional inspectors and the 13 district superintendents, but not the national inspectors, this effectively undermined the standing of the regional and national inspectors and undercut the development of the strategic evaluation capacity of the senior executive team in the inspectorate.

One explanation for this politics of incapacity building was that the minister invited the district superintendents to attend when he felt that his message was "not getting through" the regional directors and regional inspectors. He certainly reinforced his point by awarding the district superintendents new cars, but this was also widely interpreted as playing favorites. Another explanation was that aid agency competition, ministerial micromanagement, the conflation of structures, the exclusionary language policy, the absence of systematic implementation planning after ministerial meetings and the tightly centralized control of operational funds were the primary causes of the inappropriate organizational politics bridging the communication gaps, confusion and patches of paralysis.

Finally, there were other effects of blending the two structures that were felt most acutely at the school level. The overlapping roles of regional inspectors, district superintendents and school inspectors meant that school directors were expected to report to many chefes simultaneously and to a district coordinator, as well as to a school inspector. In addition, school inspectors were expected to monitor, evaluate and advise school directors, as well as direct them without a formal line of authority to do so.

The upshot, as at other levels, were waves of structural confusion and role conflict as leaders at various levels took the initiative to get things done until they bogged down and despaired in organizational politics and defaulted to East Timorese pragmatism. In sum, they did what they could, when they could, with what was at hand whenever opportunities arose, and otherwise, kept their heads down.

The key implication of this case study of post-conflict reconstruction is that an appropriate politics of organization must be conceptualized after the most appropriate blend of political ideologies has been decided, which are consistent with the purposes of the institution or system. In the case of Timor Lester, purposes, responsibility and commensurate powers were actually allocated systematically as part of establishing a new nation state. The purposes of the public school system were embedded in Section 59 of East Timor's Constitution:[2]

1   The State shall recognise and guarantee that every citizen has the right to education and culture, and it is incumbent upon it to promote the establishment of a public system of universal and compulsory basic education that is free of charge in accordance with its possibilities and in conformity with the law.
2   Everyone has the right to equal opportunities for education and vocational training.
3   The State shall recognise and supervise private and co-operative education.
4   The State should ensure the access of every citizen, in accordance to their abilities, to the highest levels of education, scientific research and artistic creativity.
5   Everyone has the right to cultural enjoyment and creativity and the duty to preserve, protect and value cultural heritage.

Responsibilities and powers were also allocated centrally to implement these rights. The Decree-Law No. 2/2008, dated January 16, 2008, determined that the Ministry of Education was to be "the central body of the Government responsible for the design, execution, coordination and evaluation of the policies defined and approved by the Council of Ministers for the areas of education and culture, as well as the areas of science and technology" (p. 1). Article 24(1) of the same Decree-Law gave the minister the power to approve, by way of a specific ministerial diploma, regulations for the structures of its central services.

The challenge identified by this chapter is that Timor Leste pragmatism has evolved in the Ministry of Education to cope with turbulent internal politics. This political ideology is impeding support for communitarianism across the system intended to give carriage to the national reconstruction policy featuring reconciliation and development through independence.

Notes

1   See http://en.wikipedia.org/wiki/List_of_countries_by_Failed_States_Index.
2   The English translations of the Constitution and laws enacted by the National Parliament and the Government since independence was restored in May 20, 2002, are available at http://www.eastimorlawjournal.org/East_Timor_National_Parliament_Laws/Index. html.

7 Becoming a director-general of education and training in New South Wales

Is it reasonable for an ex-drug pusher and political spin doctor to be appointed by political patronage to lead a state's public education system? Answering this question must inevitably review the political criteria and processes used to make the appointment. Recall, political philosophy is an appropriate means of making a disciplined and critical evaluation of the nature and justification of the politics and political infrastructure implicated in such decision making. The following case study describes and evaluates practices to uncover the actual political values in use, and then to evaluate the extent to which embedded ideals or principles justify current political arrangements.

A new director-general of education and training (DGET) was appointed in early 2007 to serve as the most senior educational administrator in NSW, Australia. The Department of Education and Training (DET) is one of the largest centralized state education systems in the Western world. It spends one quarter of the state's budget and employs about 120,000 people, of whom about 50,000 are teachers, teaching about 750,000 students. This makes it about the same size as New Zealand's national integrated school system. The politics of the DGET's appointment provides an opportunity to evaluate the quality of the criteria and processes used.

On April 5, 2007, the *Sydney Morning Herald* intimated that the newly appointed minister for education and training, Mr. John Della Bosca, had "long wanted the education portfolio and has already moved to install one of his own men to head the Department of Education" (Patty, 2007). His proposed DGET was the current director-general of commerce, Mr. Michael Coutts-Trotter. Although this intimation was an aside in an announcement proposing the introduction of merit pay for teachers, the DGET's appointment quickly achieved far high saliency in the politics of NSW, if only for three weeks.

A "war over schools director" was declared on the next day by Sydney's tabloid newspaper, *The Daily Telegraph* (McDougall, 2007). The headline referred to the blunt warning given by the Public Schools Principals Forum to Premier Morris Iemma's recently reelected Australian Labor Party (ALP) state government; that they could expect "turbulence if another noneducator was appointed DGE." This relatively small and maverick group of principals was reportedly "outraged over speculation" that a senior public servant would be appointed ahead of an educational professional, adding that they regarded the current noneducator DGE as ineffective. They urged Iemma "not to make the same mistake twice." He ignored them.

Coutts-Trotter's appointment as DGET was confirmed by Della Bosca on the April 10, 2007. A media storm broke the following day. The then current DGET, Mr. Andrew Cappie-Wood, was posted to the premier's displaced officers' list to await reassignment or redundancy. As permitted by current legislation in NSW, the DGET's post had neither been advertised nor publicly clarified as regards selection criteria or processes. Custom and practice in the matter had been established by making two prior appointments of noneducators as DGETs. Appointments to chief executive posts in NSW departments of state are deemed by current legislation to be public service appointments. The same legislation, however, so under defines the process as to render appointments to be in the personal gift of the responsible minister. Further, an appointment may be changed without notice and without incurring any reporting or accountability requirements.

One result is that the use of this legislation is subject to varied interpretation. In this case, the then Liberal Opposition Education spokesperson in NSW, Mr. Brad Hazzard, swiftly provided his view as a rhetorical (and thus legally safe) question and answer, "How is it, that someone who had a nine-year jail sentence for drug importation and who has no educational qualifications ends up as the director-general of public education in NSW? And the answer might well be that he's a Labor mate" (Welch & Patty, 2007).

The same report noted that Coutts-Trotter made a public appeal, early on April 11, 2007, on Sydney Radio 2UE, to be given a fair go. He used popularist rhetoric to portray himself as a "little Aussie battler." Ironically, in the absence of any declared criteria and process, he also argued for procedural fairness, albeit post facto;

> I've been lucky enough to encounter people along the way who have been prepared to give me the benefit of the doubt, allow me to prove myself and to reserve their judgment, and I hope Hazzard will do that and give me a chance to really get into this job.

Hazzard was soon replaced in this role by the leader of the National Party, Andrew Stoner, for unrelated reasons, who renewed the attack on the appointment.

It was confirmed on the same day that Coutts-Trotter was being "screened for his suitability to work with children due to a criminal conviction for a serious drug offence." He had spent three years in jail after being convicted in 1986 of heroin distribution, but cited him approvingly as saying that it was "utterly legitimate in the public interest" for questions to be raised about his criminal background (*The Daily Telegraph*, 2007). No one had raised this dimension of legitimacy. It was a disingenuous spin. Coutts-Trotter was inviting the public to focus on his long past of criminality and redemption. It proved to be a partially effective red herring.

A coordinated effort to keep criminality and redemption in the foreground followed. In a national radio interview on ABC on the same day (Macey, 2007), Minister Della Bosca emphasized that:

> The Working with Children Check is a matter for the Commission for Children and Young People. Mr. Coutts-Trotter is not a prohibited person under the Act, but he will undergo the standard check that everyone who holds a position of trust in the Department of Education does.

Alan Jones, an iconoclastic right-wing public broadcaster, ran the redemption line hard later the same day on Sydney Radio 2GB when he editorialized using exaggerated claims.

> Michael Coutts-Trotter has faced the bottom of the birdcage in his life. He's lifted himself off it, gained outstanding academic credentials after it, and offered himself for public service in the face of it. And I don't know of anyone who has yet found fault with the quality of that public service. I said yesterday in my opinion Michael Coutts-Trotter has been promoted on merit. It's to be hoped that the confines of the public service allow such a person to use the lessons of the past, academic and social, to direct children through education to the better future that parents seek for them. (Jones, 2007)

Although the *Daily Telegraph*[1] and the *SMH* blog sites[2] confirmed the early success of this public relations campaign based on redemption, the president of the New South Wales Teachers Federation (NSWTF) then pointed out that the DGE,

> Needs to be a person with a demonstrated commitment to the value of public education . . . for individual students, the community and Australia . . . [with] . . . a strong understanding of public schools and TAFE colleges, their purposes and their operations. Unfortunately, Mr. Coutts-Trotter (like his predecessor) does not bring that type of experience to the department which is regrettable. (O'Halloran, 2007)

Although the NSWTF affirmed the principles of rehabilitation, O'Halloran (2007) went on to stress the need for equity in and adherence to professional standards in the DET.

> A person in similar circumstances who wished to enter the teaching profession would find it very difficult. A stringent assessment would be made as to the person's suitability and character. The role of the teaching profession is crucial to society and therefore the standards exacted of the profession are very high.

The Institute for Senior Educational Administrators (ISEA), which represents about 200 of the state's top education officials, attacked the

Third straight placement of a career public servant, as opposed to an appropriately qualified and experienced educator, to the position. . . . He may claim to
be an efficient manager . . . [but he] . . . does not have qualifications in the study
of management at a time when the government is demanding that all teachers
up-grade their qualifications. . . . His major task, and one for which he is totally
unprepared or qualified, is to provide educational leadership to the teachers,
principals and students of the NSW government schools." (Ikin, 2007b)

The ISEA also pointed to the explicit cronyism involved and the absence of an
international search for a visionary educational leader. Ikin (2007b) also recalled that,

When former Premier Greiner tried to place Dr. Terry Metherell, a displaced
minister of education, in a senior, highly paid government departmental position, for which he was not qualified, Metherell did not last in the position and,
in time, Greiner's action was declared corrupt by the Independent Commission against Corruption.

A follow-up article in the *Daily Telegraph* on April 12 (Farr & McDougall, 2007)
was headlined "Liberal Outrage: Ex-jailbird Has the Right ALP Mates, Jobs for the
Bad Boys." It cited the Liberal Opposition leader, Mr. Barry O'Farrell, as saying,

He is about to take on 750,000 school kids, 100,000 employees, 50,000 of
whom are school teachers, one quarter of the State budget, and he has no
educational background. Is that sound management and good judgment? I
don't think so.

Nevertheless, the front page of the *Telegraph* featured a huge and obviously posed
photograph of a loving couple—Coutts-Trotter and his wife, Ms. Tanya Pilbersek,
a federal Australian Labor Party member of Parliament and columnist for the
Sydney Morning Herald. It was accompanied by a detailed article in which Pilbersek
reiterated the redemptionist line by claiming that "He's an inspiration . . . that
might give hope to other families struggling with having a teenage child in similar
circumstances."

They were apparently fully confident that this redemptionist spin would prove
successful because Coutts-Trotter's entry as DGET appeared in Wikipedia on the
same day.[3] They had good reason to be confident. They had allies at the state public service union level as well as at the federal ministerial level on the other side of
politics that both declared support.

The NSW Public Service Association's general secretary, Mr. John Cahill, was
clear on the nature and appropriateness of Coutts-Trotter's expertise as a senior
public servant. He affirmed that the new DGET was:

A first-rate manager and a strong leader . . . PSA members who have worked
under Mr. Coutts-Trotter during his time as director-general of commerce
have only good things to say about him . . . the PSA has found him to be

accessible and reasonable . . . [and further, that] . . . running a department is a lot different to running a classroom, and a proven public sector manager is the right person for this position. (*Sydney Morning Herald*, 2007b)

The Liberal Federal Minister of Education, Ms. Julie Bishop, "declined to criticize the NSW government's appointment . . . provided his criminal record would not cause parents to lose confidence in the education system . . . [and] . . . he has the qualifications for what is a very sensitive and important job," although adding lamely that "I haven't seen his CV; I don't know enough about the detail of his position" (*Brisbane Times*, 2007).

There was then a major setback to Coutts-Trotter's media campaign on the 12th when a caustic editorial noted that the "Issue Is Not Drugs but Know-How" (*Sydney Morning Herald*, 2007a). It criticized the NSW Liberal Opposition as being "out of touch" and dismissed the conviction and rehabilitation story as "old news." It traced Coutts-Trotter's career from his journalism degree to first press secretary, then to chief of staff to the then NSW treasurer, Mr. Michael Egan, and then to director-general of commerce for the then Minister of Commerce, Mr. John Della Bosca. It dismissed one of Coutts-Trotter's early justifications for his appointment as irrelevant—having a daughter at a public school. It targeted the issues of educational expertise, cronyism and the absence of public accountability by the government. It noted the absence of relevant qualifications and experience in education, or managing a large organization, and asked why "instead of a doctor in education, NSW schools get a former spin doctor?" It was particularly critical of the post appearing to be "another job for the boys" when "public schools are losing students" and "under attack from a doctrinaire federal minister," and how "such appointments are made behind closed doors by governments with no obligation to explain their thinking."

The national daily newspaper, *The Australian*, agreed. On the April 14, 2007, its editorial noted that:

> Hardly any time [in the debate] has been devoted to an underlying trend that has nothing to do with Mr. Coutts-Trotter's tale of redemption after a troubled youth. The new departmental chief on $387,000 a year is just one of a hand-picked group of senior NSW public servants with impeccable NSW Labor Party credentials . . . he crossed the divide from being an ALP apparatchik to becoming a public service mandarin paid to run a department with a quarter of the state's budget. . . . Former NSW Auditor-General Bob Sendt said yesterday that politically aligned staff in the Labor and Liberal parties commonly made a transition to the ranks of the public service. "I don't think there's necessarily a problem with it providing they have the experience and the qualifications," Mr. Sendt said. "You can't ban people who've had a political role." But Mr. Sendt said that governments did expose themselves to criticism if they did not use a transparent selection process in choosing their top bureaucrats. Mr. Coutts-Trotter was chosen as his state's top education bureaucrat without the position being advertised and without full screening checks. (Norington, 2007)

The response from Coutts-Trotter was news management by repetition. On April 15, the *Sunday Telegraph* gave the controversy another full-page and hagiographic treatment, with another huge and posed loving couple photograph of Mr. and Mrs. Coutts-Trotter. It reiterated the self-reported details of the new DGET's pathway from his father's death when he was 12; to heroin addict, importer and pusher; to his terrified time in jail and the supportive role of family, friends and the Salvation Army; to his degree in journalism and employment in public relations; and finally to his personal sponsorship by Egan and Della Bosca. The article ended with a hopefully neutralizing acknowledgement that the debate had shifted away from drug convictions to *nepotism* and lack of teaching experience, but allowed Coutts-Trotter to run a catch-all rebuttal; his experience in running a large organization would enable him to provide support to classroom teachers doing "one of the golden jobs" (Silmalis, 2007).

Only one interest group maintained its rage past this point. The ISEA issued a Letter to the Editors of all daily newspapers on April 15 (Ikin, 2007a). It noted that,

> At the same time as the government was defending the placement of Mr. Coutts-Trotter, it was advertising nationwide for a new police commissioner on the basis that it was such an important position that every effort must be made to find the best person for the job. On that basis how does the government rate education? To add to the hypocrisy, the NSW attorney-general, John Hatzistergos has labeled the federal government's appointment of Mr. Donald McDonald to the post of director of the board that classifies films as "a corrupt process" (*Sydney Morning Herald*, 2007). He then goes on to say that he, "does not have any evidence that Mr. McDonald is the best person for the position." Perhaps the attorney-general could provide the general public with what evidence he has that Mr. Coutts-Trotter is the best person for the position of director-general for the NSW Department of Education and Training, and if he cannot provide any such evidence, why he has not declared his placement a corrupt process?

Later the same day, the ISEA released a set of public questions for Minister Della Bosca that summarized their concerns, adding a new question, "Is there now a new 'glass ceiling' in education in that highly experienced and well-qualified educators can no longer aspire to lead the NSW Department of Education and Training unless they join the Labor Party or marry a member of Parliament?" (Ikin, 2007c). In their fourth press release, also issued on the 15th, the ISEA argued (Ikin, 2007d) that:

> One can concede that through his Labor Party affiliations he has impressed Mr. Egan and Mr. Della Bosca to the extent that they have placed him first in Commerce and now to Education. And, yes, from Mr. Coutts-Trotter's point of view this may constitute merit promotion. The sad part is that he has completely failed to understand the principle of merit promotion as it applies to the NSW public sector, namely an ethical and transparent recruitment

and selection process involving open advertisement of jobs and competitive selection of applicants . . . What is so sad is that Mr. Coutts-Trotter and the government fail to see that the director-general must be more than a chief accountant. The director-general must understand education, be able to articulate a coherent educational philosophy, and not only lead education in NSW but know where he is leading it and why.

At no point did Coutts-Trotter reply directly to the issues raised by the editorials in the *Sydney Morning Herald* and *The Australian*, to the arguments raised by the NSWTF or to the penetrating critique from the ISEA. He did not need to. They were only reported in passing in minor articles and were barely referred to at the *Daily Telegraph* and the *Sydney Morning Herald* blog sites. Their impact was minimal. There was also little opportunity for the opposition in the NSW Parliament to fan the controversy because the House only meets about 50 days a year.

Coutts-Trotter was also able to rely on the political quiescence of two major interest groups in NSW public education. The NSW Primary School Principals Association and the NSW Secondary School Principals Council made no public comment on the controversy. Indeed, within days of the DGET's appointment, both groups sought appointments with him; it was "business as usual." By April 20, readers' comments on the controversy at the blog sites had dried up. The story was dead and buried, largely at the hands of a demonstrably capable spin doctor.

There was a possibility for a period that the story may have been exhumed. Questions continued to be asked in the NSW Parliament, largely without being answered. For example, on May 10, the Honorable Jenny Gardiner asked the minister of education, without notice,

> What were the minister's grounds for deciding to dismiss Andrew Cappie-Wood from the position of director-general of the Department of Education and Training? Is Mr. Cappie-Wood still employed by the New South Wales Government in any capacity? If so, what is that capacity? In seeking a replacement for Mr. Cappie-Wood, did the minister receive any advice about the type of qualifications and experience that would be expected of a director-general of education and training? If so, what was that advice? What were the grounds for the decision not to publicly advertise both nationally and internationally for a replacement for Mr. Cappie-Wood given that the position of New South Wales Police Commissioner was recently advertised nationally? Since Mr. Coutts-Trotter's appointment, have there been any other changes in senior staffing within the Department of Education and Training?

Minister Della Bosca briefly confirmed that Cappie-Wood was "on the displaced officers' list" and being "matched to positions" that he might want to pursue. He then reiterated his right and responsibility to appoint the most suitable person as DGET, with or without advertisement, and extolled the skills, intelligence and integrity that Coutts-Trotter brought to the post. He guaranteed that the DGET and he would work together to ensure "great benefit for teachers and leadership support to make the New South Wales public education system world class." Coutts-Trotter, he said, had his and his government's "complete confidence" (New South Wales Legislative Council, 2007).

How is this case study to be interpreted? It depends on the perspectives used to analyze the information provided. The most evident perspectives are those used by the participants. They used three unique sets of political, managerial and educational values, as summarized below.

The problem revealed by Table 7.1 is that the public discussion of the issues of the case could not advance past the clarification and reiteration of positions based on one of three mutually exclusive ideologies. The reason is that an ideology is typically an organized and comprehensive network of ideas of three parts: a vision of the way the world should be; a perspective for viewing the world; and a set of norms that legitimate the imposition of this set of selected values onto reality, most commonly through political action. Recall, an ideology is typically closed in that it either does not recognize the existence of any other ideology, or if it does, it does not admit any legitimacy to its claims.

Once each interest group or member of the media had stated their positions, attacked others and then accommodated the appointment, the state government simply assumed the legitimacy of the appointment based on their electoral mandate, and moved on, confident in its use of majority power and in the rightness of its cause. It was also presumably comforted by the DGET's demonstrated capacity to manage the swift death of the controversy and restore quiescence to the portfolio, a relatively common political objective of the state, as demonstrated in Saskatchewan (Sackney, 1993).

Hence, while clarifying the ideological perspectives of participants and commentators is interesting enough in itself, it is not a form of analysis that can systematically evaluate the justifications offered by a minister and his DGET, as well as weigh up the alternatives suggested by their critics, and then offer systematic advice. This is where political philosophy begins.

The political arrangements revealed by the appointment of the DGET were found to be wanting in a number of senses. They were not justified by reference to the collective benefits of public schooling or how they would impartially promote the welfare and prosperity of all citizens, as required by communitarian values. The appointment criteria and process were driven by the values of realpolitik and could not be "truly described as being for the peace, order, and good government of the dominion concerned" (The Trustees Executors and Agency Co. Ltd v. Federal Commissioner of Taxation, 1933). Indeed, the combination of cronyism, poor transparency and rejection of public accountability violated the principles of the government's own Code of Conduct and Ethics for Public Sector Executives (New South Wales Premier's Department, 1998).

The justifications offered by the minister and his DGET for their actions were particularly unsatisfactory. The appointment criteria and process were not publicly justified in terms of the common good. As Ikin and the ISEA pointed out with precision, they violated the principles of merit selection in the public service, especially when appointing visionary strategic leaders for public education. The extent to which some stakeholders followed the direction of the spin, or remained cravenly

Table 7.1 Dimensions of the case using the participants' analytic perspectives

	Political	Managerial	Educational
Stakeholders grouped by primary perspective	Minister of Education and Training The NSW Cabinet Mr. and Mrs. Coutts-Trotter	NSW Public Service Association NSW Primary Principals Association NSW Secondary Principals Association	Public Schools Principals Forum NSWTF ISEA
Key purpose of selection	To project ministerial power across public education through the DET	To help formulate and implement public education policy effectively through the education system	To provide strategic leadership to public education
Key selection criteria	Loyalty to the minister Public relations expertise Ability to implement the minister's wishes Ability to obtain quiescence in the portfolio	Effective manager of a giant bureaucracy Political neutrality Public policy implementation	The wisdom, higher education, proven skills and mature attitudes of an educational *philosopher king*
Appropriate selection processes	The private gift of the responsible minister	Generic public service criteria using senior executive performance indicators	International search with public criteria and accountability
The nature of the DET	A political system comprising governance structures and political processes; the interplay of interests, conflict and powers; and the authoritative distribution of scarce public resources	A management system comprising functions and structures that deliver planning, organizing, staffing, directing, coordinating, reporting and budgeting (Gulick & Urlick, 1937)	A support system for teachers, learners and schools comprising political advocacy for public education, resource acquisition and distribution, and quality assurance
Appointee archetype	Key adviser on the politics of education to the responsible minister of state	Neutral and senior public servant who facilitates policy making and policy implementation processes	An Aristotelian "philosopher king" of public education
Meta-values indicated	Realpolitik Puissance	Effectiveness Efficiency	Learning Liberal democracy

submissive or morally indifferent, confirmed the need for an urgent inoculation of political philosophy if such realpolitik is to be resisted.

Coutts-Trotter's four main justifications for his appointment all appealed to personal desert and promissory merit, not public merit. The first was that he

had a child in a public school. Second was that he had demonstrated full rehabilitation and now deserved the rewards of redemption. Third, setting aside the
nature of the appointment, he now deserved a fair go, particularly as a little Aussie
battler. Fourth, he had "successful experience" running a government department,
although it was tiny compared with the DET. Relatively few commentators questioned these idiosyncratic and spurious claims in the public interest. The fact that
only the ISEA displayed more than a distant acquaintance with the nature of a
common good justification confirms how little political philosophy has a presence
in the education policy community of NSW or in Australia's media.

There were even fewer intimations of capacity in the policy community to
question the quality of the NSW government's "social contract" with the people concerning public school education. Neither the minister nor his DGET
appeared to relate their appointments or the legitimacy of the state to their delivery on voluntary (or projected) agreements entered into with the public. There
were some bottom-up hints of social contract expectations when commentators
noted that the strong whiff of corruption had left a stain of illegitimacy on the
offices of the minister and his DGET. The deep offense felt by the educationalists over the actions of the minister, and the self-interested spin on merit from
the DGET, will inevitably result in negative political expression, even though the
minister had the legal power to personally determine the outcome using any old
criteria and process.

The politically critical evaluations conducted by the ISEA, NSWTF, the *Sydney
Morning Herald* and *The Australian* did touch on the quality of government. They
shared the view that appointment criteria and process must value strategic educational leadership; avoid any perceptions of cronyism, nepotism, or corruption;
and deliver public accountability by the government. They all made it clear that
the minister's actions failed to satisfy their inchoate view of good government and
that the controversy had added fuel to a crisis of legitimacy.

The danger to the government was that such critique can only be assuaged by
longer-term electoral dynamics, especially if the questioning of the DGET, minister and their government had been more sophisticated. For example, common
good and social contract concerns on communitarian lines could have led to questions about how the appointment would guarantee that public education in NSW
would systematically improve its contribution to society through social, cultural
and economic development and demonstrably add value to the life chances of
students as engaged citizens.

From even more critical perspectives, such as those offered by communicative
rationalism and egalitarian liberalism, the minister and his DGET might have been
asked to clarify how public schooling would contribute to the just and equitable
distribution of wealth and resources, global justice, gender equity, the legitimacy
of political authority, the balance between personal freedom and democratic rule,
acts of violence in schooling and war, and the toleration and accommodation of
plural ethical positions.

These are not irrelevant or uncontroversial issues in NSW; it is one of the most
multicultural states of Australia (Rizvi et al., 1990). It was also 20 years since

the Scott Reports (Scott, 1989a, 1990) had recommended the administrative decentralization of its education systems and the democratization of its schools, to almost no avail, despite a considerable degree of organizational surgery and genetic engineering at the time (Macpherson, 1993d).

The greatest concern of many stakeholders was that the DGET's preparation and experience focused on the production and management of news, not knowledge, in an ongoing context of realpolitik. It does not appear to be a satisfactory basis for providing strategic leadership to the institution of state that guarantees that students will acquire the authorized knowledge and culture of its people and the knowledge, skills and attitudes they require for life in the 21st century.

Given the marked degree to which the DGET's career trajectory was the result of close political patronage by two members of a particular faction in state politics, many stakeholders doubted his capacity to understand and respond appropriately to the complex array of policy issues facing public education and to provide sophisticated education policy advice. In such conditions, they argued, the children and their schools are at risk.[4]

The other problem here is that moral and political propositions often have no factual or logical status—they are simply believed to be so. Policy analysts must inevitably deal with "essentially contested concepts" (Gallie, 1956). Policy researchers with philosophical training accept that reasoned reflection may not have the capacity to provide definitive answers about which political proposals and arrangements should be supported, ignored, or resisted by educational administrators. What appropriately trained policy researchers can do, however, is regularly test the justification for educational governance and infrastructure, and teaching and learning, and directly inform the basis for reflective practice and continuous improvement of educational and administrative services.

The existence of fundamentally contested concepts is not, however, a reasonable justification for using the dynamics of realpolitik to select and spin an educational or administrative policy, and then expect subordinate educational administrators managing regions and schools to stay on message. In a professional world that accepts the responsibility of creating, teaching and critiquing knowledge, such an approach would be regarded as intellectually tyrannical and ultimately futile.

The advice to statespersons since Greek times has been to provide dialectical philosophical leadership to leaders at all levels, so that they will engage actively in the development of their own wisdom, services and organization. This would offer more to public education than peddling simplistic certainties determined by political patronage and then downloading political myths using the black arts of spin doctoring.

What leaders trained in political philosophy could also offer NSW public education is a critical analysis of the key concepts used in everyday discourse, such as power, authority, policy, administration, management, rights, responsibilities and accountability, with a view to achieving far greater precision when continually teasing out administrative policy. They can also test the internal coherence of assumptions and arrangements used in NSW, compare them with those used in other states of Australia and other nations and point out the consequences of options.

This means accepting that political philosophy is as ideological as any other type of discourse, and that people will tend to accept from it whatever coheres with their prior core beliefs and values. On the other hand, sophisticated advice can't be unheard, and it has a way of resurfacing once articulated. And offering and sustaining access to "essentially contrasted" ideas is essential to the ongoing and rigorous review of beliefs; otherwise known as learning.

This case study of the appointment of a DGET in NSW has drawn attention to the potential value of positioning political philosophy central to the field of educational administration. Recall, the subdiscipline focuses on justifications for the structures and exercise of power. It enables questions about the quality of current political arrangements by moving past contested ideologies and seeking justifications in terms of the common good, the presumed social contract between people and their state, and other critical bases deemed to be reasonable in a local polity. This case study demonstrated the limited use of political philosophy in the NSW public education polity, and in Australia's media, to their evident detriment.

Finally, this and the previous two chapters clarified the potential of political philosophy as a research methodology. By unpacking the nature and value of political arrangements in becoming a primary school principal in New Zealand, a school director in Timor Leste, or the DGET in the NSW DET, it was able to suggest how future practice and structures might yet better serve the interests of stakeholders and education in liberal democracies.

The next chapter is the first of three that provides case studies of political crises in educational institutions and systems. Chapter 8 is principally a case study of a legal inquiry set up to deal with a crisis of governance in an institute of higher education. The arbitration did not penetrate below the legalities, and further, it is shown to have been delimited by the imperatives of the wider current political order. In Chapter 9, political philosophy is employed to unpack a case where the legitimacy of governance evaporated in a new university in the Middle East. Chapter 10 examines what happened when the state's school education system lost the confidence of both major political parties in New Zealand.

Notes

1 http://www.news.com.au/dailytelegraph/readerscomments/
2 http://blogs.smh.com.au/newsblog/
3 See http://en.wikipedia.org/w/index.php?title=Michael_Coutts-Trotter&action=history.
4 On April 1, 2011, Mr. Michael Coutts-Trotter was appointed Director-General of the New South Wales Department of Finance and Services, retrieved February 16, 2012, from http://en.wikipedia.org/wiki/Michael_Coutts-Trotter. He survived a change of state government in March 2011, when the ALP was swept from power by the liberal or national coalition—the same year his wife was appointed Federal Minister of Health. He was subsequently appointed Director-General of the Department of Finance and Services in NSW in April 2011, and in July 2013, to lead the state's Department of Family and Community Services.

Part III

Case studies of political crises in educational institutions and systems

8 A crisis in institutional governance in Hong Kong

In early 2007, material posted to various web sites by the senior management of the Hong Kong Institute of Education (HKIEd) triggered intense public disquiet. The alleged violations of academic freedom and institutional autonomy named two government officials: Professor Arthur Li Kwok-cheung (Professor Li), secretary of education and manpower (SEM), and his permanent secretary (PSEM), Mrs. Fanny Law Fan Chiu-fun.

The then chief executive of the Hong Kong Special Administrative Region (HKSAR) of the People's Republic of China (PRC), Mr. Donald Tsang, promptly set up a Commission of Inquiry (2007, 15 February) into their alleged interference into the affairs of the HKIEd. Of particular interest to this text, the commission was also asked to recommend how the government might better advise the institute concerning the use of its powers to achieve its purposes, thus formally requiring an evaluation of current political arrangements. This chapter examines a crisis in the quality and legitimacy of governance in higher education in Hong Kong.

To begin, I examine the arguments presented and findings concerning three allegations, within the discipline of law. I then use the tools of political philosophy to show that the nature and quality of governance related to educational administration in the HKIEd is intrinsically related to and subordinate to the wider political order in Hong Kong.

This chapter is a little longer than the others due to the complexities of this dual approach to analysis. Throughout it is important to recall that the commission limited its justifications to what was deemed to be in the common good and made no reference to a social contract between the governors and the governed in higher education or Hong Kong, or to criteria that might have been drawn from communicative rationalism or egalitarian liberalism.

Nevertheless, the analysis concludes with awkward questions about how governance is going to accommodate changes in the political economy of Hong Kong and to deliver on the promise made by President Jiang Zemin during Hong Kong's reversion of sovereignty to the PRC on July 1, 1997, specifically that, "Hong Kong will, in accordance with the *Basic Law*, develop democracy gradually with the ultimate aim of electing the chief executive and Legislative Council by universal suffrage" (*South China Morning Post*, 1997).

The Commission of Inquiry was instructed to investigate the allegations made by Professor Bernard Luk Hung-kay (Professor Luk), who, until April 30, 2007, had been vice president (academic) of the HKIEd. His allegations were published in an undated letter on HKIEd's intranet on February 4, 2007, and again on the internet web site of *Ming Pao News* on February 5, 2007. The allegations were that:

1   In January 2004, during a telephone conversation, Professor Arthur Li Kwok-cheung [Professor Li], SEM, attempted to persuade, Professor Paul Morris [Professor Morris], president and CEO of HKIEd, to take the initiative to propose a merger of the institute with the CUHK [Chinese University of Hong Kong]. The SEM also indicated that if he failed to do so, the SEM would then allow his permanent secretary for education and manpower [PSEM] to have a free hand in cutting the number of students of HKIEd.
2   In the past few years, whenever some members of the institute published articles in local newspapers that criticized the education reform or the education policy of the government and its implementation, shortly afterward senior government official(s)[1] repeatedly called to request Professor Morris to dismiss such members of the institute.
3   In late June 2004, in relation to a protest, the SEM requested Professor Luk to issue a statement to condemn the teachers concerned and the Hong Kong Professional Teachers' Union that assisted those teachers, as such assistance would inhibit the employment of fresh graduates of the institute. To Professor Luk's refusal, the SEM said, "I'll remember this. You will pay!" (Yeung & Lee, 2007, pp. 22–23)

Two commissioners were appointed by the chief executive in executive council and given statutory powers to summon persons, request documents and take evidence on oath. The commissioners were also given two directions. They were to determine if there had been any "improper interference by the SEM or other government officials." They were also directed to "make recommendations on the ways and manner in which advice by the government to the institute, with respect to the exercise of the institute's powers or the achievement of its objects, might be given in the future" (Yeung & Lee, 2007, pp. 112–113). The second direction, specifically requesting advice on governance arrangements, potentially had a much wider impact across the Hong Kong's higher education system. Indeed, the chief executive reiterated that academic freedom was a core value that must not be eroded. The commissioners were asked to report within four months.

The commission appeared to be independent, transparent and impartial. The first judge appointed as chairman withdrew when he was challenged to remove any perception of potential bias (Justice Woo, 2007). The commission posted terms of reference, judicial orders and directions, witness statements, closing submissions and its final report to a web site (Commission of Inquiry into Allegations Relating to the Hong Kong Institute of Education, 2007). On the other hand, some paragraphs were deleted from some written statements prior to posting without explanation.

The commission requested all e-mails between the SEM and the PSEM pertaining to the allegations in May but was told that there were none (Gooch, 2007). The transcripts of the cross examinations and reexaminations of witnesses and the taped conversation between the president, Professor Morris, and the SEM, and a videotaped presentation involving the PSEM, were not posted to the web site but were cited extensively in the closing submissions, extensively cross-referenced and summarized in the final report.

Seventy witnesses provided written statements, and twenty-four were heard on oath or affirmation between March 6 and May 26, 2007. Each witness was subjected to cross examination by the legal representatives of Professor Morris and Professor Luk, the HKIEd Council, the SEM and PSEM, and the commission, and then reexamined by the counsel of the party that called them. The more significant witnesses were obliged to make multiple appearances.

Closing submissions were made by the four parties and Counsel for the Commission on June 5 and 6, and the final report presented to the chief executive on June 20, 2007 (Yeung & Lee, 2007). It was accepted without change.

The commission excited a great deal of public attention and commentary, with the SEM and the PSEM being satirized in the annual Cheung Chau Bun Festival parade (Wong & Tsui, 2007). The English newspaper in Hong Kong with the largest circulation, the *South China Morning Post*, ran over 50 articles during the course of the inquiry. The nature of the public commentary suggested that the commission was seen as a litmus test of Beijing's intention to honor President Jiang Zemin's promise.

Hence, the following analyses attempt to reveal the nature of, and evaluate the justifications used by, HKIEd's senior management, the HKIEd Council, the University Grants Council (UGC), the Education and Manpower Bureau (EMB) and the commission itself, for current political arrangements in educational administration in higher education in Hong Kong.

Senior management members were first to speak to the allegations. Professor Morris clarified the nature of the HKIEd's institutional autonomy as:

1   Autonomy from the government's civil service systems including funding responsibility that was transferred from the EMB to the UGC
2   Autonomy as defined in the UGC's Note on Procedure, that, within the restraints of the laws of Hong Kong, specifically as

   a   Academic freedom and institutional autonomy to select staff, select students, set curricula and academic standards, accept research programs and allocate funds within the institution.
   b   A legal entitlement to freedom of action in managing their own affairs with unfettered rights in the selection, promotion and dismissal of staff, and the authority to approve new programs and change in programs internally instead of having to rely on external accreditation agencies (Morris, 2007).

Regarding the first allegation, Professor Morris described an "unsuccessful" campaign by Professor Li from March 2002, when he was vice chancellor of the CUHK, first to merge the CUHK, the Hong Kong University of Science and

Technology (HKUST), and the HKIEd, and second, once he became SEM, to merge the Hong Kong Polytechnic University and the City University of Hong Kong and to merge the HKIEd with the CUHK.

Much was made of the threat allegedly made in 2002, when Professor Li was still at the CUHK, specifically that the HKIEd would be "raped" if it did not agree to a merger, and the coercive nature of the SEM's behavior since his appointment. Morris contrasted the term *merger* with *federation*, *deep collaboration* and *loose affiliation* as defined in the Niland Report (UGC, 2004).

Evidence was provided to argue that the SEM's campaign for mergers did not have government support, included threats to make the HKIEd unviable, ignored advice from HKIEd's council and undermined relationships between the EMB and the HKIEd. Professor Morris then submitted the transcript of a telephone conversation that he had with the SEM, apparently taped without his knowledge, in which the SEM said that if the HKIEd continued to press for university title, he would set up a committee to decide the future of the institution; whether it should be merged into another university or disbanded altogether.

Regarding the second allegation, Professor Morris documented the deteriorating relationship with the PSEM, her reactions to public criticism by academic staff (faculty to Americans) and her attempts to obtain research proposals and to have four academic staff sacked. He also claimed that the chairman of council acted as an agent of the SEM from 2005 by pressing for a merger, and that his noncompliance then led to his non reappointment as president, with effect in September 2007. Regarding the "ways and manner" in which advice might be given by the government to the institute; Professor Morris criticized the power exercised by the EMB through the UGC without appropriate representation.

In his witness statement, Professor Luk explained how he had come to learn (a) that the SEM's merger proposals were not government policy, (b) about the PSEM's attempts to dismiss colleagues, (c) that the SEM's coercion had led to a "deep collaboration" agreement with CUHK and (d) that their council chairman was not ready to help defend the autonomy of HKIEd (Luk, 2007). He described the dominant role of the EMB in setting student places for the 2005–2008 Triennium and claimed that they were adjusted to the detriment of the HKIEd by the PSEM at the behest of the SEM. He claimed that it was the corruption of the presidential review process, the SEM's public support for the chairman's actions concerning the nonrenewal in January 2007, and a press conference called in early February by council officers and a group of external council members, that had triggered his independent posting of the allegations that led to the inquiry. His purpose was, he reiterated, to bring to the government's attention that the pressure exerted by the SEM and PSEM had been inconsistent with policy, unfair and unprofessional, and that the PSEM's behavior had been inappropriate.

Professor (and Dean) David Grossman, and one of two staff council members appointed to the ad hoc committee on the reappointment of the president, cited events that they believed had indicated that the SEM's merger strategy had moved from open to stealth tactics after his appointment and that due process had been violated during the presidential review. Grossman saw the "central issue as one of governance;" whether the HKIEd council had the constitution to meet established standards of university operations, including the ability to operate independently of government pressure, and to follow proper protocols in the review of senior appointments. His conclusion was that there had been "undue pressure" from the SEM and PSEM in operations, and that the chairman had "failed to protect the interests of the HKIEd" when he promoted actions that contradicted its policies (Grossman, 2007).

In his initial written statement, Dr. Thomas Leung Kwok-fai (Dr. Leung), a member of HKIED's council since 1994 and chairman since April 2003, traced the council's frustrated demands for change at HKIEd, despite the accumulating advice of the Sunderland Review, an internal Taskforce on the Future Development, the UGC's review of Hong Kong higher education system (known as the Niland Report) and a joint Working Party on Deep Collaboration with CUHK (Leung Kwok-Fai, 2007). He noted the negligible strategic progress achieved by the HKIEd's senior management, and instead, the gradual evolution of a "siege mentality."

In particular, Dr. Leung described a sharp deterioration in relationships after his breakfast meeting with Professor Morris on June 10, 2006. The three purposes of this meeting had been to ascertain the president's interest in reappointment, discuss the review and decision making processes, and provide preliminary feedback from the council on the president's performance over the last four years. His feedback was that Professor Morris would find it a challenge to win two thirds support from eligible external members, given their concerns over the last two to three years, which were apparently specified. From then on, Dr. Leung claimed the president construed all requests for strategic leadership toward a federation as pressure to initiate a merger as a condition of his reappointment.

Dr. Leung's second and third submissions denied claims made concerning interference by the SEM or PSEM and violations of due process by the council, and clarified his "death by 1,000 cuts" comment made in an opening address at the first retreat and how the council came to fully support the outcomes of the second retreat.

Mr. Michael Stone, the secretary general of UGC, confirmed that

> The Administration gives, *inter alia*, specific manpower requirements covering disciplines, including teachers. These are not "instructions," although conventionally it is understood by all parties that the UGC and the institutions will try and meet them if possible. Nevertheless, it has happened in the past that the UGC has reverted to the Administration on specific manpower requirements for one reason or another, with a view to having changes. (Stone, 2007)

His subtle, studiously neutral and uncritical explanation claimed that the UGC played a largely facilitative role in the accommodation of interests in higher education.

The main submissions from the EMB were made by the PSEM and the SEM. The PSEM's initial submission (Law, 2007c) explained how changes in the administrative policy context of higher education had sought to improve quality while also having to deliver 11% savings over five years, with tertiary and vocational sectors suffering disproportionate cuts. The UGC was given 10% less for the 2004–2005 year for its eight institutions, with steady-state funding thereafter for the 2005–2008 triennium. Whereas the 15% contraction of the primary school population between 2000 and 2005 had released some expenditure for the education reforms, she said, it increased pressure on the viability of some schools and the HKIEd, which primarily trained early childhood and primary school teachers. In this context, the PSEM clarified how the EMB had projected education manpower requirements and actively engaged with its stakeholders, including "frank exchanges" with academic critics in an open and pluralistic society. Her habit of calling individuals reflected her

> firm belief that, in an open government, civil servants have the responsibility to reach out to stakeholders to gather views, explain policies, and receive feedback. I believe that academics have an open mind and should welcome discussion of different points of view. A direct approach by civil servants to exchange views should not therefore be seen as interfering with academic freedom.

Regarding the first allegation, she denied any bias, lack of transparency, or variance from policy. Regarding the second allegation, that she had repeatedly demanded the dismissal of four academic staff, she denied on three grounds: they were implausible given known dismissal procedures; they were illogical if the alleged repeated demands led to repeated failures over four years; and they bore no relation to the processes actually used to manage redundancies in the HKIEd since 1994. She denied any knowledge of the conversation referred to in the third allegation.

The PSEM's second written submission sought to rebut Professor Morris's oral claims that she demanded the dismissal of four academic staff (Law, 2007b). Her third written submission (Law, 2007d) clarified the policy and methodology of allocating student places. Her fourth written submission responded to the expansion of allegations made and new matters raised during the course of the inquiry, and rejected "offensive" statements attributed to her in international settings as "preposterous and incredible" (Law, 2007a).

Professor Li, the SEM, provided a written statement that refuted the first and third allegations and cast doubt on the second (Li, 2007). He rejected the first allegation:

> In fact my suggestion was to the contrary. What I said was that, since the institute already knew that it would be facing significant cuts due to a general cut in government funding, and the institute's front-end loading would come to an end, the institute should seriously consider their future positioning in order to cope. Moreover, I said there would be additional funding from UGC to encourage restructuring and collaboration between the institutions. (Li, 2007, para. 3.2)

He went on to state that:

> My bureau's direct input on student number targets in respect of teacher education comes at a very early stage in the process. . . . My personal influence, or that of the PSEM, if any, is certainly not sufficient (on any reasoned view) to amount to a "free hand" in cutting the number of students of the institute. (Li, 2007, para. 3.8)

In another general observation, he noted that:

> As both Professor Morris and Professor Luk acknowledge, there has to be a balance between autonomy and accountability. Inevitably our respective views on where the fulcrum should be differ. . . . SEM's remit and that of the bureau require us to take broader interests into account in policy formulation. The government's resources are not infinite and the bureau must consider the interests of all educational institutions, not just those of tertiary institutions or the narrow interests of any single tertiary education institution . . . [on the other hand] (Li, 2007, para. 3.22) . . . I do use quite properly the prospect of additional funding from UGC . . . for an institution as an encouragement for it to embrace changes which the bureau believes, based on independent advice, would deliver an improved education system . . . [although] . . . I did not and would not threaten to cut an institution's funding if it refused to change, even if I was able to do so single-handedly. (Li, 2007, paras. 3.19–3.20)

He refuted the third allegation noting that it was based on the mistaken premise that the bureau's relations with the teachers' unions were poor.

The closing statements of all parties tended to focus on legal issues of interpretation, the materiality and quality of evidence, the relative credibility of witnesses and the most plausible explanations for the refuted allegations using extensive citations and interpretations of statements revealed under cross examination. They are not examined in technical detail past this point, with attention focusing instead on matters pertaining to governance, with such matters continuing to be discussed exclusively in legal terms.

The SEM and PSEM's joint closing statement and executive summary (Li & Law, 2007a, 2007b) drew heavily on the Sutherland and Niland reports to reassert the role of the EMB in policy making and implementation, issues taken up below. The closing statement of the counsel for the HKIEd council (Hong Kong Institute of Education Council, 2007) affirmed the council's policy of no full merger and deep collaboration, and that it had formally approved the process used to evaluate the president's performance. They rejected suggestions of "impropriety" or breach of procedure or law and noted that all but two witnesses had "affirmed the integrity of [the] council when it voted 10–3 against the reappointment of the president" (Hong Kong Institute of Education Council, 2007, p. 22). They confirmed that the council as a whole had never exerted pressure on Professor Morris to agree to a merger and that Professor Morris and Professor Luk had failed to notify or consult the council regarding the allegations or prior to the allegations being posted to web sites.

Counsel for the HKIEd council drew attention to the deliberate exclusion of council officers from consultations with CUHK in October and November 2006 in which Professor Luk's team proposed to replace the HKIEd council with a HKIEd board of trustees with cross membership with the council of CUHK that would lead to full federal integration by 2015 under the CUHK council. They reiterated that they had requested an explanation from Professor Morris of this unauthorized exploration of a full merger but were yet to receive a response.

In their closing statement, the senior managers reiterated the evidential base for the allegations and commented on revelations and interpretations, but as with the council, made relatively little comment on the nature and quality of extra institutional governance arrangements.

Counsel for the commission provided advice regarding legal methodologies of fact finding and evaluating standards of proof, the details of the factual and chronological context and the relative reliability and credibility of the witnesses, and offered suggestions concerning governance that are examined below (Counsel for the Commission, 2007). There was no equivalent advice provided concerning the analysis of governance.

The Commission of Inquiry announced its findings on June 20, 2007, in almost exclusively legal terms. It found that, contrary to the first allegation, there was "no concerted effort to force HKIEd to agree to a merger with CUHK by improperly reducing the student numbers of HKIEd in order to render it unviable" (Yeung & Lee, 2007, p. 107). Although it found that the second allegation was "partially established," it considered it reasonable to reach further and conclude that the PSEM's actions, "even if well-intended, were improper and constituted an improper interference with . . . academic freedom." With regard to the third allegation, "there was insufficient evidence to show any improper interference by SEM or other government officials with the institutional autonomy of HKIEd" (Yeung & Lee, 2007, p. 107). The commission's findings concerning governance arrangements are addressed below.

In its conclusion, the commission expressed the hope that improved communication between the EMB and TEIs would reduce their mutual misunderstanding and distrust, and would enable them more effectively to serve the education sector and the public at large. The general inference that could be taken was that the Commission of Inquiry had encountered a case of "good system, poor interpersonal relationships." The use of political philosophy now shows that taking such an inference without question would be naïve.

How the parties addressed governance issues was most revealing. As noted above, the senior management and the council of the HKIEd focused on the three allegations. They showed relatively little interest in the nature and quality of governance infrastructure. In sharp contrast, senior government officials and the Counsel for the Commission went to considerable length to suggest improvements that would both tighten and justify current arrangements regarding state governance of higher education. The commission adopted all of these suggestions, ostensibly in the public interest, without evoking the wider and growing crisis in state governance being driven, as it will be shown, by changes in the wider political economy.

The SEM and PSEM's joint closing statement and executive summary (Li & Law, 2007a, 2007b) made heavy use of the Sutherland and Niland reports to assert eight justifications for the department's central role in policy making and implementation in higher education:

- Given the degree of public funding involved and the importance of higher education, the government and the community has a legitimate interest in the operations of institutions with regard to quality and cost efficiencies.
- The UGC acts as a buffer to safeguard both academic freedom and autonomy of institutions while ensuring value for money for taxpayers.
- Triennial recurrent block grants and strategic capital investments are two major mechanisms used to reconcile the academic freedom and autonomy of institutions with government policy and economic objectives endorsed for the HKSAR.
- The academic freedom and autonomy of institutions are negotiated freedoms balanced by the acceptance of responsibility, the constraints of public funding and the need for public accountability.
- There is a legitimate role for government and the UGC in setting the framework in which the higher education sector pursues its roles and missions.
- Where public funds are static or in decline, and where sources of private funds are seriously limited, public policy can be expected to take a closer interest in how resources are allocated and the outcomes.
- The SEM is the gatekeeper of the public interest and represents the interests of the government.
- The SEM's prerogative and duty is to have a large say in how those interests are to be pursued, to ensure that public interests take priority over the vested interests of the few—even when the few allege violations of academic freedom and institutional autonomy.

The Counsel for the Commission tacitly endorsed these assertions by proposing a strengthening of state control mechanisms. They proposed the activation of Section 8(1)(d) of the ordinance in order to allow the chief executive to appoint from one to three public officers to the council of the HKIEd, supposedly to improve communications with the EMB. They offset this by recommending the reactivation of representation from tertiary education institutions (TEIs) on the EMB's Advisory Committee on Teacher Education and Qualifications (ACTEQ). The counsel also suggested the formalization of communications on all issues of concern in the future.

Finally, the Counsel for the Commission recommended the establishment of a formal avenue for redress, that is, a committee that would be perceived to be independent of government and enjoy the trust and respect of the TEIs (Counsel for the Commission, 2007), curiously without reference to the UGC's current role as an honest broker.

The commission's findings with regard to governance advisory and implementation functions then focused on the need for more effective relationships between the EMB and the HKIEd (Yeung & Lee, 2007, pp. 108–111). The two grounds for this argument were the former's responsibility in meeting the needs and expectations of society, and the latter's unique position as the sole institution of higher education dedicated to teacher training. The commission explicitly determined that the EMB is entitled in law to exercise control over HKIEd within policy and to improve the quality of teachers and education, while acknowledging that the degree of control is a sensitive and difficult issue that involves balancing conflicting interests. Indeed, the commission predicted growing conflict between TEIs, the EMB and the UGC over funding arrangements but oddly gave no advice on the effectiveness or legitimacy of problem solving criteria and processes. However, by attributing blame to poor interpersonal relationships between participants, the commission rendered the political and bureaucratic conditions that had contributed to the crisis all but invisible.

Instead, the commission explicitly reinforced current political arrangements without evoking their quality. It endorsed the EMB's view of its powers and its right to trade off academic freedom and institutional autonomy against responsibility, resources and accountability. Further, it endorsed all of its own counsel's recommendations, and went further by recommending that the chief executive in ExCo consider his reserve powers under Section 5 of the Hong Kong Institute of Education Ordinance (Cap 444). This enables the chief executive in ExCo, if need be presumably, to give HKIEd directions with respect to the exercise of its powers or the achievement of its purposes in the legal certainty that the HKIEd would comply with any directions given.

This was sharp rebuff to President Morris's arguments concerning the development and violation of institutional autonomy. Indeed, the recommended appointment of up to three more public officials from the EMB to HKIEd's council was explained in terms of their need to be "proactive" in explaining government policies with respect to HKIEd's development, and that such participation should be viewed as an attempt to help improve communications and not as interfering with institutional autonomy. It is, however, much more likely that this change would be seen by members of council, senior management, academic staff and potential international members of academic staff as a significant strengthening of the EMB's power to influence the HKIEd's council, at inevitable cost to its autonomy.

The commission then sought to reinforce the ambiguous independence of the UGC, by noting that its decisions are not susceptible to further formal review or appeal. It then lamely affirmed the UGC's relative powerlessness, as a buffer between the EMB and TEIs, but then undermined its standing as an honest broker by proposing another new board to serve as an avenue of redress between the EMB and TEIs. This board was to advise the government on policies and development plans of TEIs and hear appeals from TEIs on UGC funding arrangements, while somehow being moderated by the UGC. At the very least, this arrangement would lead to structural ambiguity and, at the worst, undermine the development of any coherent alternative to EMB policy proposals by the UGC. More power had shifted to the EMB.

The commission endorsed the proposal that the EMB reactivate the ACTEQ with representatives from all TEIs, symbolically turning the clock back to a more consultative era. With regard to procedures, the commission recommended that the EMB's messages be given formally and with proper documentation, presumably to prevent power plays around deniability or policy directives being "dead handed" by deliberate inattention. It also recommended that the EMB consult TEIs on teacher education and training issues, including manpower planning and requirements, before advising UGC regarding triennium planning or rollover arrangements. In sum, the EMB's hand in policy advisory and implementation functions had been procedurally finessed, legally legitimated and politically strengthened, albeit with the public sacrifice of the PSEM.

As noted above, the commission concluded its findings by expressing the somewhat pious hope that improved communication between the EMB and TEIs would result in a reduction in their mutual misunderstanding and distrust. Whereas the declared intention was to remind them of their shared responsibility to serve the education sector and the common good, the next sections show that the antagonism is not so much the result of poor interpersonal relationships, but a consequence of tensions in the wider political and administrative order, and that the nature of governance in institutions of higher education is subordinate to the wider political infrastructure in Hong Kong and in the PRC.

The commission systematically reaffirmed the current distribution of power in the HKSAR of the PRC. To clarify, the power to make public policy in Hong Kong is vested in a nonelected ExCo, whose members are appointed and chaired by the chief executive, with the bureaucracy long having achieved preeminence in policy formulation. The commission quite correctly noted that the chief executive has the authority in law to direct the HKIEd, and that his authority has been delegated to the SEM to advise policy making in higher education and to the PSEM to manage policy implementation. It also noted the delegation of power to the council of the HKIEd for institutional policy making and to the president and CEO to manage policy implementation, all within wider government policies. The primary justification for this structure of delegated authority, as stressed by the SEM and the PSEM, and affirmed by the commission, were that these arrangements were to serve the public interest or the common good.

It is interesting that none of the parties to the inquiry or the commissioners referred to a social contract between the governors and the governed in higher education at any level, or gave any other justification for the distribution and mechanisms of power than the public interest. For example, the commission limited its justification for academic freedom on the grounds that the "Active and uninhibited dissemination of ideas is a vital mechanism for the production and preservation of knowledge, crucial not just for HEIs but also for society as a whole" (Yeung & Lee, 2007, p. 91). The nature of society as a whole was left undefined in communitarian terms, and President Jiang Zemin's vision concerning its governance was never evoked, possibly to prevent it becoming a political lightning rod. When the commission justified its findings in regard to autonomy, it argued that

> Whilst the government must not interfere with the substantive autonomy of TEIs in their knowledge production and dissemination, the government's steering of HKIEd towards institutional collaboration, which was consistent with properly formulated education policy and public interest, cannot be considered unjustified interference with its institutional autonomy. (Yeung & Lee, 2007, p. 106)

These exclusively common good justifications raise the question as to the extent to which the wider politico-administrative order actually values a liberal democratic political ideology, or its potential handmaidens in educational administration of communitarianism, communicative rationalism, or egalitarian liberalism.

A classic set of tests for liberal democracy is available (Finer, 1970). The first test is that liberal democratic regimes typically justify the legitimacy of public policies and day-to-day decisions using the critical awareness (rather than the ignorance) of the population, and by seeking to convince them using persuasion rather than by coercion.

Although the SEM and PSEM's robust political behaviors demonstrated that persuasion can take many forms, the overriding concern of the government, through setting up an independent commission, was responsiveness to public opinion aroused by the allegations that the executive of the government had interfered with academic freedom and institutional autonomy. Other related concerns on display that emphasized the HKSAR's apparent preference for persuasion over coercion included the common interest requirements for societal continuity, strategic planning, achieving collective goals and effective administrative services provided by responsible secretaries of policy bureaus and their bureaucracies. In the background is the ongoing need for the HKSAR to finesse the reconciliation of Hong Kong's colonial and capitalist past and its position as a special administrative region in a wider state dominated by the Communist Party of China (CPC), the founding and ruling political party of the PRC.

Finer's second test for liberal democracy comprises three conditions: that government is derived from and is accountable to public opinion; that public opinion can be and is openly and freely expressed; and that the majority of opinion prevails when policies are in dispute.

Although government and business in the PRC are controlled by the CPC (Hutton, 2007), it is not clear about the extent to which these conditions prevail in Hong Kong.

Finer's third test concerns the ways and manner of government. It is assumed in liberal democracies that governments operate at the margin of society. Any intervention into the autonomous, self-creating and voluntary associations that comprise society has to be justified. Society is assumed to be pluralistic in its views, values and interests, and the government is to protect minorities and promote reconciliation as it governs in the common interest. Finally, governments do not impose any creed, philosophy, religion, or ideology on society but instead tolerate pluralism, accommodate interests without compromising the common interest and facilitate change through orderly policy making political processes.

Whereas the commission sought to highlight a few instances of these operational criteria of a liberal democracy, they endorsed the enabling structures that gave rise to the highly centralist, aggressive and interventionist nature of the EMB's ways and manner, suggesting that it is a front for the HKSAR government and the CPC.

Finer's fourth and final test concerns the four general characteristics of a liberal democracy that are deliberately intended to "bring friction, delay, and the necessity for consultation and compromise into the operation of government" (Hutton, 2007, p. 72):

1   Democratic representation of public opinion and public accountability.
2   An executive that implements policy and provides expert advice on its formulation.
3   Social and economic checks and balances, such as decisions in communities, professional associations and businesses.
4   Political checks and balances, such as separating control and powers of the judiciary, the executive and the legislature, having upper and lower houses and the territorial division or devolution of powers.

Although it is obvious that the HKSAR government would currently fail many parts of this test, as would many countries internationally, it is less obvious why the common good justification for liberal democracy was given near absolute standing by the commissioners without reference to other forms of justification.

One reason is that political power in Hong Kong has long been highly centralized and bureaucratized with relatively little structure giving effect to the concept of a social contract between governors and the governed (Lau, 1984, pp. 26–28). The government of the HKSAR comprises the ExCo, which acts as a policy making cabinet, the unicameral Legislative Council (LegCo; with two chambers of members confusedly elected from geographic and functional constituencies), the judiciary and the executive. Consistent with Article 54 of the *Basic Law*, it is ExCo that assists the chief executive in policy making. Although the ministerial system of accountability introduced in 2002 deemed the members of ExCo (who were also the secretaries of policy bureaus) to be *political appointees*, and then required them to leave the civil service and appoint permanent secretaries, none of them actually had a democratic mandate. Further, when Donald Tsang was elected chief executive in 2005, he personally selected some members of LegCo and eight nonofficial or public figures to serve on ExCo, and then asked all but three of the bureau secretaries to attend only when issues related to their portfolios were being discussed.

The ostensible result was overrepresentation by elite business interests and uncompromising implementation through the secretaries of bureaus, like the SEM from the EMB, with influence by Beijing effectively shrouded. Hence, although this structure of representation led to questions in LegCo about the wisdom of "governance by business tycoons" supported by a 'bureaucratic polity' (Koehn, 2001, pp. 98, 110–112), it presented no challenge to the wider and hidden hegemony of the CPC.

One reason is that the most popular elected party in LegCo, the Democratic Party, can never achieve a majority due to the current structures of representation. It is unlikely that LegCo will vote for democratic reforms to its own structure and even less likely that the chief executive or the HKSAR government would support such a proposal if they wish to retain power in Hong Kong. It appears that, in the absence of a democratic mandate, the legitimacy of governance will continue to rest exclusively on an abstract, exclusively defined and absolute value—the public interest—unless or until broader economic forces gradually threaten societal stability and prosperity and provide the conditions for the development of a fresh social contract. There are good reasons for supposing so.

Political economists have been mapping the changing forces systematically (Lee, 1998). Hong Kong has been undergoing major changes in recent decades due to global and regional economic restructuring, the reversion of sovereignty and rising political consciousness in Hong Kong. The PRC's open door economic development policy encouraged Hong Kong to outsource its production and to substantially expand its service industries, with relatively limited need for additional public services, other than to expand welfare services for an aging population and improve communications infrastructure.

During the lead up to handover in 1997, the business sector safeguarded its long-term interests by gaining an agreement from the PRC that there would be no change to economic and political institutions for 50 years and by having Article 107 embedded in the *Basic Law*. Article 107 requires the HKSAR government to deliver no-deficit budgets that match economic growth. These two agreements alienate the public from their right to alter economic and political institutions and to make authoritative resource allocations through democratic processes, two essential components of a living social contract.

Among the long-term effects Lee noted were five major policy aims inherited from the 1990s: a fiscal policy of low tax rates; surplus budgets and substantial reserves; an economic policy of noninterventionism and economic viability of the polity; a public service policy of low expenditure, contained growth and high quality; and a political policy of public accountability, distributive justice and the democratic legitimacy of governance. These aims are partially conflicted and have been accommodated by managerial rather than political responses. Seen as management challenges by the bureaucracy, these policy goals were converted into strict budgeting and resource management, tight controls on staffing in the public service and down scaling or adjusting public capacity, as evidenced in the case study. Lee's compelling analysis showed that the net effect of the new pragmatic managerialism was to adjust the public sector to the changes in the political economy, in three specific *ways and manner*:

1   In the absence of democratic accountability, administrative accountability has become the normative basis for administrative authority.

2   The principle of living within our means has been used to legitimate the authoritative distribution of community resources by fiscal policy and centralized budgeting procedures, rather than through democratic discourse addressing distributive and social justice.
3   The expanded use of performance management techniques increased the state's capacity to improve productivity and organizational cultures in executive agencies without having to invest in democratic infrastructure.

Ironically, in a supposedly communist state, the first condition ruled out communitarianism, the second preempted communicative rationalism and the third displaced any possibility of egalitarian liberalism by the managerial pragmatism practiced by executive agents of the state.

Two preliminary conclusions can be drawn at this point. The PRC's takeover of Hong Kong had resulted in the politicization of the public service. Administrative reforms had become a substitute for political reforms, which suggests that President Jiang Zemin's promise of democratic structures is unlikely to be delivered any time soon.

On the other hand, government will have to develop in Hong Kong to accommodate changes in the political economy. The terms of the *Basic Law* and the interests of the ruling elites in ExCo suggest that the common good will continue to be stressed, even as political and economic conditions change and challenges develop to their near-monopoly on policy making and resource allocation.

To understand how this could work out in public administration, it is important to realize that there is not "one country: two systems," as ingratiated in the *Basic Law*, but "one government: multiple systems" (Koehn, 2001). In addition to the politicization of public administration, public servants are increasingly being pressured behind the scenes by the PRC government and, more overtly, by pro-democracy forces, the chief executive and ExCo, the members of LegCo and the business sector. And although the public bureaucracy has maintained its central role in policy making, at the behest of ExCo, it has been increasingly pressed by the chief executive to lift its responsiveness, while the legitimacy of its authority has waned, increasingly questioned due to its lack of a popular mandate.

The Commission of Inquiry, therefore, served ExCo well by keeping this issue of political legitimacy out of public discourse. At the same time, members of LegCo had been striving to advance their role and credibility in policy formulation, and had been pressing to reform their own internally divided chambers. The net result, as Koehn demonstrated, has been a fragmented and volatile politico-administrative environment with multiple, competing and superimposed systems of governance, one government, multiple systems.

The case study of the Commission of Inquiry showed that only a public interest or common good justification had been advanced to legitimate current political arrangements in educational administration in higher education in Hong Kong. To recall, it had been alleged that government officials had interfered with academic freedom and institutional autonomy at HKIEd to the potential detriment of academic staff, the institution and society. Although the first and third allegations were determined by the commission not to be supported by the evidence or by the balance of probabilities, the second allegation was found to be supported with regard to two of the four subjects.

The commission's recommendations, therefore, can be interpreted as an attempt to prevent violations of academic freedom using legal means, to delimit the concept of institutional autonomy and to improve relationships between the EMB and the senior management of the HKIEd—and with TEIs more broadly, by edict. As noted above, the general finding of "good system, poor interpersonals" rendered the role and legitimacy of governance invisible.

To return to the beginning, the terms of reference of the commission specifically asked for recommendations on the ways and manner in which the government might better advise the institute with respect to its use of power and achieving its objects. This was not taken to mean, yet could have been, that the government genuinely wanted advice on how it might better govern the HKIEd and Hong Kong's system of higher education institutions. The allegations, however, were shown to be couched in and responded to in ways that made no reference to the nature of society, a knowledge society, or a social contract that is typically constructed between the governors and the governed in a liberal democracy.

The commission's legal discourse only used a common good justification and did not attend to issues relating to the nature and legitimacy of governance. The commission was directed to, and subsequently reinforced, the ostensible commitment of the government of Hong Kong to the principle of academic freedom, mainly through blaming and arranging a largely symbolic public sacrifice of the PSEM.

In so doing, the commission uncritically reiterated the structures of government and power relations in higher education in Hong Kong. Understandably, the inquiry was watched carefully by the HKSAR's senior civil servants because of the potential precedents that could have been created regarding any redistribution of administrative power—or even less likely, any deployment of alternative political ideologies. They would have been reassured by the reinforcement of the EMB's power.

On the other hand, the very public nature of the inquiry and the intensity of public interest in academic freedom and institutional autonomy, as proxy indicators of the continued commitment by the CPC to President Jiang Zemin's promise, can presume that those appointed as SEMs and PSEMs will be asked to be more respectful in their relationships with TEIs in the future.

Finally, the analysis of the wider context of public administration suggested that the current politico-administrative arrangements in higher education revealed by the Commission of Inquiry cohere with but are subordinate to the CPC's wider bureaucratic hegemony that supports governance largely by business leaders, leaders who front for the CPC (Hutton, 2007). Given President Jiang Zemin's explicit promise of gradual democratization to Hong Kong, it appears that an opportunity was missed by the litigants to have the roles of academic freedom and institutional autonomy considered in liberal democracies and in knowledge societies.

This would have enabled critical questions to be asked about the legitimacy of the administrative policy context and the absence of political reforms, rather than have current arrangements faithfully rehearsed and deep structures shrouded, and all reinforced by the commission—arguably, in the common good.

Political and administrative leaders in Hong Kong could also seek to ameliorate another disadvantage that follows the application of an exclusively common good justification, an incapacity to discuss and develop the nature of the political leadership required to deliver President Jiang Zemin's promise. Gradual democratization through universal suffrage will require an educative form of political leadership that can help Hong Kong society steadily acquire appropriate political infrastructure and political culture. An educative form of political capacity building will be needed to further (1) create and justify governance policies, (2) design improvements to political systems appropriate for the changing context, (3) mobilize support for enabling legislation and political and administrative infrastructure, (4) plan implementation processes to enable the public to learn democratic rights and responsibilities, skills and appropriate dispositions, (5) enable elections and the gradual establishment of government through representation and (6) manage evaluation processes that will sustain continuous improvement.

Note

1 It transpired at the outset of the hearings, on March 12, 2007, that the sole government official to be held answerable was to be the former PSEM, Mrs. Fanny Law Fan Chiu-fun, and that the four dates on which the requests were allegedly made were on October 30, 2002, late 2004, November 2004, and April 21, 2005.

9　A crisis in the governance of a Middle Eastern University

The value of academic freedom is closely linked to the fundamental purposes and mission of the modern university. The expanding role that universities are playing in the Information Age only increases its significance. The emergence of a world-wide knowledge economy, the unparalleled transnational flow of information and ideas, and the growing number of young democracies, all make necessary the con-tinued reexamination and articulation of the nature and importance of academic freedom. Indeed, across the globe, the defense of academic freedom remains at the heart of ongoing political and economic battles over the role and the institutional autonomy in higher education.

Academic freedom benefits society in two fundamental ways. It benefits soci-ety directly, and usually immediately, through the impacts and benefits of applied knowledge, the training of skilled professionals, and the education of future leaders and citizens. It benefits society indirectly, and usually over longer periods of time, through the creation, preservation, and transmission of knowledge and under-standing for its own sake, irrespective of immediate applications.

(The First Global Colloquium of University Presidents,
Columbia University, 2005)

There were three unusual features of the Middle Eastern University (MEU, a pseudonym) where I served as chancellor and CEO that are related to the key con-cerns of this book: the confused blend of ownership, trusteeship, governance and management roles; the delayed investment into research infrastructure in favor of returns to investors; and the high turnover of senior expatriate educational administrators (Macpherson, 2008b). In this chapter, I use political philosophy to suggest that these features and the political arrangements, justified by appeal to the norms of hereditary autocracy, actually served to retard the achievement of MEU's vision, mission and strategic plans.

To begin, the political infrastructure at MEU was headed by the board of trust-ees and governors (BTG) chaired by the university patron, a senior Sheikh (Royal) in his thirties. The BTG had mandated the MEU to become one of the pre-mier higher education institutions locally, regionally and internationally. It met irregularly. The university's stakeholders were defined as comprising the BTG; the Executive Board of Governors (EBG; comprising the chairman, the chancellor and

CEO, the provost and the vice chancellor of financial and administrative affairs); the Federal Ministries of Education and Higher Education; the Commission for Academic Accreditation (CAA); leaders in higher education, government and private sectors; international partners; MEU staff members; and the media. Clients were defined as the chairman of EBG, MEU students, parents and sponsors of MEU's students and potential employers of MEU students.

Participation in governance at MEU was limited. Few stakeholders and none of the clients were represented on the BTG. Places were limited to the patron, the investors and a small number of business advisers. Executive power was channeled exclusively through the chairman who, not incidentally, was also the lead investor and member of the BTG. No contact was permitted between employees and members of the BTG. Governance at the MEU was therefore, technically, an autocracy—that is, a form of "absolute government where power is held by an individual or small group and supported by control of critical resources, property or ownership rights, tradition, charisma and other claims to personal privilege" (Morgan, 1986).

Autocracy is a tribal tradition in the United Arab Emirates. When the country was formed in 1971 by a federation of emirates soon after the discovery of oil, the places on the new Supreme Council were limited to the emirs. The Supreme Council retained governance and executive powers by nominating their more able and close relatives as the prime minister and ministers. Land ownership and citizenship was also limited to nationals. These structures were replicated when each emirate developed its own government and when the laws concerning the ownership, governance and management of private enterprises were devised.

Autocracy, therefore, became a cultural and organizational norm. Any questions by expatriates about these arrangements were defined by nationals as "culturally insensitive," and if persisted with, led to the cancellation of their contracts and residency. This chapter suggests that this cultural and organizational norm of autocracy will need to be questioned and modified if governance is to be improved in higher education in the United Arab Emirates.

The chairman of the EBG was the champion of the MEU project. He personally managed the huge capital works program, and at the end of my period there, took over as the CEO. He is a highly intelligent, deeply caring and driven national in his late thirties with an MBA from an American university. He arranged my residency permit for three years, in the first instance, a contract without term and performance targets with bonuses for me to serve as chancellor and CEO from July 2005. I was to provide strategic leadership to the university.

By March 2007, I had delivered early on all of my performance targets. Instead of negotiating another set of targets, a no-fault separation was agreed to take effect from the end of June 2007. The chairman then took over as CEO while I expended accumulated leave and completed market analyses prior to departure.

It is important to note that 18 of the 20 most senior executive, academic and support unit leaders also left MEU at the end of the 2006–2007 academic year. Networking between these leaders identified the main reasons for the abnormally high degree of turnover in this setting. The most salient issue, a political issue, was the concept of "university as autocracy." It was not considered surprising to any of us in the historical and cultural context that most stakeholders and all clients of the MEU had not been given representation in governance or that the chairman intervened to micromanage issues on a daily basis. What did surprise many of us was how autocratic norms impacted us personally, swept aside proven international expertise and violated scholarly norms.

Despite the terms of my contract, I was told by the chairman soon after arrival that I would never be trusted by him, simply because I was an expatriate. More, I would be accounting to him alone without recourse or appeal to the patron and trustees. Further, although my written contract listed his current expectations, and my job description set measures and performance targets and rewards regarding internal strategic leadership, external liaison, line management, project coordination and entrepreneurial initiatives, he made it clear that my role would be (and was) changed as he saw fit.

Hence, while I set up management systems with checks and balances concerning the use of power, in order to encourage systematic, rational and evidenced-based decision making, the chairman increasingly used his near absolute powers to make faster and faster decisions, in order to, as he explained, "boost the university's responsiveness to changing market conditions."

We began with a reasonably clear division of responsibilities. My senior academic leaders and I managed academic strategic planning and operations while the chairman managed the capital works program. As chancellor and CEO, I delivered strategic leadership by (1) participating in governance (on EBG), (2) initiating collaborative strategic planning processes, (3) establishing and chairing the University Council to engage all academic and support unit leaders, (4) establishing or reforming university management systems, (5) line managing the senior executives, (6) initiating improvement projects (such as developing two new schools and faculties in engineering and design, and medical and health sciences), (7) establishing short-life working parties for policy development and action research tasks and (8) nurturing external and international relationships to the university's benefit.

At the same time, the chairman managed the capital works program, a massive undertaking on multiple campuses. However, every now and then he unilaterally launched additional autonomous and entrepreneurial businesses intended to exploit market opportunities in English language, continuing education, bridging education and executive education. The combined results included a steep growth in student numbers from 400 to about 4,000 equivalent full-time students in two years and massive windfall profits, but they also generated structural conflict, turf wars, resource conflicts and increasingly, organizational schizophrenia.

University development strategies were identified by the early workshops of stakeholders and academic and support staff, and, as might be expected, had much in common with the strategies found to be effective elsewhere (Millar, 1995). They included the coordinated development of multiple income streams consistent with a comprehensive set of university purposes. The scope and collaborative development of these strategies, however, did not cohere with the chairman's prior working assumptions. He held the university to be a business, his corporation, and that strategic planning in MEU was therefore to be managed top-down using a "balanced scorecard" planning technology (Kaplan & Norton, 2004) to determine a short list of achievable objectives for focused implementation. His cancellation of the planning processes used by the senior academic leaders, and his rejection of an academic balanced scorecard, sharply highlighted the differences between two political ideologies: autocracy and liberal democracy.

The growing tension between these two sets of assumptions about appropriate governance and management in a university took many forms and increasing disturbed all participants. For example, once the chairman had arrested the development of an academic balanced scorecard, he commissioned external consultants to help him edit his own balanced scorecard strategy map. When it was ready, in April 2007, he tabled it at an executive retreat for implementation. His action was greeted with silent astonishment and vocal support by his small inner circle of Arabic-speaking courtiers, and triggered the mass disengagement of senior academic leaders that occurred over the following months.

One concern shared among academic leaders was that the conflation of governance and planning had replaced the broader purposes of universities with a narrow set of business objectives. Some speculated that the university was to become a *cash cow* for the investors and part of a wider real estate business venture to be financed by an initial public offering (IPO). They were probably proved right when the chairman considered, but turned down for undisclosed reasons, a proposal that members of the university community be given access to shares in any IPO to boost ownership.

A second collective concern was that the power grab by the chairman, to become an all-powerful CEO, undermined the administrative and academic policies and procedures that relied on the careful diffusion of power to prevent tyrannical behavior. A third common concern was that autocratic rule by decree, increasingly informed by the advice of his courtiers, could not be reconciled with open, expert and relatively trustful educational administration, or with strategic leadership services and line management and support systems that were designed to be managed using liberal democratic norms (Raphael, 1970).

A fourth widespread concern was that the internal "business takeover" gave top priority to enrollments in entrepreneurial and vocational education programs in order to achieve and sustain a 20% return on investment in perpetuity. Many quickly realized that this would mean significant delays in funding for research infrastructure, the very infrastructure that was needed to develop human capital with the higher order learning required for human, social and economic development in the region. Instead, by the end of the 2006–2007 academic year, the student profile of the MEU had become very like that of a British college of further education, an Australian college of technical and further education, or an American community college. In effect, the business takeover had significantly reduced the possibility of MEU achieving its vision, delivering on its comprehensive mission and becoming a leading regional university.

A fifth concern was the growing damage to the psychological contracts between academic staff and the university, normally evident in mutual beliefs, perceptions and informal obligations, which both underpin the dynamics and the practical details of service delivery (Conway & Briner, 2005). Most expatriate academic staff had taken the MEU's statement of key values at face value; respect for people, productive environment, quality and excellence, leadership, international standing, customer-centric, scholarship, sustainability, equity, integrity and teamwork. Most expatriate Arabic staff with international PhDs saw these values as legitimating an approach to teaching and learning that traversed Islamic and Western understandings. They also saw them as requiring research that could create fresh blends of Islamic and Western knowledge and values, such as intercultural tolerance, an important agenda in the region. Most expatriate, non-Arabic and non-Islamic staff saw these values as preconditions for effective teaching and research, and for a tolerable lifestyle for their typically young families in the Middle East. When it became known that the chairman's business strategy was to replace a comprehensive university development strategy with an integrated business plan, and be implemented using autocratic norms, many took this to be a violation of MEU's values and a good reason to revise their own psychological contract with the MEU.

A sixth common concern to international academic and support staff was the damage that could be done to personal careers by continued association with an institution of increasingly doubtful academic credibility. All staff members were appointed in full knowledge that the MEU was a self-funded and self-managed university—that is, a private, for-profit enterprise. Many staff and students were attracted by MEU's brand values that equated private and elite standing in the country with international quality, as repeatedly stressed through architectural symbolism and the institution's public relations campaigns. These brand values were further reinforced by meeting national standards for institutional licensure and financial accountability, building much publicized international partnerships, aligning all curriculum with international standards and responding positively to all extra evaluations and capricious interventions by officials, sometimes at the behest of ministers.

This proactive approach to compliance regarding quality assurance was informally contrasted with inconsistent applications of the country's law, the uneven commitment to stakeholder representation in public and private institutions and the largely silent yet substantial and growing doubt in the legitimacy of governance in the MEU. It was widely asserted that the MEU stood for the best international quality practices and standards. However, once it became clear that short-term business objectives were to displace long-term modern and international university values, and that autocracy had displaced the liberal democratic norms internationally asserted in Western-style university governance and management, the brand values of private elitism took on new and less fortunate meanings.

These trends culminated over two years, and since they all happened within the law and cohered with the priorities and norms of the ruling elite in the emirate and in the country, it begged culturally critical questions about the nature and justification for political arrangements at the national level. The nation may need to countenance managing its strategic development in wiser ways. As I note below, there is good reason to believe that ministers at the federal and emirate level have the capacity and determination to carry through such reforms.

When the country was founded, as a monarchic federation of tribal emirates, education was deemed to be a federal responsibility and to be discharged through a ministry. In turn, the ministry established the Commission for Academic Accreditation (CAA) to assure the quality of higher education institutions, which, at the outset, were all public institutions solely for national students. The two primary mechanisms used by the CAA, institutional licensure and relicensure and program accreditation, were copied from the United States, but sometimes without a commensurate belief in the need for checks and balances regarding the use of power. There were gaps in the CAA's establishment legislation, and regular violations of its procedures occurred in 2005–2007. For example, the CAA did not have the authority to expect legal compliance from the higher education institutions in the various "Free Zones" set up in some of the emirates. Branches of prestigious international universities, that had their establishment sponsored by various emirate royal families, were arbitrarily exempted from the CAA's quality assurance requirements. Other start-ups evaded the CAA's national licensure and accreditation processes by being sponsored by a "shell university" that, ironically, was established by the postsecondary Higher Colleges of Technology whose governing council was chaired by the Minister of Education.

Despite these corruptions to policy and due process, and explicit conflicts of interest, the CAA was aware of the trends at the MEU and knowingly permitted the university to depart from its licensed role and its formal commitments to the state. The key point is that the CAA and its ministry were not using effective methods to clarify, deliver and sustain the state's social contract with its people regarding the role of higher education in the nation's development.

There are many methods of steering higher education systems that have been well-tested internationally (Clark, 1983). One method is to establish a sector funding council in order to hardwire purposes and accountability measures and targets to the allocation of public monies, for teaching and research purposes. Funding incentives for research development, such as infrastructure grants and research scholarships, would probably have triggered a strategic switch at the MEU into postgraduate and postdoctoral activity.

Another method is to expect institutional governors and managers to accept responsibility for the quality and productivity of teaching and learning and research outcomes, as compared against international benchmarks. Funding can be hardwired to agreed institutional mandates and service profiles, and commensurate performance measures and targets set with incentives developed to achieve compliance. Yet another is to introduce public-private partnerships (PPPs) in order to enable private investment and improve efficiencies in public higher education institutions (HEIs), and to encourage further switching by private sector investors into organizational solutions that can avoid conflicts of interest and legal ambiguities.

The fundamental problem was that autocracy is not well-disposed ideologically to use expert systems and policy contestability to steer the development of higher education and to build capacity. It is, after all, about serving the interests and gaining compliance with the perspectives of a ruling elite.

Fortunately, the first president of the country, HH Sheikh Zayed Bin Sultan Al Nahyan (1918–2004), embedded service to the people as a primary aim of government and as the basis for its legitimacy. Benevolence became a hallmark of government in the country and led to the democratization initiatives that were intended to blend with traditional and tribal methods of government. As indicated above, liberal democratic governance deliberately distributes power and embeds checks and balances to encourage the accommodation of pluralism. It insists on solutions that are justified by reference to the common good, to the substance of the social contract between the governed and the governors and to other dimensions considered critical to the development of a knowledge society, such as religious and cultural principles.

It is unlikely that the unfortunate trends at MEU will cause a shift in the national approach to governance in higher education. The trigger for review and reform is much more likely to be the growing crisis in the funding, quality and legitimacy of public higher education. It was widely known that the expenditure per public higher education student place had been falling, although unsatisfied demand by nationals had been rising, with inevitable falls in proportionate access, quality and satisfaction. While the annual ad hoc ministerial interventions and arbitrary announcements of additional places appeared to reflect concerns over the growing crisis, and temporarily absorbed complaints, they did not indicate the existence of long-term political or administrative strategies. The United Arab Emirates may be reaching the limits of benevolent autocracy in higher education.

A strategically critical issue for higher education in the country is that ministry policy makes no reference to the needs of the vast majority of the population that do not have rights as citizens, the expatriates. The expatriate members of society, residents for up to two generations without property or electoral rights, and quite unlike nationals, are expected to accept full responsibility for educating their children at all levels. Ironically, this has resulted in a distinct advantage for expatriates, through the working of market forces. The quality of private kindergarten, primary and secondary schools' curricula and pedagogy tend to compare more than favorably with international standards, and therefore attract many national children from professional families.

In sharp contrast, national primary and secondary schools were found, by courageous research commissioned by the minister of education, HH Sheikh Nahyan Bin Mubarak Al Nahyan, to be obsolete in terms of their management, buildings and facilities, teaching methods, curriculum, assessment and outcomes. On November 19, 2005, the readers of the most popular Arab newspaper in the country, the *Al-Ittihad Daily*, were startled to read about 11 major problems in the nation's education system, including unsuitable curricula, collapsing school buildings and low salaries.[1] In the following days, the readers were told that AED

46 billion ($13 billion in USD) would be spent in the next 10 years on rectifying the problems,[2] that current spending was 60% less than international standards,[3] that new salary scales and a long-term contract system were to be introduced,[4] and most surprising, that the state intended to modernize its Islamic curricula.[5]

It was rare for the public in the country to be told that one of their key public services had become obsolete. It was unusual for any education minister to demonstrate the need for radical reform using research and then to immediately obtain billions to carry through the reforms. It was extraordinary for the nationals of a country only 35 years old, that two generations ago were living in desert tribal Bedouin communities and today comprising about 20% of the total population of their country, to knowingly set about transforming their knowledge, skill base and culture. The decision was made by the nation's Executive Council chaired by the president, HH Sheikh Khalifa Bin Zayed Al Nahyan. The decision was based on comprehensive research commissioned by the then minister, HH Sheikh Nahyan Bin Mubarak Al Nahyan. The reform agenda was adopted in 2006 by his determined successor, HE Dr. Hanif Hassan Ali.

A sophisticated reform program was then planned and funds allocated (Macpherson et al., 2007). The radical modernization of schools followed, at the behest of the minister of education, setting aside obsolete leadership traditions and introducing a modern blend of indigenous and educative forms of leadership for schools and the beginnings of democratic processes in the governance of local authorities and professions (Macpherson & Sylvester, 2007; Macpherson & Tofighian, 2007).

However, with the funding-per-student falling in public TEIs, and the press from ministers on institutions to take even more national students, albeit with generous capital investment, there was little evidence to believe that these institutions would be able to respond quickly or effectively to the uneven outcomes of national schooling or to the broader strategic needs of all of the people living in the country. It was therefore timely, on both strategic and equity grounds, to comprehensively review the quality, funding and role of the public in the provision of higher and tertiary institutions.

Having briefly reviewed the national education policy context, I now turn to the distribution of power as evident in the organization and nature of teaching and learning in MEU. The academic organization of the MEU I inherited reinforced a particular view of teaching, that is, as "instruction by an individual teacher." Responsibility for teaching each course was allocated to an academic staff member. Anonymous student feedback was then collected automatically, processed by the Office of Institutional Research (OIR), and returned via a dean who determined appropriate action. Teachers also answered to their deans for the grades they gave to students. Deans moderated the grades awarded, that is, they sometimes altered them to fit some predetermined normal distribution, sometimes without consultation—both controversial practices. Students were broadly accepting of teacher-centered instruction. Teachers were in general tolerant of decanal power, probably because autocratic norms were so pervasive. The relatively few complaints made focused on unusual teacher behavior, such as the absence of handouts or teachers using highly accented English, or on the intellectual arrogance of some nonconsultative deans.

More broadly, the politics of teaching and learning during 2005–2007 were skewed by the twin press of facilities development and financial productivity. The key targets at the university level were to cater for the full range of possible pedagogies in facilities design and, as noted, to achieve a 20% return on equity in perpetuity. At the program level, the key targets were to staff every course with specialist PhD level expertise and to achieve the required return on income. So, when a person took up an academic appointment at MEU, their dean typically allocated a standard teaching load of 12 contact hours per week in their area of expertise, for each of two standard length semesters per annum. Those with program and other leadership roles were given fewer contact hours as compensation. Those who volunteered to teach a summer school class were given an additional and proportionate stipend. All salaries and stipends were tax free and benchmarked against the most attractive and already high salaries in higher education in the country, although inflation was a persistent concern. Academic staff members were provided free accommodation, increasingly on campus as the capital works program advanced, ostensibly to help create a knowledge community.

A new academic staff member was also typically offered a university orientation program by the human resources department and inducted into their college by their dean and program coordinator(s). Each appointee was provided with a modern air-conditioned office for their sole use with a view into an open area that received direct light, a desk, chairs, filing cabinet, a personal computer and high-speed access to the Internet.

Academic teaching staff had immediate access to glass-fronted student interview rooms where students were met and advised according to Islamic norms. Teaching staff were provided with modern teaching facilities that catered for the full range of teaching modes: mass lectures; tutorial spaces; group work; Harvard-style tiered settings for problem-based learning; and as appropriate, bookable computing, science and engineering laboratories. All teaching spaces had excellent lighting, large whiteboards, ICT links for laptops, a datashow and student seating that could be rearranged for group work. The library had a foundational collection that was growing steadily with the advice of the academic staff and a range of study spaces. Although teaching spaces were designed to accommodate a full range of teaching and learning preferences, most teachers limited their teaching style to instruction: A limitation reinforced by the distribution of power and the nature of leadership provided in MEU.

Most academic leadership in 2005–2007 was concerned with the design, organization and productivity of courses and programs, not with pedagogy or professional development. The annual planning process required all continuing courses (and any proposed new courses) to have convincing academic and business cases, prior to provisional approval and budgeting. The academic case for a course had to demonstrate that the course syllabus was coherent, comprehensive and essential to the degree program(s) it contributed to. The business case for a course was expressed on a spreadsheet template as a statement of income and expenditure, and would not normally gain approval unless it forecasted at least a 20% return on income. Deans were expected to consult the responsible colleagues and establish the quality, relevance, demand and financial viability for all continuing courses annually, and schedule delivery accordingly, as well as sustain the overall academic quality and productivity of programs.

It was discomforting to some international colleagues to take part in such planning, and sometimes marketing, to help guarantee the sustainability of their courses, and thus their continuing employment. Some initially saw no link between their course enrollments and their remuneration. The reason typically given for insisting on this link was that a private university can't allow cross subsidies, because they are an unfair imposition on colleagues, on other courses, programs, or colleges and require the biased deployment of scarce resources. It was particularly uncomfortable for some deans to have to accept responsibility for eliminating such cross subsidies and demonstrably improving college productivities, in particular:

- Developing convincing academic and business cases for courses with colleagues and program leaders
- Aggregating them into provisional college budget proposals
- Justifying and improving proposals through rigorous budget challenge processes
- Inventing solutions to problems revealed by the challenge process in order to gain approval
- Taking lead responsibility for right sizing staffing and other resources for effective program delivery, in collaboration with the provost's office, human resources and general services departments
- Coordinating operations to deliver on approved budgets

Hence, while the start-up of teaching systems focused on managing productivity factors to guarantee specific minimum returns on income and equity, and thus institutional sustainability, many other forms of teaching and learning infrastructure normal in universities were at an early stage of development or did not exist.

The issue commented on most unfavorably by academic staff was the absence of research budgets. A draft research policy was approved by EBG for consultations with academic colleagues. This was intended to signal an intention to honor the promise made to early academic appointees; that investment in research would occur in the second five years of the university's development. Academic staff were, however, acutely aware that there was no research development unit engaged in capacity building and some interpreted the slow pace of policy evolution as no more than symbolic action. Funded research opportunities has been found to be a key concern for academic staff internationally (Trowler, 1998).

The effective management and improvement of teaching and learning depended heavily on the performance of the MEU's academic court, school deans and program coordinators. The academic court was initiated soon after the university was established by the provost. Its purpose was to coordinate academic leadership services intended to implement academic policy. The academic court was expected to coordinate academic review, planning and budgeting, teaching programs, program development and accreditation, and quality assurance. It was to maintain oversight of academic leadership services in colleges; the quality of teaching and learning, courses and curricula; academic evaluation and assessment; and research, scholarship and professional development. The provost chaired the academic court which comprised the deans of colleges, the directors of English and a distant campus, chairs, program coordinators, the registrar and the provost's office staff. The academic court established six standing committees to act as advisory bodies to exchange information and opinion among students, faculty and administrators, and to produce resolutions for attention by the academic court.

The effectiveness of the academic court and the standing committees in the period 2005–2007 was badly disrupted by the move to the new campus, staffing levels in the provost's office and in the OIR, the relatively unstructured nature of academic court meetings, very few meetings being called of the standing committees and the wide variance in discursive norms and manners of leaders. The college and program advisory committees were all at a very early stage of development, and with accelerating turnover, became implausible.

Further, the authority of the academic court and university council, and the line management system of the university, were both disrupted from mid 2006 when the centers for continuing education and executive education were established, and their leaders campaigned successfully to be made answerable solely to the chairman. A major accomplishment of the academic court in the period under discussion was its development, trialing and systematic improvement of intra- and intercampus and cross-gender use of video conferencing technology (VCT). The results were so encouraging that permission was successfully sought from the accreditation agency to extend the pilot into an intercampus mode from September 2006, with full sign off eventually achieved. VCT was used extensively to form financially viable intergender and intercampus classes.

A unique feature of teaching and learning in higher education in the United Arab Emirates was that external professional associations were either nonexistent, forming, or very recently formed. One consequence was that many subjects were being taught without disciplinary or ethical oversight by external experts. One of MEU's responses to this anomaly was to contract teams of international and peer-acclaimed consultants and local industry experts to help design internationally benchmarked and locally relevant syllabi. But again, the dangers of autocracy became evident.

In the case of the new degrees in the College of Medicine and Health Science, two in the team were resident expatriates, and thus able to calibrate curriculum to local needs and conditions, while all members were able to embed the requirements of international program accreditation in their discipline. This medicine and health science team then mounted coherent advocacy for three conditions: the need for (1) a constructivist pedagogy, in particular for problem-based learning in preparation for professional service in local health care teams, (2) for courses that were common to all or some health science degree programs into the third year and (3) to give priority, when selecting appointees, to those who would actively develop professional associations and codes of ethics, and scope professional practice suitable for the country.

However, once a delivery partnership was signed with a European university coprovider, who quickly saw the commercial and professional value in the edge-cutting content and pedagogy, and promptly adopted them, the chairman abruptly terminated the services of this design team to save any further development costs. Similarly, another team contracted to design four highly relevant degrees in construction engineering, construction management, landscape architecture and interior design, for an innovative College of Engineering and Design, was arbitrarily dismissed with when a courtier convinced the chairman to shave some short-term costs. The long-term damage done to international relationships by these two actions was not appreciated at court, and the norms of autocracy there made it unlikely that organizational learning would ever be able to make good the strategic blunders involved. Instead, these international disciplinary opinion leaders quietly conveyed their evaluations of MEU through global networks.

In sum, the political arrangements evident in governance and academic leadership at MEU were shown in 2005–2007 to be trending toward and increasingly justified by the norms of autocracy. Newcomers to the MEU were increasingly warned by the old hands to reflect on the unique national, instructional and cultural context of teaching and learning, as described, as they took advantage of the superb teaching and learning facilities. On the other hand, they were also advised to consider the extent to which governance and management arrangements at the MEU reflected the cultural history of autocracy in the country, and when constrained by an exclusively business development strategy, not to expect it to be understood that research was essential to the growth of knowledge.

In the light of the turnover of leaders and faculty, I asked the chairman to advise the MEU's trustees to review the concentration of trusteeship; governance and management roles; the costs of realpolitik displacing expertise in educational administration; and the consequences of automatically distrusting non-nationals and trusting nationals in key leadership and informant roles. I also suggested that they reverse particular trends that would adversely affect the international credibility of the MEU: any further imposition of autocracy; the business takeover of the institutional academic strategy; the dismantling of checks and balances on the development of internal tyrannies; the undermining of academic collectivism; the elevation of courtiers over experts; the conversion of a knowledge organization into a cash cow; the dissolution of psychological contracts; and the disintegration of academic brand values with collateral damage to careers.

A pathway toward more liberal democratic governance and management was also suggested. The first reason given was that it would provide an environment more congenial to Western-educated academic colleagues who would continue to arrive committed to international standards of discipline-governed scholarship and academic freedom. Second, such governance and management would better serve the country's interests.

This leads to my concluding advice to the government of the United Arab Emirates. The chapter above has highlighted the destructive internal institutional politics of MEU due largely to tensions between the norms of autocracy and liberal democracy. It touched lightly on the wider consequences of this tension in the country's higher education system. Nevertheless, there is enough provided to indicate that a review of higher education in the national interest is warranted in a globalizing context. The comprehensive and courageous review of national school education noted above provided an excellent model of process. It led to fundamental reforms to schooling of historic significance to the country and to the Middle East. An equally fundamental review of higher education is now warranted to traverse the private and public sectors to ensure that they help the nation take its place as a leading knowledge society in the Middle East. In so doing, it might address two dilemmas fundamental to the long-term and healthy development of United Arab Emirate society.

First is the felt need among nationals, especially the young male adults, to assume greater responsibility for the government and development of their country. This felt need has to be reconciled with the critical and long-term role that will have to be played by expert expatriates. The under currents of discomfort, dependency, powerlessness and resentment by some nationals need to be patiently explored along with requests by expatriates for more appropriate citizenship and property rights, a planned pathway to universal suffrage and other considered moves toward more appropriate governance in higher education.

There are choices available from collegial and shared forms of governance to corporate and business forms of institutional governance (Altbach, 2005). A thorough review of higher education might therefore identify blended models of governance, such as PPPs, with clear separations of powers, along with a diversification of advanced learning opportunities and cooperative relationships in a multicultural society that may gradually render the current national-expatriate divide obsolete.

The second dilemma is that investment in the quality of research in universities is being offset against investment in professional and vocational undergraduate education. Research is much more than a safety valve to maintain the engagement of creative people in universities, by catering to their idealized perceptions of self and career. It is also more than direct investment into curriculum development, and thus into the competitive advantages of courses, programs and institutions. Research is the most proven method of creating the relatively trustworthy raw material required by knowledge economies, knowledge. When the growth of a knowledge economy is complemented with wise leadership and social entrepreneurialism, it can lead to the managed development of knowledge societies. This chapter started and now concludes by stressing the strategic importance of academic freedom in nations that want to become knowledge societies.

The United Arab Emirates's heavy investment in national human capital, currently biased in favor of bridging, undergraduate, professional and vocational programs in business and ICT to serve economic development is understandable in tactical terms. National strategic needs, however, suggest that these economic manpower demands will need to be better balanced with greater disciplinary diversity, postgraduate program development and capacity building in research.

These changes would be in the common good and help deliver on the social contract between the government of the United Arab Emirates and its peoples as articulated by HH Sheikh Zayed bin Sultan Al Nahyan, to create a tolerant and multicultural knowledge society with a unique Islamic and Arabic heritage.

Notes

1 (2005, November 19). Problems face education: Unsuitability of curricula, collapsing school buildings and low salaries (translated from Arabic). *Al Ittihad*, pp. 8–9.
2 (2005, November 20). Forty-six billion dirhams will be spent developing the education system in the next 10 years (translated from Arabic). *Al Ittihad*, p. 8.
3 (2005, November 21). Spending on education is 60% less than international standards (translated from Arabic). *Al Ittihad*, p. 9.
4 (2005, November 22). New salary scales and long-term contract system (translated from Arabic). *Al Ittihad*, p. 9.
5 (2005, November 23). The full development and modernization of Islamic curricula (translated from Arabic). *Al Ittihad*, p. 9.

10 A crisis of governance in New Zealand's state school system

Systems of educational administration are conditioned by the prevailing political and educational philosophies of the societies in which they operate. As the philosophies change, so do the administrative systems. The systems respond with a lag. A major dampening influence is resistance from groups in the system which feel threatened by proposed new developments.

(Holmes, 1977)

This chapter examines the nature of the political crisis in the legitimacy of the administration of New Zealand's primary and secondary schools in the 1980s using the tools of political philosophy. The crisis occurred when the administrative culture in the education portfolio ignored historical and social imperatives and failed to provide and sustain a policy myth of equal outcomes that would sustain such legitimacy (Macpherson, 1987a). A *high politics* intervention was triggered when bipartisan demands from Parliament were ignored by the education establishment and an electoral backlash threatened the survival of the Lange Labor government (Macpherson, 1992d). The Picot Taskforce consulted stakeholders for nine months and developed a Green Paper that proposed radical changes to governance and administrative structures and processes (Taskforce to Review Education Administration, 1988). The government accepted and promulgated most of its recommendations in a white paper, *Tomorrow's Schools* (Government of New Zealand, 1988) and then directed immediate implementation. This policy process launched a new governance structure for schools and a framework for negotiating a form of a social contract between each school's elected board of trustees and the new ministry. The contract was termed a Charter of Objectives that, once agreed, would become the basis for planning, budgeting, direct funding and managing operations in each school. The longstanding Department of Education and District Boards of Education were abolished in favor of a more compact ministry with only policy development functions and board of trustees with school governance responsibilities.

This chapter reviews the evidence to identify the political ideologies evident in the processes, structures and outcomes—in particular, the attempt to simultaneously redistribute and equalize powers between legitimate stakeholders in school communities and between the government and school communities. As Sir Frank

Holmes intimated, the greatest resistance was encountered from those who felt most threatened—the symbiotic bureaucracies—the Department of Education and its replacement, the Ministry of Education and the teachers' unions, the New Zealand Institute of Education (NZEI) and the Post Primary Teachers Association (PPTA).

To begin, New Zealand has a unique social history (Oliver & Wiliams, 1981) that has always influenced how education is organized. In pre-European times, educational activities were supported by the whanau (extended families) comprising each hapu (tribe). Experiential learning was encouraged by siblings and kaumatua (elders), with some boys being later apprenticed to tohunga (experts) who taught them the more advanced forms of knowledge highly valued at hapu and at iwi (tribal federation) levels. The key forum for community decision making was the marae; the local meeting place where matters were aired and settlements negotiated or determined by rangatira (chiefs). Hence, from the earliest times in New Zealand, Maori decision making about education was generally local in scope, intergenerational in nature and communitarian in purpose.

European settlers began arriving in significant numbers from about the 1830s. When the British acquired sovereignty in 1840 with the signing of the *Treaty of Waitangi*, Maori were guaranteed various rights in perpetuity, including land rights, as tangata whenua (people of the land). The European immigrants settled in what they regarded as largely autonomous provinces, with each province establishing a legislative assembly of sorts. Many schools were built as community projects in settler society (Graham, 1981), usually supported by local Maori leaders to reinforce rongopai, the Christian peace, and to gain access to new understandings and technologies. These early schools reflected a blend of aesthetic, economic and cultural purposes in largely communitarian polities.

When, however, the settlers' demands for land outstripped the pace at which the Maori owners would sell, or disputes over multiple ownership could be settled (Sorrenson, 1981), some of the 10 provincial assemblies convinced the governor to call in military aid from Britain. But after about 25 years of sporadic battles in some regions, and the British gradually withdrew their regiments due to unsustainable costs, the farmers, merchants and political leaders in dispute gradually saw the need for new national political structures and processes to better recognize land rights, the importance of tino rangatiratanga (self-determination) and the value of national economic, legal and administrative services (Belich, 1996).

The post-conflict reconstruction phase, after the New Zealand Land Wars, saw the rapid development of national infrastructure, especially interprovincial communications, and the widespread disruption of traditional lifestyles and local rights by national settler-dominated governments (King, 1981). Many of the alienating effects are still apparent (Bray & Hill, 1973; Levine & Vasil, 1985) and have been the focus of literary comment (Hulme, 1985) and significant activism, research and scholarship (e.g., Spoonley, Macpherson, Pearson, & Sedgwick, 1984). This helps explain the persistent demands for tino rangatiratanga through iwi structures and local government, and the difficulties that national authorities have always encountered over matters of legitimacy (Belich, 2001).

It was during the 1870s that New Zealand's provincial authorities handed over the responsibility for education to the newly formed national government (Cumming & Cumming, 1978). There were, nevertheless, many concerns expressed at the time about the possibility of excessive centralism. The two antagonistic strands to debates then and decades later, were "the principle of popular sovereignty and the principle of strong and active central government" (Robinson, 1985, p. 15). One result was that the *Education Act, 1877*, did not transfer two important functions to the capital, Wellington: namely, the inspection of schools and curriculum control. These responsibilities remained provincial responsibilities until 1914, when, in a period of understandably jingoistic and Empire-centered fervor, the 1877 act was modified to centralize both the inspectorate and curriculum development.

The concerns over centralism did not evaporate. Surges in the economic cycle, in educational thought (Beeby, 1986) and a series of reports in the early decades of the 20th century saw the centrally directed establishment of universal secondary education, universities and polytechnics. The localist lobbies, nevertheless, ensured that all of these new institutions were given boards of governors, or their equivalents, with substantial powers over staff appointments and general policy directions. On the other hand, major changes over the decades to curricula, teaching methods and examinations in schools saw substantial shifts in the power to make policy and appointments to national authorities (Cumming & Cumming, 1978).

Curiously, despite these occasional shifts in the distribution of power, the structures and practices of governance and administration in school education at the center remained much as they were settled back in 1877, and indeed, hardened into a "monocratic variety of bureaucracy" (Weber, 1947, p. 329). As each era brought new problems, which in turn triggered new initiatives, the Department of Education was elaborated with new sections, new divisions and new levels, and acquired a unique organizational culture in the public service that increasingly lagged behind demands. Increasing antithetical to this bureaucratization of educational administration was the demand for responsiveness in other forms of public service (Gibbons, 1981).

The politics and the structures of state in New Zealand have long been expected to offer relatively open, fast and flexible governance, even if they were seen to be overcentralized, and to display a special regard for social welfare (Dunstall, 1981). Parliamentary decision making, for example, became incredibly swift. It reached the point where that New Zealand was said to suffer from an advanced case of hyperlexis: "the pathological condition caused by an overactive law-making gland" (Manning, 1977, p. 767). Three-year parliamentary terms were adopted. The upper house of review, the Legislative Council, was abolished in 1950. And although New Zealand was reputed to have "the fastest law in the west" (Palmer, 1979, p. 77), localism and provincialism persisted. Historian Rollo Arnold (1985) explained that "New Zealanders resent going to Wellington to get permission to live." This deep and abiding distrust of centralist politics has been reinforced by cynical political practices. As a professor of law and one-time prime minister, Geoffrey Palmer, put it:

> There is widespread disenchantment with the way the political process works in New Zealand. People no longer believe what political parties say. Political

fighting also encourages over-simplification of issues, distortion, and lies. The manner in which public decisions are made in our system does not encourage citizens to believe that broad justice is achieved. In between triennial blitz-kreigs upon their sensibilities, citizens have too little opportunity to participate in the way decisions are made on their behalf. There is a distrust in our system of government that stems from people's lack of faith in the process by which decisions are reached. (Palmer, 1979, p. 16)

In general, New Zealand's political and administrative cultures (Gold, 1985) have long anticipated responsive service, participation, or even self-management, rather than trust in a bureaucracy to provide "egalitarianism in the Outback" as has tended to be the case in Australia (Davies, 1960). This begs a crucial question: Why did the New Zealand public suspend its political antagonism to the high degree of centralism in administrative arrangements in education (Parkyn, 1954) for such a long period?

A large part of the answer is the extraordinary grip that three policy myths achieved over education policy discourse in New Zealand by becoming societal myths. Although these policy myths have served to advance many reforms, they have also helped occasionally to ingratiate doubtful practices in education, and consistently, to deflect attention from the appropriateness and lag of long-standing administrative policies and leadership services.

The director of education from 1940 until 1960, Dr. Beeby (1986), explained how the processes of administrative policy making and implementation in New Zealand education were guided last century by three societal myths: survival of the fittest, equal opportunities and equal outcomes. He claimed authorship of the second myth and that it was endorsed without change by Prime Minister Peter Frazer:

> The Government's objective, broadly expressed, is that every person, what-ever his level of academic ability, whether he be rich or poor, whether he live in town or country, has a right, as a citizen, to a free education of the kind to which he is best fitted, and to the fullest extent of his powers. So far is this from being a pious platitude that the full acceptance of the principle will involve the reorientation of the whole education system. (Beeby, 1992, p. xvi)

The main political ideology evident in this statement is egalitarian liberalism, contrasting with its social Darwinian predecessor. Although such policy myths are, of course, contestable, his point was that such policy myths, like other societal myths (Larue, 1975; Murray, 1960; Otto, 1965; Sproul, 1979), have helped control public perceptions of educational success and professionalism in New Zealand. The myths legitimated the patterns of resource and power distribution to the extent that it became very difficult for the outcomes of administrative services to be critically evaluated using the criteria from another political ideology, such as communicative rationality (Bates, 1980; Codd, Harker, & Nash, 1985). Never-theless, research into political processes and structures in state education revealed growing dissatisfaction in the quality of lay participation in school governance (Barrington, 1981) and in the degree of influence that parents have in determining their children's state education, and the pupils even less (Calvert, 1981). It also revealed the long histories of intensely centralized and bureaucratized politics in the NZEI (Ramsay, 1981), the PPTA (Webster, 1981) and the Department of Education (McKenzie, 1981). More broadly, although the closed nature of educational administration had been criticized by both well-informed New Zealanders, such as Sir Frank Holmes (1977) and international experts (e.g., OECD, 1983), it avoided reform until its legitimacy collapsed in the national political context.

According to a long-serving and widely respected Parliamentarian, the Hon. George Gair (1986), events began coming to a head in the mid to late 1970s. Sir Robert Muldoon's National Government from 1975 to 1984 gradually lost credibility in its traditional power bases, the agricultural and corporate sectors, by being so interventionist, and yet surviving by borrowing and adding to the frightening level of external debt. At the same time, Muldoon's minister of education, the Hon. Merv Wellington, shared his leader's reactionary attitudes to education and educationalists. He emphasized "getting back to basic skills" and the need for better teacher performance, vocational curriculum and greater efficiency (1985). His relations with the teachers' unions, never warm, gradually deteriorated. As the July 1984 election approached, exchanges between them became particularly chilly, especially when the teachers' unions added considerable and public weight to the campaign against Wellington's education policies and against the Muldoon government.

The election of the Rt. Hon. David Lange's Labour government in July 1984 ushered in a three-year period of naïve euphoria in education. The euphoria was due to the settling of campaign promises and to the portfolio being largely insulated from the effects of a steadily worsening mixed economy. The naivety became particularly evident as the first Labour minister of education, the Hon. Russell Marshall, mounted a series of extensive consultative exercises on curriculum, examinations and upper secondary schooling but not on administration or leadership. Large representative committees were used, and given the level of commitment to consultation and to obtaining consensus, they tended to renegotiate the status quo and to suggest complex but impracticably expensive wish lists. Some important changes were made, but not on the holistic scale generally expected, nor to the depth many outside the education establishment had apparently hoped for, as events soon demonstrated. However educationally sophisticated, they were politically naïve.

None of Marshall's committees suggested the overhaul of educational administration. Nobody questioned why the large bureaucracies in education, the Department of Education and the teachers' unions had developed such symbiotic relationships that senior officials were able to make career moves easily between them. The consultative processes they celebrated ensured the involvement of so many hands that the distribution and use of power in education was diffused centrally and difficult to link to outcomes. In other words, history and structures were all set to repeat themselves, but for events in the wider political domain.

The Parliamentarians, under steadily increasing pressure from the public, gradually ran out of patience and intervened. The largely bipartisan intervention was initially led by Noel Scott MP (Labor) and Ruth Richardson MP (National). Noel Scott chaired the Education and Science Select Committee noted above and was an ex-district senior inspector of schools of great mana (prestige) who had resigned years earlier in protest at the Muldoon-Wellington treatment of education and teachers to run for Parliament. Ruth Richardson, then the opposition spokesperson on education, used her incisive and interrogative style to full effect, and became a very influential member of the committee.

In 1986, the select committee's report on *The Quality of Teaching* (Parliament of New Zealand, 1986) not only confirmed that the third policy myth of equal outcomes had subsumed the two earlier myths as described by Dr. Beeby, but that there was a substantial and growing mismatch between the third myth and the realities and outcomes experienced by students and parents. The select committee described a crisis of confidence in education and a consensus of criticism. They found that the high level of client dissatisfaction had a long and suppressed history, signaled the need for bipartisan intervention and, in particular, questioned the quality of administrative services in education. They concluded that the quality of teaching in New Zealand was being undermined by three problems, (1) provider capture, that is, where the providers of education had captured the terms of their service, (2) a grossly elaborated structure, so elaborate that information flows and lines of accountability were confused and confusing and (3) obsolete administrative practices and attitudes.

Although the explicitness of the report surprised some, what astonished and then bitterly offended many Parliamentarians was that their bipartisan endorsement of the Scott Report was ignored by the education establishment and obligingly dead handed by the responsible agency of state. The Department of Education cynically posted it to schools for governors and councils to take action at the beginning of a school holiday (Macpherson, 1987b), also knowing that they lacked the capacity to implement changes.

As the 1987 election drew near, and the attitudes of Parliamentarians hardened, the bipartisanship of the education and science select committee collapsed. Richardson made very effective use of the select committee's report during the campaign, much to the official annoyance and private embarrassment of the Labour government, and to the alarm of one group of their supporters, the teachers' unions. She was also able to capitalize on an unseemly brawl over teachers' salary levels just prior to the election. One result was that the Labour Party suffered badly over education issues in the polling booths, and in the time-honored way of politics, it soon turned on the teachers and "their minister."

Lange's government regained power but with a much reduced majority. In the postelection shuffle, Marshall, a senior and highly respected member of the Labour Party, was given the foreign affairs portfolio. Standing was neatly preserved all round by the prime minister himself taking the education portfolio. Overnight, however, the touchstone of Russell's ministry, "consultation," became a spent word. The newly powerful metaphors were "provider capture," "responsiveness," and "client satisfaction." Lange signaled his intentions and general reform strategy in the terms of reference for a taskforce announced on July 21, 1987 to report to him 10 months later on May 10, 1988 (Taskforce to Review Education Administration, 1988, p. ix):

- A functional review of the head office of the Department of Education to maximize the clarification and delegation of responsibilities;
- An evaluation of governance to accelerate the devolution of powers and responsibilities to institutional governors;
- A review of administrative relationships and services at all levels to enhance responsiveness to community needs and government objectives; and
- Costs and benefits of recommendations and transitional arrangements to be identified to ensure "the efficiency of any new system of education administration that might be proposed."

This taskforce was one of 17 taskforces asked to provide policy advice to the Cabinet Social Equity Committee (CSEC). These taskforces had overlapping charters that straddled all social portfolio responsibilities in order to provide for contestability in the advice they gave. Overarching them all was Sir Ivor Richardson's Royal Commission on Social Policy.

The CSEC was chaired by the then deputy prime minister, the Rt. Hon. Geoffrey Palmer, noted above. Palmer was the manager of the Lange government's reform and legislative programs. The government saw reforms in the administration of education as part of more general reforms across all "caring portfolios" and as linked to the radical restructuring of New Zealand's mixed economy and public administration. Curiously, this latter agenda was publicly driven by a small group of ministers committed to *Rogernomics*, a term used to indicate the influence of the then minister of finance, the Hon. Roger Douglas. The dry economic rationalism of Rogernomics (Douglas & Callan, 1987) became a convenient straw man for those who cared not to address the need to redistribute power as part of the administrative reform agenda. Few in education saw or found it easy to appreciate the broader sweep of the government's reform agenda or the drive for coherence and efficiency in public administration.

The Taskforce to Review Education Administration itself took the broader view. Its membership ensured that a range of perspectives were considered. The chairman was Mr. Brian Picot, a millionaire director and chairman of companies, a senior member of New Zealand's corporate oligarchy (Jesson, 1987, p. 87) and the pro-chancellor of the University of Auckland. Members included Dr. Peter Ramsay, an associate professor of education at the University of Waikato, who had led research into successful and unsuccessful schools (Ramsay, 1981), and earlier as an insider, the politics of the NZEI (1981). Another member was education activist, Ms. Margaret Rosemergy, a senior lecturer at the Wellington College of Education, and one who had helped formulate Labour Party education policy. Ms. Whetumarama Wereta, a social statistician in the Department of Maori Affairs from Ngaiterangi-Ngatiranganui, was invited to join the taskforce to emphasize a Maori perspective. The fifth member, Mr. Colin Wise, was a successful businessman from Dunedin with active links with higher education and was asked to represent employers' interests.

The Picot Taskforce studiously took account of the pluralism in the politics of education. They were briefed by the prime minister, as minister of education, and given an informed, full-time and autonomous secretariat led by Mr. Maurice Gianotti. The taskforce digested its terms of reference, decided what information it needed and then called for submissions. It made contact with over 700 individuals and organizations and met part-time for nine months. From the outset, the Picot Taskforce had the undivided attention of all concerned with education services; its questions focused on how well administrative practices and structures were serving the interests of students.

In November 1987, I returned to New Zealand to continue five years of research into the politics of New Zealand education. Informants, understandably, were keen to rehearse what they were going to tell the Picot Taskforce, to rationalize past actions and to speculate on futures, their own careers in particular. Most notable was how few recognized the broader social, political and economic contexts related to the Picot exercise being managed by the CSEC nor the political potency of the select committee report. Most were, understandably, using self-interested, conspiratorial and antieconomic interpretations of the situation.

I wrote to the prime minister's office expressing an interest in helping with structural design until late April 1988. An interview there and another in the State Services Commission (SSC) indicated that personnel in the prime minister's office were "shadowing" all portfolios and taskforces, not so much to "second-guess" them, as some supposed, but to try and maximize policy coherence. This confirmed that holistic administrative reform was a major reform agenda at that time, not simply cost-cutting according to a New Right agenda as some understandably supposed, given the aggressive profile of Rogernomics. I agreed to join the team then being formed in the SSC to help provide structural advice directly to the Picot Taskforce.

The SSC is a unique organization in public administration. It is the Department of State in New Zealand held responsible for the organizational effectiveness of all other departments of state. In essence, because it has a charter to advise on the degree of adherence to, and the continuing appropriateness of the operating norms and procedures of other departments of state, it is officially expected to provide and encourage double-loop organizational learning (Schon, 1983) and to challenge dynamic conservatism (Schon, 1989), the phenomenon in organizations noted above where resources are used to prevent change.

Typically, the SSC would have only had a more downstream interest in such an exercise, but in the Picot case, the government's reform strategy had already been signaled in the terms of reference. The SSC, therefore, moved quickly to advise on more appropriate governance and management structures and practices for the administration of education at all levels. On the other hand, it must be emphasized that there were many other interests and views put to the Picot Taskforce, now briefly summarized.

Although the SSC focused on organizational structure and the distribution of power, the treasury (New Zealand Treasury, 1987) emphasized a neo-Friedman variant of market liberalism and sought to commodify education in a search of economies (Grace, 1989). Officials in the Department of Education appeared unable to discern an alternative future and tended to reiterate a Benthamite logic of centralism. Maori lobby groups tended to demand emancipation from an oppressive hegemony in education and for far greater empowerment at the local level. The teachers' unions were alternatively dismissive of yet another inquiry, and yet vigorously defensive of the status quo at the center in the name of equity. The message, however, from both sides of Parliament was blunt; there was bipartisan support for major structural reform and radical devolution in search of qualitative improvements to administration.

The Picot Review was therefore never about relocating administrative functions closer to the client, the lateral extension of bureaucratic structure that is usually and euphemistically referred to as *decentralization*. Instead, the Picot Taskforce was soon exploring the possibilities of devolving the power to govern that had accumulated at the center to elected school boards of trustees, so that the balance of power between the providers and the clients would be immediately altered in favor of parents and their children. It was also about locating leadership responsibilities for the quality of teaching and learning as close to the classroom as possible. The organizational principle involved, yet never explicitly identified, was subsidiarity; operations should be handled by the smallest, lowest, or least centralized competent authority. The general belief was that such devolution of power would provide the conditions and the incentives for more responsive administrative, curricular and pedagogical practices to develop.

The SSC's views on administrative reforms were influential. One reason was that they cohered with assumptions held by those in cabinet. So-called machinery of government (MOG) exercises had already converted a series of government departments and agencies into semiautonomous corporations called *state owned enterprises*, which, in some cases, had then been sold to retire parts of the national debt. However, although no one in Lange's cabinet wanted to privatize education, welfare, or health services at that time, it was generally accepted that radical administrative surgery was long overdue in education to raise the responsiveness and legitimacy of school governance and administration in school education.

Another reason for the SSC's influence was that the alternatives to MOG perspectives were not well-marketed. Indeed, by late 1987, a language offensive was gathering pace. Speeches, kites from the prime minister's office and leaks from informed sources were all suggesting that the Department of Education should be replaced by a new ministry with no more than policy advisory, funding, institutional chartering and audit functions. By about February 1988, Picot's team was asking direct questions that were helping to articulate a fresh devolutionary administrative policy. They were consulting in a context where MOG-based metaphors, slogans and speculative press releases were informing and guiding public policy discourse.

A third reason was that Picot's team appeared to have taken a particular view of what policy itself was. They appeared to assume that policy was essentially a contestable cultural artifact. Their practices indicated that it was held to be something that they and their associated advisers and political masters could make with talk to justify and direct initiatives. Power, structure, biography, perceptions, values and organizational mindsets all played their part, but at heart, policy only ever existed as concerted understandings about courses of action. These concerted understandings were arrived at in an iterative and holographic manner—that is, built by determined individuals; group work; extensive networking and overlapping writing exercises; simultaneous specialization and generalization; and considerable self-directed activity, much as proposed by Morgan (1986, pp. 97–98).

To summarize, intense philosophical, strategic and political debate in a range of partially controlled settings determined how the situation was to be understood, what the issues were, what purposes were to be served and how reform was to be implemented. As my six months of participant observation unfolded, it gradually appeared that policy makers were using philosophical and strategic means but mostly political tools to distill and share reasons for taking action. As Hodgkinson (1981) argued, ideas were handled in abstract, qualitative and human terms, and then transformed into a socially constructed artifact, draft policy. People were persuaded by powerful language, by the leverage that control over resources gave, and by the other arts and crafts of politics. When new scenarios were accepted as right or as inevitable, new administrative policy had been simultaneously made and marketed.

The Taskforce to Review Education Administration (1988) reported that the combined effects of new technology, changing and plural values, new cultural sensitivity and the intensifying demands on education services had outstripped the administrative capacities of the system. They called for greater responsiveness. They also assumed that this could be achieved with appropriate incentive regimes at all levels for system and institutional managers.

The management systems, according to the Picot Report, had complex and fragmented structures and processes, relied on arbitrary institutional roles and poor information, and had wasteful duplications. Accountability systems, it claimed, measured fidelity to administrative regulations rather than how effectively educational aims had been achieved. Opportunity cost and outcomes analyses were being almost totally displaced by input economic thinking. Perhaps the most telling observation put to the CSEC was that the themes of low efficiency and undermined effectiveness were causally linked to client dissatisfaction and to the alienation of disadvantaged groups.

The Picot Report opted for radical devolution, it argued, to reinforce the professionalism and dedication of individual teachers, and the participation of parents and community. It did this by focusing on the organizational context that sustains the relationship between learner and teacher, the school. As noted above, the primary strategy adopted was to alter the balance of power between clients and providers at the institutional level to gain greater responsiveness.

Key measures included reforming governance at all levels, generating local empowerment and moving as many functions as possible from the center to the school.

In the White Paper, *Tomorrow's Schools*, the Government of New Zealand (1988) formally accepted almost all of the Picot Taskforce's ideas, laid out an implementation process and set October 1, 1989, as the changeover date. As a consequence, each school community elected a board of trustees that had to negotiate a charter of objectives to reflect local aspirations and needs within national guidelines. Each charter had to be approved by a new ministry before it became the basis for operational planning, program budgeting and accrual accounting, because each school had to manage its own finances and operations. There was, it was stressed, a great deal of professional development required of leaders in schools.

A national Education Review Office (ERO) was established to provide multi-skilled teams to make transparent how well each school was using its funds to meet its chartered objectives. A parent advocacy council with a secretariat was proposed as a check on the tyrannical use of centralist power at the center, although combined lobbying by the treasury and SSC officials resulted in this mechanism being set aside, ironically on the grounds that it may enhance centralism. The upshot was that the new ministry and the teachers' unions were able to reassert their dominance in education lobbying in Wellington. The other traditional defense of localism and regionalism against centralism, the 10 provinces' education boards, were replaced by school support centers intended to provide contracted services. Further, ad hoc taskforces were eventually preferred to a national education policy council, which further consolidated the influence of the ministry and the teachers' unions. A relatively slim ministry then provided policy advice, administered property, moved funds and provided guidelines on personnel, administrative, governance and curricular matters.

There were major problems with role loss and discovery, disturbed bargaining relationships, supply crises in expertise, the loss of trust in the portfolio and fears about managerial techniques displacing educative leadership (Macpherson, 1989). Nevertheless, the meta-value of the Lange-Picot intervention remained the equalization of power in education in adverse national economic circumstances, a phenomenon not uncommon internationally at the time (e.g., Dror, 1986; Pratt, 1987).

The interplay of powers and the realignment of power structures can now be summarized. The Parliamentary select committee, the Lange Labour government, the CSEC and the Picot Taskforce sought radical and simultaneous changes to policies, structures and practices in the administration of the public school education system and in the governance of schools. It was an explicitly *high politics* intervention; the electoral threat to the government exceeded the political risks of alienating centralist and symbiotic bureaucracies. The redistribution of power reached toward but did not achieve full subsidiarity in the governance and operational management of schools. It was an intervention that was justified by appeal to a politically pragmatic policy myth of equal power that was built on and reinterpreted in two earlier myths: Beeby's equal opportunity policy and Renwick's (1986) equal outcomes policy. The scope was no less ambitious; the Lange-Picot intervention was intended to achieve what Beeby had intended, the reorientation of the whole education system. It was developed as it was embedded in the education policy community using a managed political process that responded to the electoral fallout from the Scott Report and consulted stakeholders by the taskforce, and then employed a traditional green and white paper process to announce the implementation of a new political order in state education.

What the process did not do was conceptualize and implement the fundamental shift required to move education and union system leaders away from a centralist political ideology reinforced by bureaucratic rationality toward a more educative ideology. Recall, Weber's (1947) original formulation of bureaucracy was derived from case studies of the Prussian Army, the Chinese mandarin system in imperial days and the Roman Catholic Church. It used specific political myths to legitimate bureaucratic organization: (1) apart from their official duties, members are free, (2) offices, not people, form the hierarchy, (3) each office has a legally defined area of competence, (4) offices are filled by open selection and free contracting, (5) officials are appointed purely on the basis of expertise, (6) salaries are graded by office, (7) each office requires the full-time commitment of the appointees, (8) officials are protected from politics by policies and duty statements, (9) officialdom is a career with promotions based on seniority and achievement as judged by those in more senior positions and (10) the strict discipline of office-holding coheres with a wider, rational, legal and impersonal order in society.

School system management based on such bureaucratic rationality would clearly violate New Zealand's preference for popular sovereignty and liberal democratic political norms. It would also contradict refined knowledge of excellent organization (Morgan, 1986; Peters & Waterman, 1982), which stressed eight conditions: clarity of purpose, minimum formal structures, reflective action, specialization, client-responsive, innovative, shared decisions, and a respectful and educative culture.

This suggested that educative leaders should create and sustain a productive and critical culture in which purposes, structures and practices remain contestable and responsive. A key criterion of their leadership would be the extent to which it sustains the development of members' and stakeholders' learning about the consequences of being organized. An empowerment myth could then legitimate governance and management at the system and school level if it offered to:

- Create many, simultaneous and coherent, vertical and horizontal patterns of policy making and implementation
- Design and protect feedback for double-loop learning that also helps members account regularly to stakeholders
- Replace rigid systems of rules addressing the rights and duties of employees and employers with more temporary and negotiable performance contracts and positive incentive regimes

- Displace standard procedures for dealing with all contingencies at work with zones of discretion for work teams, zones governed by policy to achieve external coherence
- Reconstruct impersonal and hierarchical relationships into open and respectful communication, responsible politics and democratic forms of representation
- Supplant selection and promotion based on seniority with more temporary and shared leadership services delivering performance and outcomes through competence
- Redefine planning, once purely a line function, to become a contested and support service that facilitates interactive and collaborative decision making across team, institutional and system levels
- Achieve coordination not through control systems but by marshaling commitment and resources in order to accomplish valued ends (Macpherson, 1991a, pp. 74–76).

Overall, this analysis and evaluation of the distribution of power attempted by the Picot process reached two conclusions. Prior centralism reinforced by bureaucratic rationality inhibited feedback on rightness and significance, objectified social reality, attempted to fixate legitimation, and offered moral absolution to functionaries in return for passive compliance. This centralism was sustainable until the accumulation of electoral risk to elected Parliamentarians outweighed the advantages of dynamic conservatism, and thus precipitated a liberal democratic catharsis in school governance and leadership. It was a classic case of a *high politics* intervention (Macpherson, 1992d) at national levels that also anticipated implementation at the school level through *low politics* educative leadership (Macpherson, 1999g).

It is important to record what the political catharsis was not. It was not a communicative rationalist liberation of public education, as long preferred by New Zealand's academic elite in education and the education establishment. It was not driven by the educative neopragmatism that I wanted to displace Kiwi pragmatism; I recommended asking school governors and leadership teams to demonstrate (a) thoughtful and evidence-related policy and actions, (b) how pedagogy, curriculum, assessment, evaluation and accountability had all contributed to the achievement of school purposes and (c) how structuration had remained a creative aspect of their work. Recall, the aim of educative neopragmatism is the development of shared moral knowledge and learning about being well-organized and productive for legitimate educational purposes. This aim would have required clarity and openness over the blend of political ideologies embedded in the educative rationality, discourse and structures employed in each institution and system, an issue taken up in the next chapter.

Instead, within a few years, the incoming national minister of education, the Hon. Dr. Lockwood Smith, started tinkering with the social contracting process that culminated in each school's charter of objectives in an attempt to gain greater steerage, I suspect at the behest of neocentralists in addition to his own political interests. His actions gradually upset the delicate balances of power

10

between local stakeholders and between each school community and the ministry, and triggered to a resurgence of factionalized and adversarial politics at local and national levels. The moral legitimacy of political infrastructure in education, initially boosted by the establishment of schools' boards of trustees, tilted back into a gradual decline.

It is appropriate at this point to turn back to the broader issues of theory development as regards educative leadership, informed by political philosophy.

Part IV

Questioning and suggesting theory

11 A politically critical review of educative leadership

> Remembering that I'll be dead soon is the most important tool I've encountered to help me make the big choices in life. Because almost everything—all external expectations, all pride, all fear of embarrassment, or failure—these things just fall away in the face of death, leaving only what is truly important. Remembering that you are going to die is the best way I know to avoid the trap of thinking you have something to lose. You are already naked. There is no reason not to follow your heart.
>
> (Steve Jobs, cited in Isaacson, 2011, p. 457)

It is one thing to propose political philosophy to help improve the practice, research and theory building in educational administration. It is quite another to use the subdiscipline to evaluate the quality of one's own engagement in the production and application of new ideas about educative leadership. Nevertheless, it was noted above that reflective critique of research outcomes using evidence to improve the quality of future work was an essential component of evaluating scholarship (Glassick et al., 1997). Such reflective critique, as Steve Jobs noted, is also essential to discovering what is truly important in one's own life.

Hence, in this chapter, I apply the subdiscipline of political philosophy to my own research projects since 1980 that have been related to the concept of educative leadership. Pat Duignan and I (1987) originally defined the term to mean leadership intended to improve learning to distinguish it from the more generic term *educational leadership* that meant any form of leadership in education. My hand in its development over two decades included action research (being an educator, evaluator and educational administrator at the school and institutional level), systematic studies intended to refine a practical theory of educative leadership and applied research (advising reforms to education systems and to institutions that required educative leadership).

This review[1] indicates that, although the concept has served as a useful organizer for my career and research, my theory building was too long restricted to education and would have been enhanced by an earlier and critical application of political philosophy. It is concluded that my ongoing scholarship concerning educative leadership should be related to knowledge organizations globally; applied in sister fields in public administration, enterprise management and adolescent health; and use political philosophy more explicitly to understand and evaluate the use of power in practice and theory in administration, leadership and policy development. This conclusion was acted on and, in part, resulted in the next and final chapter.

The aim of this chapter is to report formative evaluation of a research program in educative leadership that was integrated with a career in positions of responsibility. As noted above, leadership responsibilities came early. I trained and served as a primary school teacher in New Zealand, retrained as a secondary remedial education specialist in Scotland, graduated in mathematics and management, and then helped lead a large comprehensive school in England before I was 30.

After a period teaching mathematics in Western Australia, I was seconded to lead a professional development program for secondary principals across the state. My master's and doctoral research projects then took me into teaching, research and leadership roles at Monash University, the University of New England and the University of Tasmania, and also into two six-month periods advising administrative restructurings and accountability reforms in New Zealand and NSW education systems.

My first professorial chair was to lead the Centre of Professional Development at the University of Auckland prior to service as the CEO of Waiariki Institute of Technology in New Zealand. My second chair, in strategic leadership, was to lead the establishment of a private university in the United Arab Emirates, as described above. I then accepted a portfolio of part-time commitments in Australasian universities and education systems internationally, most notably as an adjunct professor at Macquarie University, as a capacity builder with New Zealand Aid in Timor Leste and, most recently, as the evaluator of a pilot project in England that trialed integrated health centers in secondary schools (Macpherson, 2013).

With retirement, I found the time needed to evaluate my research and theory building concerned with educative leadership with three formative purposes in mind: (1) it would further refine my strategic sense of direction, (2) it might help other leaders and aspirant leaders in education to enhance their own approach to leadership, but most important, (3) it could help position political philosophy central to critical reflection on the nature and justification for the use of power by leaders in education.

These purposes were addressed using refereed research publications as data and political philosophy for analysis and evaluation. This approach did not aspire to the standards of scholarly biography (e.g., Selleck, 1982) or even autobiography in educational administration (Macpherson, 1986b). Instead, it used selected relevant publications and political philosophy to sustain critical reflection, while seeking to avoid the account becoming an *apologia* or a self-congratulatory memoir. As pointed out earlier, political philosophy has rarely been used in educational administration as methodology, which is remarkable given the field's engagement with power. I trust that the critique of this and other chapters will lead to much more sophisticated studies.

Summaries of key research projects related to educative leadership follow, highlighting political ideologies in passing. The intention is to reveal the genealogy of educative leadership with special reference to the nature and justification of power in roles I either researched or served in. In the final section of the chapter,

I evaluate the summaries, discuss some implications, and provide tentative advice regarding future practice, research and theory building.

My master's degree research into the role of deputy principals of senior high schools in Western Australia showed that their justification for their use of power depended on the gendered nature of their roles and their career orientation and was reflected in the measured levels of role conflict they experienced (Macpherson, 1980). Female deputy principals were expected to sustain the pastoral care of students and give special attention to the needs of girls. Male deputy principals were expected to organize the school timetable and give special attention to the maintenance of discipline, boys especially.

Four career orientations to being a deputy principal were found. The *veterans* (about 50%) made a virtue of the social norms of the school's staffroom and community, avoided promotion or change and tended to value loyalty and past achievements. These restricted communitarians regarded external policies and initiatives by new appointees as temporary phenomena to be endured and stressed the value of experience in, and dedication to, their particular school. They had the least measured role conflict.

The *executives* (about 20%) were the embodiment of their school's mission, rules and adaptive and maintenance mechanisms, as determined by the principal. Largely disconnected from staffroom and community cultures, these Aussie bureaucrats saw the system as a benign guarantor of a professional administrative career and had low to moderate degrees of measured role conflict.

The *upward mobiles* or *stepping stoners* (about 20%) had instrumental, rather than caring, attitudes and solved problems to demonstrate the ability to get things done (rather than to create longer term organizational learning capacities or efficiencies). They looked ahead to a principalship close to home in Perth, the state's capital, as soon as possible. These Aussie pragmatists suffered from moderate to high degrees of role conflict due to disparate perceptions about the legitimacy of their power in a context of growing teacher militancy.

The *educative leaders* (about 10%) stressed the broad goals and philosophies of education; service to students; reconciling colleagues' and students' interests; and the facilitation of improvements through professional development, organizational development and organizational learning. Their neopragmatism typically exhibited a blend of communitarian, communicative rationalist and egalitarian liberalist assumptions, with a largely unstated mix of common good and social contract justifications. These critically reflective practitioners had the most measured role conflict of all deputies.

This troubled yet inspirational minority of deputy principals gave me many preliminary clues about what truly educative leaders might be. They were the deputies who questioned the distribution and use of power in everyday professional actions, such as classroom tyrannies and abhorrent subcultures occasionally revealed by discipline problems. They displayed a greater concern for rightness than consensus and collegial norms or compliance, and were strategic in their interventions, often seeking to improve what they and their coprofessionals had long taken for granted.

In 1982, 24 of the 85 secondary school principals in Western Australia volunteered to participate in peer process consultancy triads in order to facilitate action research in their schools (Macpherson, 1983). After reading introductory research and participating in preparatory workshops, five self-selected triads formed. Each principal had a pair of peers available to facilitate action research in his or her school. The changing pairings in each triad meant that each principal experienced being a client once and being a consultant twice. School improvement projects were developed by each triad in consultation with the professionals in each school. A number of improvements were achieved before industrial action unrelated to the one-year pilot led to a direction from the top that all principals were not to be out of their schools.

The greatest effects on the participating principals were achieved through giving rather than receiving advice. Systematic diagnosis with a peer partner and then giving feedback in a host school, prior to contracting a senior team to mount an intervention, had, in most cases, already been deeply internalized and partially implemented in the consultants' own schools.

When these triads were viewed in retrospect as temporary political coalitions, this project apparently partially suspended positional authority in favor of action research that engaged educative leaders and professional colleagues in a political culture of communitarianism and communicative rationalism, all justified rather sloppily as being in the interests of students, parents and other stakeholders, that is, in the common good. Some remarkably clever innovations were carried through that led me to doubt consensus in the staffroom or an intuitive and unchecked notion of the common good as sufficient bases for critical professionalism.

In the early 1980s, I designed then-novel doctoral research to examine what it was to be and become a regional director of education in Victoria, Australia (Macpherson, 1984a), including lengthy periods *Boswelling* these elite administrators (Macpherson, 1985a). A legitimacy crisis in public education had precipitated radical and recent regionalization (Macpherson, 1986a). The ontological data collected over a year through shadowing and interaction showed that these regional directors campaigned incessantly to embed ideas as policy for implementation and to refine structures in order to sustain policy implementation (Macpherson, 1985b). The historical data collected showed that the enhanced powers given to these leaders had a long gestation in the public education system (Macpherson, 1986a). The biographical data collected from the 12 incumbents showed that the different political styles of these powerfully reformist administrators dated from their first significant political success, indicating their styles were more learned than inherited.

It was, therefore, concluded that their power to influence was only partly reliant on their positional authority, as realized by many in their role set. It was also to do with their intellectual sophistication and coherence, managerial skills, and imaginative and resilient attitudes across each phase of policy making (philosophy, planning, politics) and implementation (mobilizing, managing and monitoring; after Hodgkinson, 1981). This array of learned capacities enabled them to talk up major improvement projects while creating and controlling knowledge about being organized using the sociopolitical arts of what Giddens defined as *structuration* (Macpherson, 1988).

Looking back, these powerful men had all been selected to reform and restore public faith in public education through regionalization in Victoria. They had each developed a passionate (albeit slightly different) belief in a new social contract between Premier John Cain's incoming state Labor government and the people of Victoria. Their shared intention was to deliver high quality public education as a form of distributive justice, principally to ensure equal opportunity, with special support for the disadvantaged. But using a rich blend of pragmatic, communitarian and communicative rationalist justifications was not enough for these reformers. Most of them came from very modest upbringings, and they were driven by an abstract Australian cultural notion of giving "little Aussie battlers a fair go" in terms of personal freedoms and equal educational opportunities, with any special help going to the worst off; they were also egalitarian liberals to their boot straps. The overall political ideology evident in their language was a pragmatic blend of ideologies, that is, neopragmatism.

In 1986, the three public school state education systems in NSW, the Australian Capital Territory (ACT) and Victoria commissioned a collaborative project to develop five sets of professional development materials to encourage the development of educative leaders (Duignan & Macpherson, 1987). Each set was to summarize the latest research in one of five designated areas in the lead chapter of a text that included additional illustrative chapters, along with a stimulus video, an audio taped lecture and other professional development materials. The design of each set was moderated by a team of expert practitioners nominated by the three systems in collaboration with leading Australian researchers and theorists. An edited text assembled a practical theory of educative leadership that was induced from their recommendations (Duignan & Macpherson, 1992).

In retrospect, a rich blend of political ideologies is evident in a synthesis of the findings (Duignan & Macpherson, 1993). To explain, the research linking educative leadership to the quality of teaching explored why and how educative leaders should facilitate the development of constructivist pedagogies, initially and principally from a communitarian perspective (Northfield, Duignan, & Macpherson, 1987). The case for ethical educative leadership stressed rule consequentialism in an implied context of neopragmatism (Evers, 1987). The case for the constructivist facilitation of curriculum development by educative leaders was also argued in a way that was also consistent with neopragmatism (Walker, 1989). The case for educative leadership in a multicultural society explicitly employed communicative rationalism as a practical method of challenging racism and promoting interculturalism (Rizvi et al., 1990). The recommended role of educative leaders when reorganizing the delivery of educational services implied a neopragmatist blend of communitarianism, communicative rationalism and egalitarian liberalism (Pettit, Duignan, & Macpherson, 1990).

Follow-up issue-focused and action research studies then extended the system-sponsored project. The first example reported the bereavement processes created by an English headteacher to help a school community come to terms with a staff member committing suicide (Macpherson & Vann, 1996). An educative micropolitical

intervention generated long-term learning about death and enhanced the cooperative problem solving and knowledge production capacities in the school community.
It was neopragmatist, employing communicative rationalism to unpack socially
critical perspectives and arbitrate emergent interpretations, insisting on egalitarian
liberalism in processes, and as the bereavement processes wound up, reinforcing
communitarian norms.

A second example was a philosophical evaluation of educative leadership itself
(Macpherson & Cusack, 1996). This project traced many of the concepts of educative leadership back to John Dewey's democratic and educative pragmatism,
which stressed scientific experimentalism, rejected dualisms in favor of mediating
and reconciling ideas, and combined fallibilism and optimistic progressivism. This
suggested that educative leaders should properly be concerned with the development of democratic communities committed to inquiry-based learning, that is, to
a strongly communitarian agenda in addition to their commitment to pragmatism,
communicative rationalism and egalitarian liberalism.

More recent research in England has shown how such educative leadership can
help democratize schooling. The Leadership for Learning project at Cambridge
(MacBeath & Dempster, 2009) mounted a number of trials to engage students
in leadership roles to explore how schools can develop as democratic communities of learning. Traditionally, instrumental justifications for student participation
have claimed that it improves their affiliation, combats disaffection and delivers a
human right. These justifications, however, tend to be light on pedagogical justification and empirical evidence of improved learning outcomes.

The former limitation regarding pedagogy has been attended to in part by
an analysis of student participation, as leaders in learning partnerships (Frost &
Roberts, 2011). It suggested that student agency could serve as the link between
learning, participation and democracy. The justification had four parts.

First, deep learning was held to empower students because it develops life-
enhancing capacities: self-awareness, critical thinking and autonomy. Such deep
learning was always achieved through social activities, which in turn implied the
need for willful and collaborative participation.

Second, such student participation was mediated by the extent to which leadership was distributed in each learning community and by the degree to which
the distribution enabled all members to govern learning strategies and comanage
practices.

Third, a holistic democratic framework for student participation in such governance and management would have to be supported by a deliberative culture in
which students have the power, voice and appropriate information to determine
the vision, strategy and day-to-day decisions about learning (Woods & Woods,
2012, forthcoming). To be effective, it was argued, this culture would have to value
critical thinking (by respecting evidence, tolerating multiple perspectives and reasoning in argument) and help students develop these capacities with induction,
scaffolding and positive interventions.

Fourth and finally, as noted, the key theoretical link between learning, participation and democracy was given as student agency. Practical examples of such

agency in schools included student consultations or voice, students participating in governance and representation, students taking up roles of responsibility, students as researchers and as teachers and other forms of student leadership. Whereas such agency was not systematically related to student learning outcomes by Woods and Woods, inevitably a key issue to educative leaders, it was proposed instead, somewhat hopefully, that:

> The future of democracy across the world may well depend on the extent to which schools can become the sort of communities in which the skills, values, and dispositions necessary for the maintenance of democratic civil society are cultivated through the pedagogy that is manifest in classrooms but also through a rich variety of modes of participation in which student leadership is prominent. (Frost & Roberts, 2011, p. 81)

There are edge-cutting examples in England that give hope. It was shown in a national report how Samuel King's School in Cumbia had used student voice to critique and improve the quality of teaching, how Ashcroft High School in Bedfordshire had placed student voice central to its successful school development plan and how Roseland Community College and Penair School in Cornwall had trained students as learning detectives to boost the quality of teaching and learning (Department for Children Families and Schools, 2008). In another three-year study in Cornwall, Budehaven Community School, Hayle Community School and Penair School decided in 2009 to empower students with the governance of their new integrated health centers. It was found three years later that their students' general capacity to self-manage their general health and well-being, and their sexual and mental health, were all positively and increasingly related to their academic progress and significantly related to a fall in youth offending (Macpherson, 2013).

Despite these examples, however, most researchers in England and in the United States remain deeply skeptical of educational leaders being able to advance the democratization of schooling, even with regard to empowering teachers, let alone students. Hatcher (2005), for example, noted persistent contradictions between how distributed leadership is being used both to improve the participation and empowerment of teachers and to secure the commitment of teachers to government reform agendas, in a context where collective self-management is prevented by the hegemonic hierarchical model of power distribution. Fielding (2006, p. 347) noted the preeminence of the "personalization and high-performance schooling . . . the new totalitarianism" of leadership and management in English schools. He compared the *impersonal* and *affective* approaches to his preference, *person-centered*. He warned that "the dominant policy context of economic neoliberalism and the prevailing intellectual motifs of performativity will ensure that 'personalization' binds us more securely and more comfortably to purposes we abhor and practices we come to regret" (Fielding, 2006, p. 349). I am not so sure about this iconoclastic prediction, especially when the driving political ideologies are taken into account.

Hatcher's and Fielding's positions were driven primarily by a communitarian ideology. Hatcher's (2005) beliefs hailed from the comprehensive school movement of the 1960s and 1970s, when teachers were allegedly entitled to democratic participation in school governance and self-management (pp. 262–263). Fielding (2006, pp. 350–355) drew heavily on the works of John Macmurray, the Scottish communitarian philosopher who stressed agency, identity and community, to develop his preferred model of schools as person-centered learning communities. Neither addressed the relativity of their driving ideology or offered systematic empirical evidence for their policy proposals.

In sharp contrast, Maxcy and Nguyen's (2006) case studies of the distribution of leadership in two elementary schools in Texas, United States, were intended to highlight implications for democratic school governance. Their evidence indicated that managerial analyses of distributing leadership were more concerned with steering local actors and channeling local activity than in improving the politics of distributed leadership. The problem was that "the characterizations of leadership distribution offered also reflect a depoliticized rhetoric that masks an antidemocratic, managerial bias" (Maxcy & Nguyen, 2006, p. 180). By focusing on the nature and dynamics of leadership, especially to do with school performance and community-building, they demonstrated the importance of distributed leadership in boosting responsiveness to, and reciprocal accountability with, local stakeholders. Hence, a particular strength of the study was that it investigated the language, processes, technologies, purposes and outcomes of distributing leadership, acknowledging and revealing the relativity of managerial and social justice ideologies. It appears that democratization through distributed leadership was more congenial in a context of communicative rationalism than where American pragmatism prevailed, with the study having nothing to say about egalitarian liberalism.

In retrospect, it is now clear that, by the mid 1990s, I was becoming increasingly resistant to any particular political ideology being allowed foundational status in the analysis or evaluation of current political arrangements in schools or in education systems. This position, as noted above, was reinforced and refined using Evers and Lakomski's (1991) nonfoundational, coherentist and pragmatist epistemology.

It was also at this point that I was invited to serve as an administrative policy advisor in New Zealand. My research in the politics of education in the mid 1980s had earlier advised the education policy community that a high politics intervention into the administration of education was imminent, and indeed, could by justified by a new policy myth of "equal power in adversity" (Macpherson, 1987a). Interesting, my suggestions were vigorously dismissed by the academic and bureaucratic elite. As Chapter 10 details, the Department of Education, the teachers' unions and the education research community, otherwise known as the "education establishment," appeared to be indifferent to the bipartisan belief held by New Zealand's politicians concerning their social contract with the people. The education establishment ignored the bipartisan call by the members of the Education and Science Select Committee of Parliament for fundamental reform in order to achieve more equal outcomes (Scott, Fraser, Gregory, Marshall, & Richardson, 1986). Continued inaction by the education establishment then led to an electoral backlash in 1987 that nearly unseated the Lange Labor government. The prime minister took personal charge of the education portfolio and established the Picot Taskforce to challenge "provider capture" and improve the governance and performance of schools (Macpherson, 1993b). The SSC contracted me to help provide structural advice, which was not entirely dismissed. The conflation of political forces described in Chapter 10 resulted in a radical redistribution of power in the system and in school governance.

Follow-up research (Macpherson, 1991c, 1993b, 1999g) found that the decentralized and neopluralist political arrangements established by the reforms were enabling schools (Macpherson & Morrison, 2001) and later polytechnics (Howse & Macpherson, 2001), to diversify, develop local governance and management capacities and more actively recognize the Treaty of Waitangi.

Reflecting today on the radical change to political arrangements in education from 1987 to 2001, it appears that the initially bipartisan intervention by New Zealand's politicians was an example where egalitarian liberalism had successfully contested the uncritical and self-serving centralism of the symbiotic systems, principally through the workings of liberal democracy. The communicative rationalism promoted heavily by the elites in the education research community in the 1980s and 1990s (e.g., Codd, Harker, & Nash, 1985; Grace, 1989) tended to be limited to discourse analysis that bundled and attacked all of these reforms as variants of New Rightism.

It was salutary to me that this technique of discourse analysis was adopted by the Te Kotahitanga Project to identify cultural impediments to success for Maori students, and thus provided a neopragmatic basis for the design of systematic interventions that have apparently made empirically measurable and statistically significant improvements (Bishop, Berryman, Cavanagh, & Teddy, 2007).

For the next six months, I was seconded to serve as an administrative policy advisor in NSW. In March 1988, during state elections, the people were promised a ministerial review of management in education by the incoming Premier Nick Greiner's Liberal government. One of five main commitments made was to enhance the quality of public education, especially to the disadvantaged people of Western Sydney. Dr. Brian Scott was commissioned to recommend how administrative structures and practices could better serve the development of teaching and learning. He spent the latter half of 1988 consulting on how effectively and how efficiently administrators were helping teachers teach and learners learn.

Scott then assembled an eight-person team, including myself, to analyze the data, debate options and draft policy proposals. The policy development process later became the subject of analysis (Macpherson, 1990), bitter contestation by a person linked to the NSW Teachers Federation (NSWTF; West, 1991) and systematic rebuttal (Macpherson, 1992c). The evidence pointed to an extreme case of dynamic conservatism in the system's head office, intensely adversarial industrial relations that were helping to prevent reform, and a governance vacuum and symbolic leadership in schools. The Scott Report's (Scott, 1989a) proposals for reform assumed that "the school, not the system" was the key organizational element providing teaching and learning, that every school was different and had different needs, and that the best judge of needs were the school's teachers and its community. The report's blend of egalitarian liberalism and communitarianism also assumed that schools would best meet their needs if they were self-managed within general guidelines and that they would become more effective if system administrators focused on providing support to schools and their leaders (Scott, 1990).

A similar set of proposals were made with regard to the Technical and Further Education (TAFE) sector (Scott, 1989b). It was not, as widely purported by the teachers' unions, simply a neoliberal plot to cut costs. Scott actually persuaded the Greiner government to guarantee continuity of funding for the reform of both systems, which they delivered. However, the Department of Education also agreed to adopt a decentralized and school-centered approach and to become both responsive and accountable at all levels, which they subsequently failed to deliver. Parents and local school communities were asked to provide more active and constructive support for their children in schools across the state, but, ultimately, were not given any political power to advance their views.

Looking back through the lens of political philosophy, the Greiner government came to power committed to an agenda of egalitarian liberalism. Scott's assumptions about how schools and TAFE colleges could self-manage better were primarily pragmatic and communitarian. His proposals initially attracted bipartisan political support and steady-state funding guarantees in real terms in difficult economic circumstances, and mobilized departmental personnel selected to assist with implementation.

Tragically, the minister's blunt style, his stress on professional responsibility and accountability at the institutional level and his difficulties with the neopluralist nature of federal politics (Macpherson, 1991b), gradually created counterforces that encouraged trenchant teacher militancy (Macpherson & Riley, 1992). The minister's eventual decision not to make school councils mandatory led to few being established and denied school communities a local font of communicative rationality and legitimacy and the political power to question and thwart rampant regionalization and eventually recentralization, in a context where most other Australasian education systems were trialing various forms of school management and devolved accountabilities (Macpherson, 1993a). The minister's decision not to establish the recommended Ministerial Council of Review eliminated the intended guarantor of policy fidelity during implementation as well as systematic feedback from major stakeholders. His interventions resulted in the gradual fragmentation of Scott's administrative policies despite the substantial degree of *system surgery* and *genetic engineering* achieved (Macpherson, 1993c). Ironically, the minister's unchecked and autocratic leadership style gradually reaffirmed the residual bureaucratic centralism in the Department of Education and the adversarial centralism of the NSWTF, until his departure from the portfolio.

Echoes of such ministerial idiosyncrasy were heard again, as examined in Chapter 7, when a new minister appointed his political associate to be the director-general of education and training in NSW. Such actions refreshed doubts about a social contract regarding public education ever being delivered by one of the largest and most centralized education systems in the Western world.

In 1995 I was engaged as an administrative policy researcher in Tasmania. By the early 1990s, the general strategy of improving the performance of schools by devolving power to school communities and building self-management capacities was occasionally resulting in near-feral and politically embarrassing outcomes (Macpherson, 1992a, 1992b). In Tasmania, the home of the self-managed school (Caldwell & Spinks, 1988), the concept of professional accountability was becoming politically incorrect (Macpherson, 1996a), that is, offensive to changing political norms in the profession. The Tasmanian Department of Education commissioned policy research intended to reconcile community, school and systemic needs for accountability, despite the collective wish in some Tasmanian school staffrooms not to participate (Macpherson, 1995c).

An international search began for educative forms of school accountability that were systematically summative, demonstrably formative and politically effective. Focus groups were used in volunteer school communities and in the department to clarify the concepts of accountability in use, to clarify differences in perspectives and to identify common ground that could serve as the basis for policy making. The common ground was then expanded in three ways. First, consultations with system and school leaders and executives were used to refine the policies and their implementation (Macpherson, 1995a). Second, advice was taken from international accountability policy researchers in education to anticipate likely challenges (Macpherson, Cibulka, Monk, & Wong, 1998). Third, surveying and consulting principals regarding policy options were used to identify performance indicators and competencies, and the professional development required (Macpherson, 1995b; Macpherson & Taplin, 1995). This process deconstructed largely summative forms of accountability using student test scores and then reconstructed an accountability framework comprising summative, formative and educative processes using both qualitative and quantitative measures of student achievement and school performance (Macpherson, 1996b, 1996c, 1996d).

The framework and developmental process offered to Tasmanian school communities was found to compare favorably with the English Office for Standards in Education (OFSTED) model at the time due to its respect for three principles of government that were highly valued in Tasmania: cooperative pluralism, liberal democracy and subsidiarity (Macpherson, 1996b, 1998). Follow-up studies during implementation in volunteer schools showed that the department leaders and school principals played a key educative role when they moved from command to neopluralist political arrangements (Macpherson, 1997c). This move also gradually convinced politically active parents and teachers that the system and their schools were moving from symbolic politics into contracted and reciprocal accountabilities with the intention of boosting school effectiveness (Ewington & Macpherson, 1998).

The most comprehensive and effective examples of educative accountability policies and practices occurred where (a) the system and school stakeholders suspended status at workshops, openly and critically debated policy options, then cooperatively built and legitimated a new customized policy, and (b) where the new school policy was put into operation by in-school professional teams coordinated by the principals (Macpherson, 1999a).

In retrospect, it also appears that the most educative accountability policy making processes at the school level in Tasmania used neopragmatism to accommodate and blend Aussie pragmatism, communitarianism, communicative rationalism and egalitarian liberalism, while stressing communitarian norms during policy implementation through professional action. The parallel international policy reviews showed that progress toward more educative forms of accountability had to deal with additional dilemmas that were unique to the governance values and politics of education in each jurisdiction. The other jurisdictions examined included the other states of Australia (Cuttance, Harman, Macpherson, Pritchard, & Smart, 1998), United States, Hong Kong (Macpherson et al., 1998) and England and Wales (Macpherson, 1997b).

The common ground between all strands of these administrative policy research findings were educative accountabilities that were simultaneously summative, formative and politically effective, in that they delivered on national and institutional social contracts and reaffirmed the importance of the connections between liberal democratic governance at state and community levels, and educative leadership in each school community.

In 1997 I was appointed professor and director of the Centre of Professional Development at the University of Auckland. The center had been established the year before to provide professional and organizational development with an emphasis on the quality of teaching and learning and on pedagogical research (Macpherson, 1997a). The early controversy over students evaluating the quality of lecturers' teaching gradually gave way to research-led organizational learning, as more sophisticated evaluation policies and methods were introduced and as human resource management policies were refined to reward empirically demonstrated improvements in the quality of teaching (Macpherson, 1999c, 1999f).

By mid 1999, empirical research was reported publicly (Macpherson, 1999e) showing that pedagogical research in the University of Auckland was (a) displacing internal and public myths of poor teaching, (b) the university had developed research-based performance indicators of its teaching, (c) teaching and assessment were demonstrably improving and that (d) the evaluation of teaching system was boosting organizational learning. In sum, students reported that less than 15% of teachers were not teaching well, that less than 20% were borderline and that more than 65% were teaching well, very well, or superbly.

Simultaneously, various organizational development projects were maturing. For example, the recovery of the Elam School of Fine Arts had been achieved through collaborative strategic planning and largely self-managed reforms (Macpherson, 1999b, 1999d). Another example was the exploitation of information and communication technology for teaching and professional development purposes, moderated with international benchmarking (Macpherson, 2000a, 2000b; Macpherson & Frielick, 2001; Macpherson et al., 2000). In sharp contrast, one faculty's business interests were advanced when it was permitted to capture online delivery rather than having the University of Auckland adopt software with open source code in order to encourage participation in international pedagogical research.

In retrospect, and in general, the political arrangements in the University of Auckland exhibited the cultural norms of a liberal democracy (Finer, 1970, pp. 58–74). As a participant observer for five years, it appeared to me that the legitimacy of professional and organizational policies and practices in the University of Auckland relied on the critical awareness and informed consent of academic staff, with academic leaders expected to create functional degrees of harmony through respectful interaction with colleagues. Leaders were also expected to avoid interfering in teaching and research in ways that could be taken as violations of academic freedom. It was widely assumed that university governance was derived from and accountable to internal and external community stakeholders and would operate at the periphery of university life. Further, any interventions into the largely self-managing, self-refining and voluntary nature of academic departments would be the exception and have to be justified. University managers were expected to protect minorities and accommodate plural views as they managed with a light touch in the common interest within their departments or faculties. Less frequent but evident and important were references made to the social contract that was presumed to exist between the university community and its wider host society.

Leaders in the University of Auckland were expected to facilitate change through orderly and systematic policy making processes and to champion due process during collaborative strategic planning. Cultural transformation had to be achieved via the open clarification and debate of policy options, and implementation had to guarantee cultural safety by using respectful consultations and allow time for people to change their positions. It appears in retrospect that neopragmatist educative leadership was particularly appropriate in such a neopluralist liberal democracy mainly due its capacity to (a) accommodate communitarianism, communicative rationalism and egalitarian liberalism, (b) respond effectively to active representation from internal and external stakeholders, (c) accept corrections from social and political checks and balances and (d) achieve demonstrably pragmatic improvements. The leadership team of the university led by vice chancellor John Hood, deputy vice chancellor (academic) Raewyn Dalziel and deputy vice chancellor (research) Tom Barnes provided some of the finest examples of educative leadership I have ever seen in academia, and with the focused engagement of faculty and support unit leaders, demonstrably turned the University of Auckland around in financial, research and teaching terms. Hood was then invited to serve as vice chancellor of Oxford University; Dalziel started planning for her retirement, and with a new regime and regime change both imminent, it was time for me to find a new challenge.

The most immediate difference I noted on arrival at the Waiariki Institute of Technology as the new CEO in early 2002 was that the institution was strongly committed to a social justice agenda, specifically, providing opportunities for Maori. The second was that its governance and management systems were in disarray. The clearest indicators were that it was operating hand-to-mouth on a shoe string, did not have an operational plan or budget for the coming year and was spiraling into deficit. A queue of debtors threatening legal action soon formed at my door. A provisional budget was quickly created, and the institution's management and information systems were reconfigured to manage and stabilize cash flows.

Te Mana Matauranga (Maori elders nominated by the main tribes of the region), the elected Council of Waiariki and the senior management team (SMT) soon agreed to focus on four priorities: the reform of governance; the reform of management systems; settle debts; and to deliver a financial turn round. Governance, thereafter, focused on accountabilities, risk management and growth strategies. The reformed management systems resulted in new programs and fresh methods of reconciling academic quality with course and program viabilities. Collaborative strategic planning processes involving stakeholders then developed a new charter and profile in late 2002, revising it in 2003 and 2004. Budgets were signed off in October each year to allow operational planning for the next year to begin. Debts were settled and surpluses were achieved from 2003.

When I left in 2005, the reforms in governance, management, debt settlement and finances was attributed to four main factors: (a) the reintegration of bicultural governance and management processes; (b) the new planning, risk management, scheduling and information systems; (c) the internal reviews that improved the productivity of support units, regional campuses and schools; and (d) the development of effective partnerships with regional secondary schools, industries and local and regional governments that improved bridging education and curriculum alignment. I would add a fifth key factor: the trustful relationship between the chair of Te Mana Matauranga, the chair of Waiariki Council, Waiariki's kaumatua (senior cultural leader) and myself.

There were two major impediments to Waiariki's survival and recovery in the period 2002–2005. First was the precarious and vicarious nature of the national funding and policy context for polytechnics, including the absence of a capital works program. Second was the Labour government's active discouragement of extra-region entrepreneurialism while allowing the establishment and free-rein expansion of two wananga (Maori TEIs) in the Waiariki rohe (region), the latter of which, Te Wananga o Awanui-a-rangi was actually sponsored and nurtured by Waiariki prior to its formal establishment and independence.

Looking back, the political arrangements at Waiariki were unique in that they enabled cogovernance by two entities using different politico-cultural assumptions and justifications. The council of Maori elders, Te Mana Matauranga, used *marae-style* procedures, including exhaustive discussions to reach consensus. They expected monthly and detailed reports from the CEO and the director of Maori advancement, although the focus of their interest was not institutional performance but on the advantages that would flow to Maori students and staff members and to the eight beating hearts (tribes) of Te Arawa.

The elected council members represented regional stakeholder constituencies alongside a significant bloc of government appointees who stressed compliance with national policy, especially financial solvency. It met fortnightly, used standard corporate meeting procedures, and sought monthly, written and verbal reports from the CEO and all directors. It delved deeply and frequently into policy and operational matters, provided regular directions, without, curiously, ever accepting any responsibility for the mess that I and the SMT had inherited.

Although the mismatch of governance expectations was ameliorated to a degree by meetings of a joint committee, the steady intensification of internal and local accountabilities were trumped by changes in the wider political context. As indicated above, the government's rhetoric encouraged cooperation between tertiary institutions but masked increasingly hostile market realities. Waiariki struggled to survive within its restricted territory, suffered from fixed or falling subsidies per student and saw demand fall due to historic lows in unemployment levels. The government proved unwilling to invest in Maori trades training at this time while simultaneously giving the two wananga significant market advantages. In this context, the members of the SMT invested whatever discretionary time they had in driving up the productivity of all courses and programs and in developing more competitive products. Their three partially contradictory objectives were to (a) cross subsidize socially critical products and services, (b) compress costs in an attempt to deliver modest institutional surpluses and (c) wherever possible, sustain staff morale and employment. In effect, the neopragmatism in leadership practices blended communicative rationalist, monetarist and humanitarian priorities.

There were, inevitably, a few casualties. Soon after I left in mid 2005 for the Middle East, the government arbitrarily imposed funding caps, and Waiariki moved into three years of deficits. A few years later, the government introduced a capital works program for polytechnics. Waiariki then boosted its intake of full-fee international students, and its finances rebounded.

In sum, although the institution's mission stressed a regional and bicultural approach to governance, the bifurcation of accountabilities added significant risk to institutional survival. As trading conditions deteriorated and the limits of cost compression were reached, cross subsidies had to be pruned back and tensions mounted locally in governance. The government's cap on institutional income then took the institution into deficit trading and required a down scaling of bicultural governance and socially critical services, until they could be cross-subsidized again by international marketing.

In 2005 I was invited to become a chancellor and CEO of a new university in the Middle East. Chapter 8 used political philosophy to describe and review the politics of governance in this institution. It showed that strategic capacity building was impaired by autocratic governance and interventions that undermined the engagement of Western-educated academic staff who expected leadership in more liberal democratic terms. The impact of these governance arrangements on teaching and learning was also reported in detail elsewhere (Macpherson, 2008b). The two key points I drew from this extraordinary experience were that:

1   The use of autocratic politico-cultural norms enabled a profoundly counterproductive politics of realpolitik that violated the liberal democratic norms associated with university governance and academic freedom needed to create and teach fresh knowledge.

2   Culturally insensitive questions must be asked in a framework of political philosophy if the United Arab Emirates is going to learn wiser ways of reaching and refreshing social contracts in the common good in order to achieve its aim of becoming a modern knowledge society.

Similarly, culturally insensitive and politically incorrect questions are apparently warranted regarding New Zealand's PLP (for *Professional Leadership Plan 2009–2012*). It was designed to deliver preparatory and succession professionalization to primary school principals. Chapter 5 provided a case study of becoming a primary school principal that suggested what appear to be serious flaws in the PLP policy and provisions. The narrow objectives focus on implementing ministerial priorities and encouraging the adoption of Kiwi pragmatism instead of advancing the communitarianism and communicative rationalism needed to underpin distributed leadership roles in self-governing and self-managing community schools. Kiwi pragmatism is also likely to limit responsiveness in schools to the national will and encourage dynamic conservatism in the ministry. Chapter 5 concluded with two interesting propositions: Neophyte leaders of primary schools are being professionalized into a political ideology of Kiwi pragmatism rather than implementing national educational policies preferred by successive governments, and power is being recentralized into the ministry and sister unions, away from school communities, national parent advocates and the team of responsible ministers. If so, history is likely to repeat itself with a gradual collapse of political legitimacy in the portfolio.

The case study in Chapter 6 was about becoming a school director in a newly independent country, Timor Leste. Again, the politically incorrect question asked was about the mismatch between the local political ideology of communitarianism and the East Timorese pragmatism that has evolved in the Ministry of Education to cope with turbulent internal politics. Sadly, this mismatch is impeding support for communitarianism across the system of school education, which is intended to give carriage to the national reconstruction policy based on reconciliation and development through independence.

A common feature of the outcomes described in Chapters 5, 6 and 7 was that, in the absence of clarity over appropriate political arrangements in schools and education systems, and the implementation of designed political structures, aberrant forms of pragmatism evolved. In sharp contrast, when three secondary schools in Cornwall, supported by the Dutchy Health Charity, the Princes' College of Medicine and Cornwall Council, decided to trial school-based integrated health centers, they engaged students closely in design and decoration to create attractive reception areas leading into modern clinical and group meeting rooms. Student ownership was then extended into the selection of coordinators and into center management and governance, alongside school, community and provider representatives. As noted above, three years later this deliberate distribution of power to students was associated with a measurably improved general ability to self-manage general health and well-being, and sexual and mental health, and to academic progress and significantly reduced youth offending (Macpherson, 2013). Although many other factors were associated with these outcomes, such as pedagogical, curricular and organizational improvements, the deliberate design of appropriate political structures for center governance and management were shown to be essential preconditions of success.

Looking back, the sequence of role studies above also imply that being an educative leader requires suspending uncritical acceptance of the pragmatic and communitarian norms in schools and education systems, tolerating degrees of role conflict and taking responsibility for the quality of professional and organizational learning. Taking responsibility in these senses requires reflecting critically on individual and organizational learning outcomes and then committing to strategic interventions such as action research and deeper genetic adjustments, such as developing educative accountability criteria and processes. It appears from the intersystem research reported above that educative leadership is evident in various ways.

- Pedagogical curriculum, knowledge and structural leadership that uses constructivist professional development to engage professionals as learners
- Moral leadership that emphasizes rule consequentialism
- Communicative rationalist leadership during policy deconstruction and reconstruction intended to contest exclusive, corrosive, or unjust ideologies, such as racism
- Politically critical leadership that seeks to improve the quality of policy making and implementation structures and processes

The cases of research in accountability and administrative policy making above suggest that political and administrative leaders can offer strategic forms of educative leadership when they use liberal democratic means to develop or refresh the social contract between the governed and the governors. They can drive up the legitimacy of political arrangements in human systems and the fairness of outcomes. Conversely, instances of command politics that serve an absolutist ideology contrast sharply with examples of forms of liberal democracy in governance that both accommodate neopluralism and deliver substantial degrees of subsidiarity. The general upshot of the review is that the concept of educative leadership needs to move beyond being simply educationally critical in nature and become ethically critical, socially critical and politically critical to achieve strategic relevance using neopragmatism. I attempt to establish the relativity of politically critical analysis and evaluation in the next and final chapter.

This takes me to the potential role that political philosophy may play in the growth of knowledge about educative leadership. The research program reviewed above indicates the importance of educative leaders being able to facilitate the construction of educational policies that reflect a neopragmatic blend of communitarianism, communicative rationalism and egalitarian liberalism, principally to provide the time and scaffolding needed to help people to reconstruct their understandings and commitments during implementation. The review also highlighted the value of communitarianism to professional educators during policy implementation, along with ongoing democratic representation by stakeholders, social and political checks and balances, and rigorous summative and formative evaluation. The cases of institutional leadership examined drew attention to the importance of strategic leaders who are politically critical of the policy and funding context, that is, able to deconstruct political rhetoric masking the drivers of change in the host political economy and, at the very least, to anticipate political interventions.

This case study of a career integrated with a research program in educative leadership suggests three important reasons why political philosophy needs to be added to the repertoire of perspectives already evident in the field of educational administration, in the sister fields of public administration, and given the growing ubiquity of knowledge organizations in the globalizing mixed economy, in management science.

The first special service it can provide, as a disciplined activity, is to help leaders who would be educative to describe the relativity of political ideologies in current arrangements, such as in governance and political subcultures, and to develop an ethical justification for using power to achieve reforms. This would help challenge political ideologies that are based on factional interests or particular commitments being given foundational status.

The second service could then follow; political philosophy could help identify and promote the political arrangements that are supportive of the growth of knowledge needed to achieve global and sustainable peace, compassion and prosperity. Because power is an evitable feature of human affairs, a healthy political philosophical discourse in institutional politics would help ensure that it is put progressively to more right ends.

Third, and finally, political philosophy would help further develop educative leadership as a politically critical component of governance and leadership in knowledge organizations in a globalizing world in order to (a) avoid any naïve adoption of pragmatism, communitarianism, communicative rationalism, or egalitarian liberalism, (b) circumvent justifications that back up into absolutist ideologies supported by a foundational epistemology and (c) explore more deeply the democratic elaboration of justifications that will further develop the social contracts between the state and the people, and the governors and the governed in institutions.

Note

1 This chapter is a revised version of a previously published article (Macpherson, 2008b).

12 The relativity of politically critical analysis and leadership

For him [Thomas Jefferson] politics was informed by philosophy, but one could achieve the good only by putting philosophy into action. To do so required the acquisition of power. He moved carefully in Williamsburg, first introducing bills in order to test "the strength of the general pulse of reformation." Satisfied that the lawmakers were, in fact, interested in a new order, Jefferson pressed on—but only after becoming sure of his ground. . . . The Founders' dream of a nation beyond partisanship was one that simply could not survive the very nature of a free politics in a culture of diverse interests. . . . It was easy to speak theoretically and idealistically about politics when one is seeking power. The demands of exercising it once it is won, however, are so complex and fluid that ideological certitude is often among the first casualties of actual governing. Jefferson had achieved something that his Federalist foes would not have thought possible: He was, to some, no longer Republican enough. Jefferson was, in other words, a man who had displeased the extremes of his day—a sign that he had been guided not by dogma but by principled pragmatism. . . . One thing is unmistakably consistent, however, in his successors' understanding of Jefferson: Like him they believed in the power of words in public life, in the molding of popular opinion—and in the centrality of presidential power to keep the nation safe and strong in the most difficult of hours.

(Meacham, 2012, pp. 121, 373, 416, 504)

The previous chapters may suggest to educational administrators, managers and educative leaders that I am suggesting that political philosophy should become a dominant component of their practice. Not so. I have argued instead that it should be an important component of their practice that should be evoked whenever power is in play to ensure that agency, dynamics and structures are justified. As Thomas Jefferson clearly understood, there are many other ways of being critical that are as equally as important as being politically critical.

This final chapter extends the point of Socrates's death to suggest that practitioners, researchers and theorists in education should not only reflect critically on their power practices and the arrangements in place, but use many ways of being critical. By *many ways*, I mean that they use ethically critical, socially critical, environmentally critical, politically critical and globally critical perspectives judiciously, appreciating the relativity of each. I illustrate what might be possible in education by referring to wider realms of leadership. I conclude with my preferred blend of Deweyan democratic and educative neopragmatism, principally because it supports many ways of being critical in educational administration and educative leadership.[1]

Recall, in 399 BC, when Socrates had been found guilty of heresy and sedition, he was given the opportunity to plead for alternatives to punishment by death, such as exile, a fine, or a period of imprisonment. His student Plato (1963) recorded that his first plea was that he be rewarded because his alleged crime—teaching the youth of Athens how to reflect on the quality of their lives and Athenian society—was actually a positive contribution to the health of the state. Seeing the futility of this argument with the jury, his second plea, for exoneration, was on the grounds that going into exile was pointless because he would face the same problem wherever he went, unless people and rulers came to understand the value of reflection and independent and critical thinking. Once again seeing that the jury was unconvinced, his third and final plea was to point out that to accept being silenced by imprisonment would be to disobey a command from God to constantly examine the goodness of life. He concluded, therefore, that "an unexamined life is not worth living." So, out of extreme piety and patriotism, Socrates decided to take the legally prescribed and lethal dose of hemlock in order to highlight the right and the responsibility of every citizen to contribute to society with independent and critical thinking.

This final chapter is for leaders in knowledge organizations who wish to consider the implications of taking up their right and responsibility to reflect on and critically evaluate the nature of their own services using many perspectives, and for teachers in academia who would want to support such learning by extending their research to such ends. To be clear, knowledge organizations comprise the rapidly growing number of firms and institutions in the public, private and blended sectors internationally that (a) rely on knowledge as their raw material, (b) employ knowledge professionals to process knowledge using information communication technology, (c) deliver valued knowledge-based goods and services and (d) achieve economic, ecological and social returns on investment (Casey, 1995; Liebowitz & Beckman, 1998). Because knowledge organizations sustain their development through the growth of trustworthy knowledge, this process needs to be regarded and refined as the central means of production and reproduction in modern economies and societies.

As touched on in Chapter 1, a distinctive feature of the growth of knowledge is that it is advanced by four interdependent and equally valuable forms of scholarship that usually, but not always, follow a never-ending cycle of discovery, integration, application and teaching (Boyer, 1990). Given the key role of scholarship in modern knowledge societies as a means of production and reproduction, we need to be clear about evaluative criteria concerning the quality of scholarship.

Sophisticated philosophical research has established that there are common criteria for evaluating quality scholarship irrespective of form (Glassick et al., 1997). The first criterion is clarity of goals: basic purposes are clearly stated; realistic and achievable objectives are stated; and important questions are defined. The second is the adequacy of preparation: prior scholarship is understood; necessary skills have been used; and appropriate resources have been deployed. Third is the appropriateness of methods: methods are appropriate to goals; methods selected are used effectively; and procedures have been modified to suit changing circumstances. The fourth criterion concerns the significance of results: the goals have been achieved; the outcomes are significant; and new areas have been indicated for exploration. The fifth criterion concerns effective presentation and communication: There is a suitable style and effective organization used to present the outcomes; appropriate forums are used to communicate to intended audiences; and outcomes are presented with clarity and integrity. Sixth, and finally, is the use of reflective critique: There is a scholarly and critical evaluation of outcomes; an appropriate breadth of evidence is used in the critique; and critical evaluation is used to improve the quality of future work.

This detail is provided to emphasize that leaders must have the strategic understandings, the tactical and technological skills, and the disposition to lead the organization, administration and the coordination of all aspects of policy making and policy implementation concerned with critical scholarship, on behalf of their governors, for their knowledge organization to flourish. The upshot is that there are at least two prior but insufficient conditions for the effective leadership of knowledge organizations: educative leaders who are organizationally critical and epistemologically critical. There are, however, many other ways in which leaders will need to be critical.

Most leaders acquire early the techniques and arts of being functionally critical, and then become more financially critical as their responsibilities for resource management increase. In contrast, despite a rich folklore and potential for improved artistry in leadership, relatively few leaders aim to become aesthetically critical (Bathurst, 2007) or get to appreciate leadership as a dramatic and ethical art that cultivates meaning, community and responsibility among educators (Starratt, 1993, 2003, 2004b).

There is also enormous value in stepping outside of education into the critical literature of business education. Interest has grown steadily in a critical pedagogy for management education in business (Reynolds, 1998), with special interest developing in less hierarchical methods and potential pitfalls (Reynolds, 1999). Most notably, this emergent field of critical management studies (CMS) in commerce is expected to relate a plurality of intellectual traditions and innovative engagements to management practice (Fournier & Grey, 2000). There have been calls for CMS to help management students in the public and private sectors to recognize profound changes to the nature of competition in business and to understand the historical, social, political and philosophical traditions underlying contemporary conceptions of organizations and management, with a greater sensitivity to the emancipatory and transformational potential of practice (Dehler, Welsh, & Lewis, 2001).

It is interesting and helpful that critical and neopragmatic management principles were proposed to advance this more socially critical than neopragmatic agenda

(Watson, 2001). The field of management education is moving from seeing a CMS simply as means of challenging immoral practices (Perriton & Reynolds, 2004) toward realizing that such discontinuous learning events can trigger higher level learning and inward critical self-reflection, and that these forms of learning are essential to the development of entrepreneurialism (Cope, 2003). An example examined above was learning about philanthropic entrepreneurialism serving educative ends in adverse social and economic circumstances.

Hence, this chapter focuses on forms of critique that are directly related to the role of leaders in knowledge organizations, and in passing, helps widen the scope of the CMS literature. To this end, it introduces concepts, tools of analysis and criteria for evaluation that would assist leaders to become simultaneously more ethically critical, socially critical, environmentally critical, politically critical and globally critical, in a context of neopragmatist practice.

We can begin with ethically critical leadership. Leadership practice in most settings involves having a decisive influence over the actions of others and events. Such practice is mediated by plural contexts; the history and current complexities of the situation, projections of options and consequences, and the personal philosophies and experiences of managers and those they manage. Leadership in knowledge organizations is especially mediated by a concern for the growth of knowledge and problem solving capacity, because they create improvements to the value-adding capacities and the sustainability of the organization. Given the centrality and yet potentially oppressive nature of creativity in knowledge organizations (Prichard, 2002), most stakeholders and those being managed will expect leaders to link human creativity to well-being as an organizational goal, and therefore to be just rather than unjust in their leadership services, to make right rather than wrong decisions and to promote good rather than evil. There appear to be three general ways in which ethically critical leadership practice might proceed.

First is leading on principle. Although Socrates's point in principle is relatively well-know, what is less well-known is that he and Buddha, Confucius and Jeremiah, the mystics of the Upanishads, Mencius and Euripides, had together, between 800 and 300 BC, pioneered a new form of human experience—a principled way of thinking (Armstrong, 2006, pp. xii–xiv). None of these philosophers displayed any interest in doctrinal or metaphysical ways of thinking, such as metaphysical naturalism as noted above, or in their followers becoming unthinking believers. All of them helped push out the boundaries of human consciousness to include transcendental, nonempirical, or spiritual dimensions. Although all were reverently silent about their experience of this dimension, they did not regard it as necessarily supernatural or impose it on others.

Instead, as Socrates exemplified, they insisted that no one should take any religious teaching on faith or at second hand, to treat what people took for granted as provisional knowledge and to test teachings empirically by relating it to personal experience. And, in any case, their common advice was that what you believed in mattered less than how you behaved and lived your life. To this end, they all advised people to behave and live in ways that are compassionate, generous and supportive of peace and prosperity, and to abandon egotism, greed, meanness and violence. Respecting the rights of all beings as sacred was the essence of their spiritual ethos, not the orthodoxies of being a believer. They offered principles to help people reflect critically on the quality of their actions, lives and community.

I am, therefore, strongly attracted by Rorty's (1989) argument that such philosophical reflection can and should enable people to (re)create themselves in diverse communities that are bound together by common commitments, commitments that straddle their public and private lives. His concept of reflective equilibrium (1991) is particularly helpful during political decision making because it describes how we can search deliberately for coherence and find balance and mutual adjustments between general principles of educative leadership, such as encouraging learning about the accommodation of interests on the common ground and by customizing judgments to unique settings, after Thomas Jefferson if you will.

Second is to lead using rationalism rather than intuition to assemble the facts, as far as possible, as well as reasonable interpretations of the situation to logically propose and justify particular courses of action. This is not to rule out the apparently nonrational factors, although it is unusual and probably unconvincing for leaders in education or managers in business today to turn to transcendental, nonempirical, or spiritual sources to justify their practices (Jones, 1980). Followers today tend to regard arational justifications as arbitrary.

Nevertheless, many ethical principles have endured, suggesting that their continued utility may have a rational basis. A prime example is the so-called golden rule of ethics, to "treat others as you would wish to be treated." The golden rule has been shown by Gensler (1996) to champion reciprocity in human affairs and require coherence between what is desired and desirable, and that it can be used to evaluate and improve behaviors on the bases of fairness and care.

This reveals two unique features of principles. First, they tend not to be conceived logically through rationalism but through critical reflection on religious, existential and ideological commitments. Second, as Hodgkinson (1996) pointed out, principles are given birth by the psychological processes that convert such commitments into a striving for action and change, rather than being gestated through more rational appreciations of consequences or the extent to which alternative courses of action are likely to be supported by consensus.

Returning for a moment to the rigor of rationalism, although evidence and logic are essential, particularly in the archetypical decision system used to arbitrate knowledge claims known as the scientific method, they are not enough on their own. Aristotle, the father of rationalism, argued that they need to be complemented by particular moral and intellectual virtues. He emphasized the moral virtues of justice, courage and temperance, and the intellectual virtues of wisdom and prudence (see Duignan, 2006). I suggest that they be adopted and integrated into a neopragmatic process of ethical decision making appropriate for educational leadership by setting aside the use of simplistic dualisms and foundational commitments and by giving high priority to reconciling the values presented in complex dilemmas on the common ground. By accepting that only language is available for political philosophy, albeit precise language about the empirical facts of the matter, one is freed to create center-less, nonfoundational and coherent webs of belief in service of educative leadership.

There is, of course, as Hodgkinson (1983) also pointed out, a third general approach to the ethical justification of leadership practice that is fundamentally different from principle-driven and rationalism-driven approaches. It is to make decisions on what feels good at the time, on personal preference, making an intuitive appreciation of what presents as "the facts of the matter." The basic psychological process triggering this type of leadership action is the uncritical engagement of feelings and suspending the use of ethical principles, rational appreciation and aesthetic evaluation. The process can indulge the ego, take the line of least resistance and make a meta-value of expediency.

The moral evaluation of leadership practice, it follows, has two basic steps: the analysis and description of values in practice, and then, arbitration of the justifications on a systematic basis. The first step, of conducting a values audit, creates clarity concerning the nature of values in use, as evidenced in actions, or more precisely, in language about actions. In Chapter Two, I commended Hodgkinson's (1978) model of the concept of value because it is based on the difference between rightness and goodness, that is, between the desirable and the desired, and thus between deontology (a logic of duties and rights) and axiology (a logic of value). Rightness is concerned with what is proper, morally sound and duty bound, and what ought to be. Goodness is about preference that comes spontaneously via impulse, immediate feelings about experience in the empirical world and innate dispositions.

On this basis, Hodgkinson identified three methods of justifying value judgments. Type III judgments are self-justifying because they rely on the uncritical application of personal preferences. They use values derived from an emotive psychological state without reference to social norms or principles in the wider context. In philosophical terms, using Type III value judgments coheres with using the degrees of reductionism inevitable with logical positivism and behaviorism, sometimes further flawed by employing the naturalistic fallacy—using evidence about what *is* to develop a claim about what *ought to be* and allowing logic and science to suborn ethics and values.

Type II justifications are different in that they are derived from an appreciation of a social or organizational context. They are derived in two main ways: by appeal to consensus or to consequences. Both methods require rational analysis and cognitive projections, albeit to build agreements and count hands, or to estimate the implications of probable outcomes. In philosophical terms, such reasoning tends to lead to an ethic of enlightened self-interest or some form of humanism embedded through compromise into a pragmatic system of moral imperatives.

Type I value judgments are different again in that they appeal to selected principles. As illustrated by Socrates, they are derived from a metaphysical position based on moral insight, religious revelation, or perhaps, an aesthetic sense of a personal drama. Because they can't be logically or empirically verified, they tend to be absolutist in nature. Type I value judgments are therefore *transrational* in that they imply acts of will based on faith and belief. Sadly, they can also be used to justify a dangerous ethic of uncritical compliance, or worse, militant fundamentalism.

Once the values in practice have been mapped, evaluation can proceed. Such evaluation really ought to begin with meta-evaluation, that is, by questioning the assumptive base of Hodgkinson's model, rather than allowing hidden assumptions to affect the rest of the evaluation without question. The first postulate is the values hierarchy itself. It indicates Hodgkinson's view that Type I values are more superior, more authentic, better justified and more defensible than Type II values, and in turn, than Type III values. Having served in many positions with considerable authority, and encountered instances where power has distorted or reconstructed principles, this hierarchy discomforts the rationalist skeptic in me and suggests that we use, yet also partially discount, each type of value according to its limitations and use the process of reflective equilibrium to embed them in our web of belief.

The second postulate is that the values in use tend to degenerate in authenticity or force over time. I have seen this happen so often that I believe that the agreements between stakeholders that underpin strategic plans should be revisited annually and that embedded political ideologies and infrastructure should be similarly reexamined using a neopragmatist mind set.

The third postulate is that people tend to avoid values dilemmas by resolving them at the lowest possible level. My experience has been that people tend to revert to a blend of the norms of their formative culture mediated by their current interests and ideologies. Hence, it is important to note that these postulates are based primarily on Hodgkinson's deep regard for the moral leadership of visionaries throughout the ages and his view that these principles have been degraded through uncritical use and moral laxity. He has a point.

Two other objections to the model have been raised by Colin Evers (1985), neither of which, in my view, seriously undercuts the utility of the model for analyzing values in practice, while awaiting his proposals for improvement. First, Evers noted, the model precludes by definition any Type II (that is, rational) defense of a Type I value and is, therefore, not able to arbitrate contested Type I principles. Although this is fair enough in a technical sense, Gensler's defense of the golden rule of ethics illustrated that principles can be found to have rational basis, implying that we may use principles on advisement. Further, given Duignan's and Starratt's demonstrations of the contemporary potency of Aristotelian virtues, I suggest we continue to use Type I values provisionally in our webs of belief but without giving them foundational status.

Evers's second objection is that Hodgkinson's hierarchy of values is a moral judgment in itself without the theory of value involved being declared. I am not so sure about this as an impediment to use because Hodgkinson did declare and justify his preference for neo-Stoicism on the grounds of aesthetic transcendentalism and scholarly modesty. Again, he may be right.

Hodgkinson (1986) rejected Evers's objections by referring to the incommensurability of the value types. However, if his value types use incommensurable criteria and scales, how can they constitute a plausible hierarchy? Evers's second objection was rejected on what were claimed to be historically validated grounds: The *intelligent will* is of a higher order than *the mind*, and that the mind is of a higher order than *the objects* being sensed by the mind. Although it is not entirely clear to me what a higher order is, and in particular how this validates the value hierarchy, Hodgkinson's general proposal was that the highly principled and ageless proposals provided by moral leaders warrant profound (yet not absolute) respect. Seeing and appreciating both Evers's and Hodgkinson's points, I will leave this ground to them and henceforth limit my use of Hodgkinson's model to audit, analysis and description.

This takes us back to how to arbitrate values, with particular attention to organizational type and values, because they offer important but not exclusive bases for the purposes and moral legitimacy of leadership practice. My starting point is that a knowledge organization is an organizational form that must value high quality scholarship related to the growth of understanding and capacity building about solving substantive problems. Hence, to proceed, I recommend four congenial postulates developed by Evers (1987) that address why and how educative leadership practices should be subjected to moral evaluation:

1   Such moral appraisal is possible and desirable, and should be conducted according to a moral theory that values problem solving and the growth of knowledge.

2   The moral knowledge used to make judgments needs to be understood as part of a person's whole web of belief that develops according to the general principles that govern the growth of knowledge. Hence, leaders can be appraised morally to the extent of the control they have over organizational life and learning, while taking into account the diffusion of responsibility and the extent to which they make contributions.

3   Because organizations face and solve problems through conjecture and refutation, their leaders ought to be educative and, therefore, ought to be held responsible for the quality of organizational learning. The appraisal of educative leaders should, therefore, focus on the extent to which they promote learning and problem solving in organizational life, as evidenced in the social relations of effective inquiry.

4   Because effective inquiry requires learning through informed feedback and rigorous process, educative leaders should promote particular values: fair distribution of knowledge and access to conditions of learning, respect and tolerance for different viewpoints and experiences, and freedom of thought, inquiry and expression.

As with Duignan's and Starratt's general approach, Evers's methodology is intrinsically Deweyan in that it is pragmatic, holist, rule consequentialist, nonutilitarian, humanist and nonfoundational (Campbell, 1995). The methodology is pragmatic in that it makes all parts of the moral theory used open to revision and permits no absolutes. The methodology is holist in that the principles permitting revision include consistency, coherence, comprehensiveness and the simplicity of the total web of belief involved. The methodology is rule consequentialist in that it makes a general rule of using rationalist problem solving and the growth of knowledge as the touchstone for the evaluation of leadership practices, especially the extent to which they help achieve long-term educational consequences. The methodology is nonutilitarian in the strict sense of not being obliged to maximize benefits to all. The methodology is humanist in the belief that it is possible to live decently without religious and metaphysical certainty, with reasonable confidence coming from the condition that all knowledge and opinion remains open to correction. Indeed, the flourishing of colleagues in a knowledge organization is held to be dependent on open communication, free discussion, criticism and consensus without coercion. Finally, this methodology is nonfoundational in that it remains deeply respectful yet skeptical of well-tried and long-standing principles, allowing them provisional standing while rejecting any absolutism—while also relying heavily on tests for coherence between principles, the moral dilemmas presenting in the situation, the best possible estimates of consequences made by stakeholders, as well as a subtle appreciation of precedents and risks.

Hence, in my view, ethically critical leaders in knowledge organizations ought to promote the continuing education of all members, seeing it as a strategic means of organizational learning that can blend science with aesthetics and cultural development with liberal democracy. The crucial conditions include freedom of thought and opinion, the full development of intelligence, applied research in science and technology, and a supportive organizational context that is characterized by liberal democratic social and political systems, and a socially critical and environmentally critical awareness of external contexts.

We can now turn to socially critical and environmentally critical leadership. The idea that leaders should be held responsible using values external to their enterprise is not new, particularly in the private sector. This may come as a surprise to leaders and theorists in education, especially those who persist in reiterating the processes of structuration, even to the point of rebadging them as "biopolitical production" (Hardt & Negri, 2000, p. xiii), freely elaborating the concept without evidence (Collin & Apple, 2010, pp. 27–29), and then seeing neoliberalism as the driving force behind every shift in education policy in contexts as diverse as Japan, Israel, Palestine and across Latin America.

The concept of social responsibility in corporate management was highlighted by research into the separation of ownership and control in the context of American capitalism (Berle & Means, 1932). A new class of professional managers were found to be acting as the stewards of the enormous resources controlled by large and vertically integrated firms. This stewardship was also being expected by owners to maximize profits and to serve the needs of an increasingly complex society. Since then, stewardship has accepted degrees of social responsibility and other bottom lines, resulting in plural evaluation criteria for performance management.

The justifications for managers accepting social responsibilities have since tended to be either ethical or instrumental in nature (Jones, 1999). The ethical justifications were derived either from religious or metaphysical principles or from prevailing social norms (Freeman & Gilbert, 1988; Goodpaster, 1984). After Hodgkinson, Type I advocates argued that managers must act in a socially responsible manner because it is the morally correct thing to do. Type IIA advocates agreed on the basis that managers should be held accountable for the consequences of the business sector controlling the bulk of society's resources. Type IIB scholars believed that ethical behavior is positively related to business performance, with many supporting such behavior even where there was unproductive expenditure involved (Vogel, 1991).

Instrumental arguments for managers taking social responsibility tend to be based on Type IIA rational calculations that it will benefit the organization, at least in the long term. For example, accepting social accountabilities can help position an enterprise to anticipate political dynamics; suggest alternatives to hostile government regulations; exploit opportunities arising from increasing levels of cultural, environmental and gender awareness; and differentiate its products and services from less socially responsible competitors (Freeman, 1984).

A Type IIB view would acknowledge that, while corporations have significant powers due to their resources, knowledge and influence, they also have more stakeholders than owners in mixed economies, and these internal and external stakeholders have moral (and increasingly legal) rights that means that their views and interests must be taken into account when refining policy and leaders' practices.

Arguments against managers accepting social responsibility tend to be based on privileging property rights and organizational efficiency. For example, it was argued (Levitt, 1958) that not-for-profit organizations exist to deliver social responsibilities and that managers of large private sector corporations do not have the time, expertise, or mandate to levy a de facto tax on the shareholders in order to deliver and account for social outcomes, which is, in any case, more properly the responsibility of democratically elected politicians. Allowing or encouraging managers to change their institutional role according to principles of social responsibility is to allocate inappropriate degrees of autonomy in a society without democratic accountability. Other attacks were even blunter; managers had no legal or moral right to do more than act as the owners' representative, and ought to focus on increasing share values while remaining within the law and being respectful of social conventions (Friedman, 1962, 1970).

Despite these objections, as intimated above, the concept of management accountability has broadened in recent decades from single to double and to triple-bottom-line (TBL) accountabilities that are globalizing in scope. Traditionally, managers accounted to owners for changes to the bottom line of profit or loss over a period of time. They accounted for variances to budgets regarding the components of the Accounting Equation, that is, Assets + Expenses + Disbursements = Liabilities + Owner Equity + Revenue. Wherever owners started asking managers to account in any sense for indications of the social return on their investment, it inevitably triggered attempts to develop a double-bottom-line accounting methodology. Binary thinking followed about the nature of value so created; it could be either economic, as created by for-profit companies, or social, as created by not-for-profit or nongovernmental organizations (NGOs). This binary thinking finally collapsed when a *blended value proposition* was proposed that assumes that all organizations create value that consists of economic, social and environmental components (Emerson & Bonini, 2004). Hence TBL accountability conceived wider responsibilities to *stakeholders*, rather than just to shareholders, with stakeholders defined as anyone who is influenced or otherwise affected, either directly or indirectly, by the actions of an enterprise (Elkington, 1994, 1998). The proprietary rights of owners were thereby diluted by the political rights of stakeholders, and wherever it was implemented, governors and managers had to articulate and balance the scope of stakeholder interests against shareholder interests in financial returns on investment.

TBL was initially challenged on at least four grounds (Norman & MacDonald, 2004). First were the technical limits of auditing and measuring social performance and impacts, and then aggregating them convincingly into a net social profit or loss. Second was the absence of evidence that measurement leads to social performance and to better profits. Third was the elusive justification for obliging firms to demonstrably maximize or improve their net positive social impact and transparency to all stakeholders. Fourth and finally was the incommensurability of the scales used to measure economic, social and environmental values, and the severe limits implied regarding the degree to which trade-offs could be calculated.

Nevertheless, the globalization of socially critical and environmentally critical management were significantly advanced when the United Nations (1987) adopted a policy of sustainability to stress intergenerational justice and the changes required in national politics. TBL then became an international sociopolitical movement challenging reactionary nationalism and promoting values and criteria for measuring organizational and societal success in terms of economic prosperity, social responsibility and environmental sustainability. TBL was formally adopted by the United Nations in 2007 as the standard for urban, community and public sector full-cost accounting, with similar standards endorsed for the measurement and reporting of natural, human capital and ecological footprints.

Four broadly compelling justifications for TBL could well become evaluation criteria for socially critical and environmentally critical management in education. First, TBL proposes a methodology for establishing social and natural deficits as a basis for national and global fiscal policies that could eventually help achieve global monetary reform. Second, global reform is self-evidently needed urgently to avoid a catastrophic breakdown of nature's services. Third, such reform is becoming technically possible, given the emergent consensus regarding (a) full-cost accounting of natural capital and social capital, (b) formal metrics for ecological and social loss or risk and (c) an evidence-related understanding of how communities rely on contributions of volunteer and professional capital in addition to financial capital. Fourth, parallel studies of nature's services are also providing evidence-based metrics of the *value of earth* and *value of life*. For example, the Kyoto Protocols and Euro Currency Integration processes appear to have provided first generation steps, despite recent setbacks, toward the standardization of units of accounting and global ecosystem reporting, with international liabilities and benchmarking (Milne, Tregidga, & Walton, 2007).

Despite broad international agreement on the value of fair social conditions and the sustainability of the environment, there are five main criticisms of TBL (Bendell & Kearins, 2005). The first is that TBL embodies naïve functionalism; it blurs the efficiencies and distributable surpluses that have been gained through deliberate divisions of labor, concentrations of expertise and resources, and the specializations of enterprises. It could force plural accountabilities on organizations outside of their areas of expertise at cost to efficiency. The second criticism is that TBL has undervalued the role of Adam Smith's invisible hand and the need to keep faith in the creativity of free individuals in private enterprises in a mixed economy. The third criticism is that TBL is politically naïve in that it underplays the role of nationalism and nation states, where the plural interests of citizens are arbitrated as policy settlements with the active political engagement and support of many sectors. The fourth criticism is that TBL is globally naïve; simultaneous global policy agreement and implementation is unlikely to overcome political inertia centered on nationalism and could render agreements unenforceable. The fifth criticism is that TBL is currently still too complex to support business, government and global decision making, especially if it is to be implemented through reforms to a global economic system that will continue to be monetary-based.

With these criticisms, or more accurately, current limitations of TBL in mind, it is recommended that socially critical and environmentally critical management focus on (a) correcting social and natural deficits, for example through national and global fiscal policies that might contribute to global monetary reform, (b) urgently accelerating environmental interventions, initially to correct global warming and (c) standardizing global units for accounting and reporting international liabilities in ecosystems. Finally, as TBL evolves internationally, educational administrators might anticipate their educational accountabilities broadening to include social, economic and environmental criteria.

We can now turn to politically critical leadership. For leaders to be critically aware of how they employ power, and justify current political arrangements, it requires a working knowledge of the major theories of power, forensic skills of analysis when there are crises of legitimacy in governance or leadership and a disposition to question the norms and assumptions of operating political systems that enable policy making and dispense privileges. Much of the knowledge of politics in education is, however, cast in simplistic dualisms. For example, capitalism is an economic theory or system based on the private ownership of the means of production, distribution and exchange. This theory or system is characterized by the freedom of those with financial capital to operate or manage their property for profit in competitive conditions. In direct contrast, socialism is an economic theory or system in which the means of production, distribution and exchange are owned by the community, usually through the state. This theory or system is characterized by production for reasonable use rather than for profit, by equality of individual wealth, by the absence of competitive economic activity, and, theoretically, by government determination of investment, prices and production levels.

Political theories in education tend to depict capitalism and socialism in dualistic terms, either as potentially productive and liberating or as destructive and oppressing.

This dualistic approach to analysis has been extended to the weighing of benefits: business or society, owners or employees, property rights or human rights. Such dualisms, however, are increasingly seen as too crude to sustain helpful analysis.

One obvious reason is that most countries have mixed economies comprising privately, publicly, jointly-owned and voluntary or association-owned enterprises. Apart from the shareholders in an enterprise, different stakeholders can have diverse interests and objectives, and their cooperation in an organization can also be provisional or temporary. Whose interests and objectives are met and whose not in most organizations also tends to be a matter of power internally as well as in the wider host society, and a matter of degree. In a capitalist society, most power resides with the owners of capital and their representatives, the managers. In a democratic society or public organization, most power resides with those with significant numbers and voice in policy making, and their representatives, the managers.

These ubiquitous managers, however, confront four persistent dilemmas in complex democracies or organizations with mixed economies. One is how meaningful democracy is in situations where most economic resources and powers are concentrated in a relatively small number of firms, households, or individuals (Bowles & Gintis, 1985). Another is how meaningful ownership is in situations where the views of many stakeholders have to be taken into account (Lindbloom, 1977). A third dilemma is the extent to which government should intervene to ensure that the plurality of interests is represented in policy decisions (Barrow, 1993). A fourth is the extent to which business, social, environmental and global interests should influence governments in democratic countries or organizations (Miliband, 1969).

The result in most countries is a symbiotic relationship between government and business. The state is dependent on economic activity for tax revenue to fund its programs and payroll. Government and business share a political reality where reelection chances correlate with the economic climate that provides for growth in income and employment while controlling inflation. The support and goodwill of the business sector is crucial to maintaining this climate.

Alongside this, because key personnel in government and business typically interchange over time, and the business sector retains control over far more resources than any other sector, there is a convergence of organizational structures and rationalities between major societal institutions and corporations. This convergence is also mediated by the plurality of interests in the business sector due to differences in sector, size and position in domestic and export markets, with different positions taken on market liberalization, antitrust enforcement, currency valuation and government subsidies.

On the other hand, businesses tend to have similar views on the basic institutions of the state, specifically as regards private property, wage labor and managerial prerogative. And once party political ideologies, electoral mandates and ministerial responsibility have been synthesized, usually as portfolio policies, priorities and programs, the managers of public institutions and PPPs are delegated authority and responsibility and held accountable for implementation. In general, whatever the sector, managers exercise power that is legitimized through forms of governance. They manage people at work using forms of organization, including forms of coercion, all of which can reasonably be expected to be justified using politically critical analysis and evaluation.

As introduced in Chapter 1, a range of political ideologies have been developed over time to interpret the econopolitical context of management and to propose the focus of appraisal, although they can suffer from crude use and obsolescence. To reiterate briefly, Marx proposed historical materialism (Tucker, 1978)—that is, history defined as struggles between classes, the state as an instrument of oppression by one class over another, with changes in the economic infrastructure causing changes in the institutional and ideological superstructure. He therefore expected managers to serve the leaders of a revolution that would replace the capitalist state with a dictatorship of the proletariat—that is, the working class without property, followed by a withering of the state. Neither happened, although the prior structural conditions continued and morphed into contemporary structures, largely due to the widespread growth of middle classes with property and political rights, and the impact of new technologies and their embedded ideologies.

Mosca proposed elitism (Finocchiaro, 1999) on the grounds that the nature of human social life makes true democracy impossible to attain and, indeed, may enable anarchy. Hence, he argued, political decisions are inevitably in the hands of the elite, and organized minorities rule their host societies. He called for the development of democratic political systems that use the principle of *juridical defense* to prevent any person, class, force, or institution from dominating others.

> Juridical defense is the high discipline of the moral sense, brought about through social mechanisms, which prevent the uncontrolled aspirations of individuals from governing society. It is the condition of a government characterized by established and regular rules. (Grazia, 2012)

Hence the need for educative leadership that takes juridical responsibility for the quality of structuration in educational governance and decision making.

Antithetical to the project of educative leadership, Bakunin argued openly for collective anarchy (Miller, 1984), taking the view that the individual is sovereign, authority is an unjustified repression of will and that attempts to resolve individual and common interests through institutions or the threat of force are futile. He called for coordinated resistance against coercion and for managers to facilitate the development of nongovernmental collectivism based on voluntary cooperation without private property or religion, and with rewards according to contribution. Hence, I argue the need for morally defensible forms of coercion in education and for neopragmatic educative leaders who can nurture policy discourse, narratives of professional practice and webs of belief built on the common ground about what is the interests of learners.

All such grand narratives were rejected by postmodernists (e.g., Lyotard, 1979) who saw an open multiplicity of incommensurable language games in society and therefore declared that the values of the Enlightenment (critique, tolerance and rational consensus) were redundant. The declaration was premature. Postmodern conditions certainly require educative leaders to assist with the development of many first order and neopragmatic narratives as the touchstone of democratic freedom. Libertarians will disagree and argue, instead, that since individual will and initiative have created the economy and social life, it is important to protect the rights of individuals and to develop processes incrementally that demonstrate the appropriateness of piecemeal actions taken independently of conceptions of final outcomes (Nozick, 1974). Managers, by these lights, should seek to develop a minimal state in support of self-determining individuals in free-market capitalism. However, in a complex society and mixed economy, educative leaders of systems and institutions aware of the limits of the context are needed to revisit and regenerate policy settlements and to sustain the conditions for effective problem solving and the growth of knowledge.

In sharp contrast with both postmodernism and libertarianism, the ideology of communitarianism values social life, identity and relationships; insists that the collective provides rights and obligations to individuals; and advances the integrity and value of traditional practices, such as the social construction of meaning (MacIntyre, 1984). Managers, it follows, are to refine institutions and practices to promote and serve the community and the public good and to champion cooperative practices and values such as reciprocity, trust and solidarity.

Communicative rationalism took this further by focusing on control and understanding emancipation in organization and society with a view to boosting communicative rationality, as opposed to instrumental rationality (Habermas, 1984–1987, 1992). Appropriate analysis, Habermas argued, was to reveal the disruptive effects of market and bureaucratic systems, the intersubjective notions of practical reason and the discursive procedures used to justify universal norms. By these lights, managers should be held accountable for the development of an open, participative and deliberative democracy for a complex modern world. To this end, they should use the values of the Enlightenment, legitimate law and discourse ethics, and provide a defense and critique of institutions using public practical reason.

I am sympathetic to common good justifications, warmly disposed to communitarianism at the group and institutional level, and appreciate the penetrating tools of analysis provided by Harbermas's communicative rationalism. Similarly, I appreciate the general thrust of John Rawls's egalitarian liberalism (1999, 2005) while doubting its plausibility in practice because it requires governors and leaders of organizations to develop a new hypothetical social contract derived from an original position of not knowing socially significant facts or what a good life is.

Clearly, such a deliberate veil of ignorance could help undermine the dynamic conservatism of nationalism and factionalism with its equal concern for everyone and distributive justice, but is such a suspension of political ideology and the heroic suppression of interests really wise, feasible and likely? I doubt it.

Hence I suggest instead that educational leaders, administrators and policy advisors develop other means of delivering Rawls's principled aim of justice as fairness—that is, equal liberty and equal opportunity, with inequalities only justified if they benefit the worst off.

Given the unique nature of knowledge organizations, and the potential for global knowledge societies, special consideration needs to be given to Dewey's democratic and educative pragmatism (Campbell, 1995). He demonstrated the potency of scientific experimentalism in education, rejected dualisms in favor of mediating ideas and combined error correction and optimistic progressivism. He, in effect, called for educative leaders to develop increasingly democratic communities and learning organizations committed to the growth of knowledge through inquiry-based learning.

In sum, a politically critical educative leader would be able to evaluate justifications for current political arrangements using political philosophy and to articulate a personal educational ideology or a specific blend of ideologies when proposing improvements. To be convincing, the person would use descriptive-explanatory and ethically normative methods to unpack, reveal and justify the nature and use of administrative power. Further, a personal political ideology would need to be demonstrably relevant to the context, principally by offering a sophisticated blend of principles, consequences and rationality on the means and ends of justifiably exercising power. Given the special nature of knowledge organizations, the blend I recommend would combine Rawls's concept of justice as fairness with Dewey's democratic and educative pragmatism, but advance it with neo- or linguistic pragmatism and set aside absolutism, epistemological foundationalism, or expect to comprehend the world with complete objectivity. Educative leaders are, therefore, to be understood as linguistic practitioners who learn by systematically elaborating their webs of belief, including their knowledge of, and responsibility for, political infrastructure and process in education at all levels.

The next candidate is globally critical leadership. As noted above, educational administrators are increasingly likely to confront dilemmas due to the rapid globalization and integration of economies, enabled in large part by the pace of innovation in ICT, compared with the much more modest pace at which the globalization of governance is proceeding. Although the immediate task of the World Commission for Culture and Development (WCCD; UNESCO, 1996) was to articulate globally responsible ethics, their recommendations can be used to project potential responsibilities for managers in nine areas. These areas offer exciting possibilities for fresh research, theory and practice in educational administration.

One area for initiative concerns the potential sources of global ethics for educational leaders. Cultural traditions internationally can provide useful ideas, such as the ubiquitous golden rule. International crises can highlight the vulnerability of people and their need for security and support. An emergent global civic culture is developing as an appropriate basis for all forms of collective enterprise, public, private, or mixed. It is a suite of normative ideals, purposes and moral legitimacy provided by the United Nations (Kell, 2005) that is especially conscious of the earth's interdependent ecosystems and the interlinked principles of human rights, democratic legitimacy, public accountability and legal judgments being based on evidence. Together they provide potential sources of global ethics appropriate for educational leaders.

A second area is the potential nature of global leadership ethics. The WCCD proposed five elements for a new global ethic for management practice that might be refined for use in education. Their driving concern was to integrate the protection of human rights with collective and personal responsibilities. This meant protecting individual physical and emotional integrity and providing the minimal social and economic conditions for a decent work life, fair treatment and equal access to the mechanisms for remedying injustices. Equally important was combining these rights with duties—that is, combining options with bonds, choices with allegiances and liberties with ligatures. The aim of the WCCD was to ensure that liberty within an enterprise is not libertine, authority is not authoritarian and personal choices are real and bonds of engagement are reasonable.

Global leadership ethics could be added to the processes of policy making and implementation in education, specifically in each of the phases Hodgkinson identified: (a) philosophical leadership regarding concepts and values used to analyze and justify organization, (b) strategic leadership regarding the systematic identification and appraisal of options, such as new international PPPs, (c) cultural innovations that can reconcile diverse perceptions of human and collective rights, (d) creative political and legal solutions that can transform existing traditions and institutions, (e) imaginative management that implements policies and improvement plans in sensitive ways and (f) educative evaluation that sustains the growth of knowledge about a just, global civil society in which peoples and their enterprises flourish.

A third area proposed for exploration is how educative leaders might advance the role of democracy as an element of an integrated civic and enterprise culture in organizations (Dryzek, 1999). One challenge is to provide organizational participants, especially adolescents and teachers, with significant degrees of political discretion and empowerment as stakeholders, so that they have a voice in determining the purposes and organization of the collective, and the policies it will adhere to. Democratic managers will need to sustain participative governance that engages the citizenry of each organization, see freedom of expression as both a means to creative engagement in a common enterprise and as an end in itself, recognize grievances early and offer conciliatory problem solving processes and bring moderation to organizational politics.

A fourth area suggested by the WCCD for exploration is how leaders of global democratic enterprises might help sustain humane safeguards for political, ethnic and other minorities against the tyranny of the majority, in addition to free, fair and regular elections of representatives and freedom of information, dissent and association (Altvater, 1999). Educational leaders can help other leaders to avoid reacting to micropolitical movements seeking greater self-determination with discrimination and repression and, instead, offer new political solutions. These solutions might give priority to three conditions: (a) minorities should have the same basic rights, freedoms and safeguards granted to all, (b) the human rights of all members of majorities and minorities must be guaranteed by the form of governance designed, and take precedence over any claims to cultural integrity advanced by communities and (c) tolerance, cultural conviviality, mutual understanding and respect should all be promoted, accepting diversity and encouraging interculturalism.

A fifth area for investigation is how leaders in global enterprises might establish a culture of peace for conflict resolution and fair negotiation, promoting justice in global ethics. Although the problems of justice and fairness are central to global civic and business ethics, there is no widely accepted or universal principle of justice available that can be imposed (Singer, 2002). The challenge for educative leaders is to ensure that all affected parties are represented and have a voice in what principles or rules should decide the matter. Their role here is to neutralize threats to peace, security and human improvement and enterprise development; expose the interests and political ideologies behind militancy; and cultivate the skills of conciliation, cooperation and tolerance.

A related area is how educative leaders might improve equity within and between generations (Attfield, 1999). An obvious challenge is how to deliver universal human rights irrespective of class, gender, race, community, organization, or generation. Less obvious is how to accept responsibility for humanity's common natural, genetic and cultural heritage, its relationship to the earth and its unborn generations. Leaders who would be educative may need to invent new forms of guardianship that strengthen and integrate intergenerational equity in civic, business and joint enterprises.

The potential relationship between public, private and voluntary global ethics is problematic, as explained by the WCCD. Because nation states provide the legal and political framework for advancing global ethics, the managers of their judicial and executive organs, such as education systems, have opportunities to review the current legal structures of international society—international and intergovernmental organizations—including transnational blocks that are less than global and regional unions, and yet outstrip their own jurisdictions. Such initiatives have tended to be patchy and disconnected (Kettl, 1997). Some have achieved a great deal by advancing criteria of moral conduct during reviews of policies in public and private organizations, organizational structures and agencies. Significant successes have followed fresh governance that has challenged power politics with moral principles and enabled the freer international movements of goods, services, capital, people and ideas. This dynamic coheres with the purpose of this book: to enable educative leaders to challenge power politics in education with moral arguments to facilitate the freer movement of ideas about professional practice.

An eighth emergent area for research is how managers of transnational corporations, international organizations, global civil organizations and blended variants that have educational responsibilities, might advance ethically critical practice that is commensurate with their influence over consumer choices and their resource power, power that frequently exceeds that of many nation states. It has been shown by Haufler (2001) how private sector managers can deliver on global ethics through self-regulation, and it appears, help corporations with global reach prepare for a coming era of global incorporation, taxation, and accountability. Educational leaders of larger institutions and public systems are well-positioned to help intergovernmental agencies limit the abuse of their power, steer its use to the public good, and through more sophisticated forms of stakeholder control, accountability and transparency, achieve far wider participation by voluntary societies, religious congregations, trades unions, private firms, professional organizations and women's and youth associations. The aim would be help develop the moral conscience of an integrated global knowledge society.

A ninth area is how educative managers of global NGOs, voluntary societies, grassroots organizations, churches and other religious associations, action groups, professional societies, interest groups and similar institutions might advance global ethics and achieve their aims through collaboration with government agencies and corporate enterprises. There are many examples emerging (Eade & O'Bryne, 2005). Social entrepreneurship is one. Officials, managers, teachers and professors, consumers and citizens without a great deal of positional political power can influence their government and corporate leaders. How? Professional societies can articulate moral principles for self-regulation, social control and international relations. Global groups can affirm trust, loyalty, solidarity, altruism and love as the basis of association. International aid can help discharge the obligations of the rich to help the poor through both the alleviation of suffering and capacity building. Corporations, as global collectives of citizens, can respond more quickly to crises than politicians who tend to be constrained by the interests of polities.

In sum, this section indicates that globally critical managers can and ought to confront ethical dilemmas created by the growing mismatch between the globalization and integration of economies, enabled by information communication technology and the globalization of governance, retarded in large part by various forms of politics of nationalism and self-interest. On the other hand, there are many potential sources of global ethics available—with growing clarity over the potential nature of global leadership ethics and how democracy might help integrate global civic and enterprise cultures in knowledge organizations. There is growing certainty how leaders of global enterprises might provide safeguards for minorities, sustain a culture of peace and improve equity within and between generations. These global ethics should be developed and supported by democratic and educative neopragmatism, principally because of its utility in the leadership of public organizations, transnational corporations, international organizations, civil organizations and blended variants such as partnerships and networks.

This book has stressed the role that political philosophy can play in refining educational administration and educative leadership. This final chapter has aimed at articulating the relativity of politically critical leadership by stepping outside of education and proposing a range of ways of critically managing knowledge organizations. The book and this chapter can now be summarized.

Leaders of knowledge organizations are invited to take up their right and responsibility to improve their capacity to reflect on and critically evaluate the nature of their powerful practices. Knowledge organizations are increasingly a blend of public, private, charitable and mixed enterprises that rely on the growth of knowledge and capacity building in problem solving. Scholarship is the basis for quality assurance in the production of goods and services in knowledge organizations, and thereby essential to many types of returns on investment expected and the sustainability of such enterprises. Leaders have been alerted to concepts, tools of analysis and criteria for evaluation that could assist them to become more ethically critical, socially critical, environmentally critical, politically critical and globally critical.

The invitation comes with advice on process. Knowledge organizations such as schools and education systems will need ethically critical managers that understand the relativity of principles, consequentialism, consensus and preference when auditing values and arbitrating optional actions. Educative leaders are advised to focus on the language of policy making and implementation to identify political ideologies in education using the constructs developed through pragmatism, communitarianism, communicative rationalism and egalitarian liberalism. They are advised to mediate their understandings of the meanings in the language of leaders using neopragmatism. Moral justifications are then to be tested as knowledge claims using coherence checks with all other warranted claims held provisionally in a web of belief. Finally, educational leaders are urged to promote continuing education as a strategic element of organizational learning in order to blend science, aesthetics, cultural development and political capacity building.

Socially critical and environmentally critical leaders of knowledge organizations are encouraged to help correct social and natural deficits. Politically critical leaders of knowledge organizations are asked to map and evaluate justifications in the language of leaders for current political arrangements and to progressively refine their personal political ideology and social contracts that value justice as fairness and democratic and educative neopragmatism.

Finally, globally critical leaders of knowledge organizations are urged to confront ethical dilemmas generated by the different pace at which economics and governance are globalizing, largely due to the early advantages accruing to neoliberal entrepreneurs, uneven exploitation of information communication technology and aberrant forms of nationalism. A provisional global ethics of leadership was recommended to managers of public organizations, transnational corporations, international organizations and civic organizations, to help them integrate global civic and enterprise cultures in knowledge organizations, provide safeguards for minorities, create a culture of peace and improve intergenerational equity. They are advised to anticipate the impact of environmentalism and a TBL approach to accountability in increasingly integrated ecosystems.

To conclude, this chapter and book started with an invitation to leaders in knowledge organizations and management educators to reflect critically on the nature of their services using the discipline of political philosophy. This chapter elaborated the invitation by clarifying a number of ways of being critically reflective. It justified the invitation primarily using neopragmatism primarily because it can serve both as a meta-ideology, to appreciate the strengths of particular blends of ideologies, while also facilitating their integration in context and using the common ground to mediate extremism. It ends with the thought that, if the invitation remains unaccepted, then it means living with the implications of Socrates's career-threatening conclusion—that unexamined leadership may not be worth practicing and perhaps should not be allowed.

Note

1 This chapter is a modified version of an article published earlier (Macpherson, 2008a).

References

Abbot, M. G. (1965). Intervening variables in organizational behavior. *Educational Administration Quarterly, 1*(1), 1–14.

Altbach, G. P. (2005). Patterns in higher education development. In P. G. Altbach, R. O. Berdahl, & P. J. Gumport (Eds.), *American higher education in the twenty-first century: Social, political, and economic challenges* (2nd ed.). Baltimore, MD: The Johns Hopkins University Press.

Altvater, E. (1999). Restructuring the space of democracy: The effects of capitalist globalization and the ecological crisis in the form and substance of democracy. In N. Low (Ed.), *Global ethics and environment* (pp. 283–309). London, England: Routledge.

Anderson, G. L. (2004). William Foster's legacy: Learning from the past and reconstructing the future. *Educational Administration Quarterly, 40*(2), 240–258.

Angus, L. (1994). Educational organization: Technical/managerial and participative/professional perspectives. *Discourse: Studies in the cultural politics of education, 14*(2), 30–44.

Angus, L. (2008). The politics of community renewal and educational reform: School improvement in area of social disadvantage. In E. A. Samier & A. G. Stanley (Eds.), *Political approaches to educational administration and leadership* (pp. 204–220). New York, NY: Routledge.

Apple, M. (2012). *Education and power* (3rd ed.). Abingdon, Oxon: Routledge.

Aristotle. (1912). *Politics* (W. Ellis, Trans.). London, England: Everyman.

Armstrong, K. (2006). *The great transformation: The world in the time of Buddha, Socrates, Confucius and Jeremiah*. London, England: Atlantic.

Arnold, R. (1985, August). Personal communication, interview, Victoria University of Wellington.

Attfield, R. (1999). *The ethics of the global environment*. Edinburgh, Scotland: Edinburgh University Press.

Baldridge, J. V. (1989). Building a political model. In T. Bush (Ed.), *Managing education: Theory and practice* (pp. 57–65). Milton Keynes, England: Open University Press.

Ball, S. (2012). *Global education inc.: New policy networks and the neo-liberal imaginary*. Abingdon, England: Routledge.

Ball, S., & Junemann, C. (2012). *Networks, new governance and education*. Bristol, England: Policy Press, University of Bristol.

Balls, E. (2008, June). Ed Balls's speech to the National College for School Leadership Annual Conference. Retrieved from http://www.dcsf.gov.uk/speeches/search_detail.cfm?ID=802

Baron, G. (1980). Research in educational administration in Britain. In T. Bush, R. Glatter, & J. Goodey (Eds.), *Approaches to school management* (pp. 3–25). London, England: Harper and Row.

Barrington, J. (1981). The politics of school government. In M. Clark (Ed.), *The politics of education in New Zealand* (pp. 43–65). Wellington, New Zealand: New Zealand Council for Educational Research.

Barrow, C. W. (1993). *Critical theories of the state*. Madison, Wisconsin: University of Wisconsin Press.

Bates, R. J. (1980). Educational administration, the sociology of science, and the management of knowledge. *Educational Administration Quarterly, 16*(2), 1–20.

Bates, R. J. (1983). *Educational administration and the management of knowledge*. Geelong, Australia: Deakin University Press.

Bates, R. J. (2006). Educational administration and social justice. *Education, citizenship and social justice, 1*(2), 141–156.

Bates, R. J. (2008). The politics of civil society and the possibility of change: A speculation on leadership in education. In E. A. Samier & A. G. Stanley (Eds.), *Political approaches to educational administration and leadership* (pp. 173–188). New York, NY: Routledge.

Bathurst, R. (2007). *A tiger by the tail: The artistry of crisis management*. Research Working Papers Series, 1: Massey University, Department of Management and International Business.

Beck, C. (1999). Values, leadership and school renewal. In P. T. Begley & P. E. Leonard (Eds.), *The values of educational administration* (pp. 223–231). London, England: Falmer Press.

Beck, L. G. (1999). Metaphors of educational community: An analysis of the images that reflect and influence scholarship and practice. *Educational Administration Quarterly, 35*(1), 13–45.

Beck, M. (2008a). The context and history of the education sector in Timor-Leste. In J. Earnest, M. Beck, & L. Connell (Eds.), *Rebuilding education and health in a post-conflict transitional nation: Case studies from Timor-Leste* (pp. 3–8). Rotterdam/Taipei, The Netherlands: Sense.

Beck, M. (2008b). First of its kind: A pre-service graduate programme for primary school teachers. In J. Earnest, M. Beck, & L. Connell (Eds.), *Rebuilding education and health in a post-conflict transitional nation: Case studies from Timor-Leste* (pp. 39–54). Rotterdam/Taipei, The Netherlands: Sense.

Beeby, C. E. (1986). Introduction. In W. L. Renwick (Ed.), *Moving targets. Six essays on educational policy* (pp. xi–xlv). Wellington, New Zealand: New Zealand Council for Educational Research.

Beeby, C. E. (1992). *The biography of an idea. Beeby on education*. Wellington, New Zealand: New Zealand Council for Educational Research.

Begley, P. T. (1999a). Academic and practitioner perspectives on values. In P. T. Begley & P. E. Leonard (Eds.), *The values of educational administration* (pp. 51–69). London, England: Falmer Press.

Begley, P. T. (1999b). Introduction. In P. T. Begley & P. E. Leonard (Eds.), *The values of educational administration* (pp. 1–3). London, England: Falmer Press.

Begley, P. T., & Leonard, P. E. (Eds.). (1999) *The values of educational administration*. London, England: Falmer Press.

Belich, J. (1996). *Making peoples: A history of the New Zealanders from polynesian settlement to the end of the nineteenth century*. Auckland, New Zealand: Allen Lane, Penguin.

Belich, J. (2001). *Paradise reforged: A history of the New Zealanders from the 1880s to the year 2000*. Auckland, New Zealand: Allen Lane, Penguin.

Bendell, J., & Kearins, K. (2005). The political bottom line: The emerging dimension to corporate responsibility for sustainable development. *Business Strategy and the Environment, 14*(6), 372–383.

Bentham, J. (2002). *Rights, representation, and reform: Nonsense upon stilts and other writings on the French Revolution*. Oxford, England: Oxford University Press.

Berle, A. A., & Means, G. C. (1932). *The modern corporation and private property.* New York, NY: Macmillan.

Bird, C. (2006). *An introduction to political philosophy.* Cambridge, England: Cambridge University Press.

Bishop, R., Berryman, M., Cavanagh, T., & Teddy, L. (2007). *Te kotahitanga phase 3 whanaungatanga: Establishing a culturally responsive pedagogy of relations in mainstream secondary classrooms.* Report to the Ministry of Education. Hamilton, New Zealand: University of Waikato, School of Education.

Blackmore, J. (1992). *Making educational history: A feminist perspective.* Geelong, Australia: Deakin University.

Blackmore, J. (2006). Social justice and the study and practice of leadership in education: A feminist history. *Journal of Educational Administration and History, 38*(2), 185–200.

Bossetti, L., & Brown, D. J. (1999). The future of public education. In P. T. Begley & P. E. Leonard (Eds.), *The values of educational administration* (pp. 232–245). London, England: Falmer Press.

Bottery, M. (2008). Supranational organisations and their impact on nation state education: The case of the International Monetary Fund. In E. A. Samier & A. G. Stanley (Eds.), *Political approaches to educational administration and leadership* (pp. 269–284). New York, NY: Routledge.

Bowles, S., & Gintis, H. (1985). *Democracy and capitalism.* New York, NY: Basic Books.

Boyd, W. L. (1982). The political economy of public schooling. *Educational Administration Quarterly, 18*(3), 111–130.

Boyd, W. L. (1992). The power of paradigms: Reconceptualizing educational policy and management. *Educational Administration Quarterly, 28*(4), 504–528.

Boyer, E. L. (1990). *Scholarship reconsidered: Priorities of the professoriate.* San Francisco, CA: Jossey-Bass.

Bray, D., & Hill, C. (1973). *Polynesian and Pakeha in New Zealand education: Volume 1, the sharing of cultures.* Palmerston North, New Zealand: Bennett.

Brisbane Times. (2007, 12 April). Bishop has no issue with Coutts-Trotter. Retrieved from http://news.brisbanetimes.com.au/bishop-has-no-issue-with-couttstrotter/20071412-74q.html

Brooking, K. (2005). Boards of trustees' selection of primary school principals in New Zealand. *Delta, 57*(1 & 2), 117–140.

Brooking, K. (2008a). The future challenge of principal succession in New Zealand primary schools: Implications of quality and gender. *International Studies in Educational Administration, 36*(1), 41–55.

Brooking, K. (2008b). Principal appointments data report. Retrieved from http://www.nzcer.org.nz/default.php?cPath=122

Brooking, K. (2008c). *Worrying trends in principal appointments survey.* Media release. Wellington, New Zealand: New Zealand Council for Educational Research.

Brown, A. (1986). *Modern political philosophy: Theories of a just society.* London, England: Penguin.

Bull, B. L., & McCarthy, M. M. (1995). Reflections on the knowledge base in law and ethics for educational leaders. *Educational Administration Quarterly, 31*(4), 613–631.

Burnett, J. (1936). *Aristotle on education. Extracts translated and edited from Ethics and Politics.* Cambridge, England: Cambridge University Press.

Bush, T. (1986). *Theories of educational management.* London, England: Harper and Row.

Bush, T., & Crawford, M. (2012a). Mapping the field over 40 years: A historical review. *Educational Management, Administration and Leadership, 40*(5), 537–543.

Bush, T., & Crawford, M. (Eds.). (2012b). *Special 40th anniversary issue: Educational management administration and leadership*. London, England: BELMAS, Sage.

Button, H. W. (1966). Doctrines of administration: A brief history. *Educational Administration Quarterly, 2*(3), 216–224.

Caldwell, B. J., & Spinks, J. (1988). *The self-managing school*. London, England: Falmer Press.

Callahan, R. E. (1962). *Education and the cult of efficiency*. Chicago, IL: University of Chicago Press.

Calvert, B. (1981). Parent power and pupil power. In M. Clark (Ed.), *The politics of education in New Zealand* (pp. 89–102). Wellington, New Zealand: New Zealand Council for Educational Research.

Campbell, J. (1995). *Understanding John Dewey*. Chicago, IL: Open Court.

Capper, C. A. (1994). "We're not housed in an institution, we're housed in the community": Possibilities and consequences of neighborhood-based interagency collaboration. *Educational Administration Quarterly, 30*(3), 257–277.

Capper, C. A. (1998). Critically oriented and postmodern perspectives: Sorting out the differences and applications for practice. *Educational Administration Quarterly, 34*(8), 354–379.

Casey, C. (1995). *Work, self and society after industrialism*. London, England: Routledge.

Chin, R., & Benne, K. D. (1984). General strategies for effecting changes in human systems. In W. G. Bennis (Ed.), *The planning of change* (4th ed.). New York, NY: Holt, Rinehart and Winston.

Clark, B. R. (1983). *The higher education system: Academic organization in cross-national perspective*. Berkeley and Los Angeles: University of California Press.

Codd, J., Harker, R., & Nash, R. (Eds.). (1985). *Political issues in New Zealand education*. Palmerston North, New Zealand: Dunmore Press.

Coleman, J. S. (1990). *Foundations of social theory*. Cambridge, MA: Belnap Press, Harvard University Press.

Coleman, M. (2012). Leadership and diversity. *Educational Management Administration and Leadership, 40*(5), 592–609.

Collin, R., & Apple, M. (2010). New literacies and new rebellions in the global age. In M. Apple (Ed.), *Gobal crises, social justice, and education* (pp. 25–60). Abingdon, England: Routledge.

Collins, G. (2006, April). *The career pathways of teaching principals*. Paper presented at the New Zealand Educational Administration and Leadership Society Conference, Nelson, New Zealand.

Columbia University. (2005, January). *First global colloquium of university presidents*. Chaired by the UN Secretary-General, Kofi Annan, New York, NY: Columbia University.

Commission of Inquiry. (2007, February). Commission of inquiry appointed. *Commission of Inquiry into Allegations Relating to the Hong Kong Institute of Education*. Retrieved from http://www.info.gov.hk/gia/general/200702/15/P200702150197.htm

Commission of Inquiry into Allegations relating to the Hong Kong Institute of Education. (2007). Press Releases. Retrieved from http://www.commissionofinquiry.gov.hk/eng/preleases/preleases.htm

Connell, L. (2008). Teaching the arts to pre-service primary teachers in Timor-Leste. In J. Earnest, M. Beck, & L. Connell (Eds.), *Rebuilding education and health in a post-conflict transitional nation: Case studies from Timor-Leste* (pp. 55–68). Rotterdam/Taipei, The Netherlands: Sense.

Conway, N., & Briner, R. B. (2005). *Understanding psychological contracts at work: A critical evaluation of theory and research*. Oxford, England: Oxford University Press.

Cope, J. (2003). Entrepreneurial learning and critical reflection: Discontinuous events as triggers for 'higher-level' learning. *Management Learning, 34*(4), 429–450.

Corrigan, D. (2000). The changing role of schools and higher education institutions with respect to community-based interagency collaboration and interprofessional partnerships. *Peabody Journal of Education, 75*(3), 176–195.

Council of Chief State School Officers. (2003, February). Interstate school leaders licensure consortium (ISLLC). Retrieved from http://www.umsl.edu/~mpea/Pages/AboutISLLC/AboutISLLC.html

Counsel for the Commission. (2007, June). Closing Submission by B. Yu S. C. & Y. Cheng. *Commission of Inquiry into Allegations Relating to the Hong Kong Institute of Education*. Retrieved from http://www.commissionofinquiry.gov.hk/pdf/submissions%20of%20counsel%20for%20the%20Commission.pdf

Cowie, M., & Crawford, M. (2009). Headteacher preparation programmes in England and Scotland: Do they make a difference for the first year head? *Educational Management, Administration and Leadership, 29*(1), 5–21.

Crawford, M. (2012). Solo and distributed leadership: Definitions and dilemmas. *Educational Management, Administration and Leadership, 40*(5), 610–620.

Crick, B. (1982). *In defence of politics* (2nd ed.). Middlesex, England: Penguin.

Cumming, I., & Cumming, A. (1978). *History of state education in New Zealand 1840–1975*. Melbourne, Australia: Pitman.

Cuttance, P., Harman, G., Macpherson, R. J. S., Pritchard, A., & Smart, D. (1998). The politics of accountability in Australian education. *Educational Policy, 12*(1–2), 138–161.

Daniel, L. (2006). *National school roll projections: July 2006 update*. Wellington, New Zealand: Ministry of Education, Central Forecasting and Modelling Unit. Retrieved from http://www.educationcounts.govt.nz/themes/national_school_roll_projections/national_school_roll_projections_2006

Davies, A. F. (1960). Problems of decentralisation of state government in Australia. In E. L. French (Ed.), *Melbourne studies in education, 1958–1959*. Melbourne, New Zealand: Melbourne University Press.

Dehler, G. E., Welsh, M. A., & Lewis, M. W. (2001). Critical pedagogy in the 'new paradigm.' *Management Learning, 32*(4), 493–511.

Department for Children Families and Schools. (2008). *Going the extra mile: How schools succeed in raising aspirations in deprived communities*. London, England: Department for Children Families and Schools.

Diket, R. M. (2008). The politics of education in museums. In E. A. Samier & A. G. Stanley (Eds.), *Political approaches to educational administration and leadership* (pp. 189–203). New York, NY: Routledge.

Douglas, R., & Callan, L. (1987). *Toward prosperity*. Auckland, New Zealand: Bateman.

Dror, Y. (1986). *Policymaking under adversity*. London, England: Transaction Books.

Dryzek, J. S. (1999). Global ecological democracy. In N. Low (Ed.), *Global ethics and environment* (pp. 264–282). London, England: Routledge.

Duignan, P. A. (2006). *Educational leadership: Key challenges and ethical tensions*. Cambridge, England: Cambridge University Press.

Duignan, P. A., & Macpherson, R. J. S. (1987). The educative leadership project. *Educational Management and Administration, 15*(1), 49–62.

Duignan, P. A., & Macpherson, R. J. S. (1993). Educative leadership: A practical theory. *Educational Administration Quarterly, 29*(1), 8–33.

Dunn, J. (2003). *East Timor: A rough passage to independence*. Sydney, Australia: Longville.

Dunstall, G. (1981). The social pattern. In W. Oliver & B. Williams (Eds.), *The Oxford History of New Zealand* (pp. 396–429). Oxford, England: Clarendon Press and Oxford University Press.

Eade, J., & O'Bryne, D. (Eds.). (2005). *Global ethics and civil society*. New York, NY: Polity.

Educational Administration Abstracts. (2001). Categories used to classify research findings in educational administration, *36*(4).

Elkington, J. (1994). Towards the sustainable corporation: Win-win-win business strategies for sustainable development. *California Management Review, 36*(2), 90–100.

Elkington, J. (1998). *Cannibals with forks: The triple bottom line of 21st century business*. Stony Creek, CT: New Society Publishers.

Emerson, J., & Bonini, S. (2004, February). The blended value map: Tracking the intersects and opportunities of economic, social and environmental value creation. Retrieved from http://www.blendedvalue.org/publications/index.html#glossary

English, F. W. (2007). Unintended consequences of a standardized knowledge base in advancing educational leadership preparation. *Educational Administration Quarterly, 42*(3), 461–473.

English, F. W. (2008). The new McCarthyism: The right wing's assault on American academic thought. In E. A. Samier & A. G. Stanley (Eds.), *Political approaches to educational administration and leadership* (pp. 252–268). New York, NY: Routledge.

Ermarth, E. D. (2000). *Postmodernism: The concise Routledge encyclopedia of philosophy* (pp. 699–700). London, England: Routledge.

Etzioni, A. (1993). *The spirit of community: The reinvention of American society*. New York, NY: Simon and Schuster.

Evers, C. W. (1985). Hodgkinson on ethics and the philosophy of administration. *Educational Administration Quarterly, 21*(4), 27–50.

Evers, C. W. (1999). Complexity, context and ethical leadership. In P. T. Begley & P. E. Leonard (Eds.), *The values of educational administration* (pp. 70–81). London, England: Falmer Press.

Evers, C. W. (Ed.). (1987). *Moral theory for educative leadership*. Melbourne, Australia: Victoria Ministry of Education.

Evers, C. W., & Lakomski, G. (1991). *Knowing educational administration: Contemporary methodological controversies in educational administration research*. Oxford, England: Pergamon Press.

Evers, C. W., & Lakomski, G. (1996). Three dogmas: A rejoinder. In C. W. Evers & G. Lakomski (Eds.), *Exploring educational administration: Coherentist applications and critical debates* (pp. 238–246). Kidlington, Oxford: Pergamon.

Ewington, J., & Macpherson, R. J. S. (1998). Parents' perceptions of school effectiveness: An investigation into the effectiveness of Tasmanian public schools. *Leading and Managing, 4*(1), 32–48.

Farr, M., & McDougall, B. (2007, 12 April). Drug lesson: Wife of new school boss tells: He's an inspiration. *The Daily Telegraph*, p. 1.

Fazzaro, C. J. (2008). Democratic ideals, ethics, Foucalt, and the hegemony of modern thought in American education: A critical enquiry. In E. A. Samier & A. G. Stanley (Eds.), *Political approaches to educational administration and leadership* (pp. 123–136). New York, NY: Routledge.

Fielding, M. (2006). Leadership, personalization and high performance schooling: Naming the new totalitarianism. *School Leadership and Management, 26*(4), 347–369.

Finer, S. E. (1970). *Comparative government*. London, England: Penguin.

Finocchiaro, M. A. (1999). Gaetano Mosca. In R. Audi (Ed.), *The Cambridge dictionary of philosophy* (2nd ed., p. 591). Cambridge, England: Cambridge University Press.

Flew, A. (1984). *A dictionary of philosophy* (2nd ed.). Basingstoke, England: Pan Books.

Foster, W. P. (1986a). *Paradigms and promises: New approaches to educational administration*. Amherst, NY: Prometheus Books.

Foster, W. P. (1986b). *The reconstruction of leadership*. Geelong, Australia: Deakin University.

Foster, W. P. (2004). The decline of the local: A challenge to educational leadership. *Educational Administration Quarterly, 40*(2), 176–191.

Foucault, M. (1980). *Power/knowledge*. New York, NY: Pantheon Books.

Fournier, V., & Grey, C. (2000). At the critical moment: Conditions and prospects for critical management studies. *Human Relations, 53*(1), 7–32.

Freeden, M. (2000). Ideology. In *The concise Routledge encyclopedia of philosophy* (pp. 381–382). London, England: Routledge.

Freeman, R. E. (1984). *Corporate strategy*. Boston, MA: Pitman.

Freeman, R. E., & Gilbert, D. R. (1988). *Corporate strategy and the search for ethics*. Englewood Cliffs, NJ: Prentice Hall.

French, J. R. P., & Raven, B. (1959). The bases of social power. In D. Cartwright (Ed.), *Studies in social power*. Ann Arbor, MI: University of Michigan Press.

Friedman, M. (1962). *Capitalism and freedom*. Chicago, IL: University of Chicago Press.

Friedman, M. (1970, September). The social responsibility of business to increase its profits. *New York Times Magazine*.

Frost, D., & Roberts, A. (2011). Student leadership, participation and democracy. *Leading & Managing, 17*(2), 66–84.

Furman-Brown, G. (1999). Editor's Foreword. *Educational Administration Quarterly, 35*(1), 6–12.

Gair, G. (1986, August). Personal communication, interview, Parliament House.

Galbraith, J. K. (1983). *The anatomy of power*. New York, NY: Houghton Mifflin Harcourt.

Gallie, W. B. (1956). Essentially contested concepts. *Proceedings of the Aristotelian Society, 56*, 167–220.

Galvin, A. (2006). *Teacher supply key statistics report: May teacher loss rates*. Wellington, New Zealand: Ministry of Education, Demographic and Statistical Analysis Unit, Data Management and Analysis Division. Retrieved from http://www.educationcounts.govt.nz/publications/series/teacher_loss_rates/teacher_loss_rates_2006

Gamage, D., & Ueyama, T. (2004). Professional development perspectives of principals in Australia and Japan. *Educational Forum, 69*(1), 65–78.

Gaskin, J. C. A. (2005). Marcus Tullius Cicero. In T. Honderich (Ed.), *The Oxford companion to philosophy* (Vol. 2, p. 142). Oxford, England: Oxford University Press.

Gensler, H. J. (1996). *Formal ethics*. London, England: Routledge.

Getzels, J. W., & Guba, E. G. (1957). Social behavior and the administrative process. *The School Review, 65*, 423–441.

Gibbons, P. J. (1981). The climate of opinion. In W. Oliver & B. Williams (Eds.), *The Oxford History of New Zealand* (pp. 302–330). Oxford, England: Clarendon Press and Oxford University Press.

Giddens, A. (1984). *The consitution of society: Outline of a theory of structuration*. Berkeley: University of California Press.

Giddens, A. (2010). *The Third Way and its critics*. Cambridge, England: Polity Press.

Glass, T. E., Mason, R., Eaton, W., Parker, J. C., & Carver, F. D. (Eds.). (2004). *The history of educational administration viewed through its texts*. Lanham, MD: Scarecrow Education, Rowman and Littlefield.

Glassick, C. E., Huber, M. T., & Maeroff, G. I. (1997). *Scholarship assessed: Evaluation of the professoriate*. San Francisco, CA: Jossey-Bass.

Glatter, R. (1980). Educational 'policy' and 'management': One field or two? In T. Bush, R. Glatter, J. Goodey, & C. Riches (Eds.), *Approaches to school management: A reader* (pp. 26–39). London, England: Harper and Row, Open University Press.

Glatter, R. (2012). Persistent preoccupations: The rise and rise of school autonomy and accountability. *Educational Management, Administration and Leadership, 40*(5), 559–575.

Gold, H. (Ed.). (1985). *New Zealand politics in perspective.* Auckland, New Zealand: Longman Paul.

Gooch, L. (2007, May). Law's words come back to haunt her on the stand. *South China Morning Post.*

Goodpaster, K. E. (1984). The concept of social responsibility. *Journal of Business Ethics, 2,* 1–22.

Government of New Zealand. (1988). *Tomorrow's schools: The reform of education administration in New Zealand.* White Paper, Wellington, New Zealand: Government Printer.

Grace, G. (1989). *Inaugural professorial address.* Wellington, New Zealand: Victoria University of Wellington.

Grace, G. (1995). *School leadership: Beyond education management. An essay in policy scholarship.* London, England: Falmer Press.

Graham, J. (1981). Settler Society. In W. Oliver & B. Williams (Eds.), *The Oxford History of New Zealand* (pp. 112–139). Oxford, England: Clarendon Press and Oxford University Press.

Grazia, A. D. (2012). Political organization. Chapter 2 Law and constitutionalism. Retrieved from http://www.grazian-archive.com/politics/PolOrganization/PO_C02.htm

Green, T. H. (1999). *Lectures on the principles of political obligation.* Kitchener, Ontario: Batoche Books. Retrieved from http://socserv2.mcmaster.ca/~econ/ugcm/3ll3/green/obligation.pdf

Greenfield, T. B. (1975). Theory about organizations: A new perspective and its implications for schools. In V. Houghton, R. McHugh, & C. Morgan (Eds.), *Management in education, Reader 1: The management of organizations and individuals* (pp. 59–84). London, England: Ward Lock Educational and Open University Press.

Greenfield, T. B., & Ribbins, P. (1993). *Greenfield on educational administration: Towards a humane science.* London, England: Routledge.

Greenlees, D., & Garran, R. (2002). *Deliverance: The inside story of East Timor's fight for freedom.* Crow's Nest, Australia: Allen and Unwin.

Grey, A. (2004). The quality journey: Is there a leader at the helm? *New Zealand Research in Early Childhood Education, 7,* 91–102.

Griffiths, D. E. (1977). The individual in organization: A theoretical perspective. *Educational Administration Quarterly, 13*(1), 1–18.

Grogan, M. (2004). Keeping a critical, postmodern eye on educational leadership in the United States: In appreciation of Bill Foster. *Educational Administration Quarterly, 40*(2), 222–239.

Gronn, P. (1982). Neo-Taylorism in educational administration? *Educational Administration Quarterly, 18*(4), 17–35.

Gronn, P. (1983). Talk as the work: The accomplishment of school administration. *Administrative Science Quarterly, 28*(1), 1–21.

Gronn, P. (1984). On studying administrators at work. *Educational Administration Quarterly, 20*(1), 115–129.

Gronn, P. (2003). *The new work of educational leaders.* London, England: Paul Chapman.

Gronn, P. (2008). Hayek, leadership and learning. In E. A. Samier & A. G. Stanley (Eds.), *Political approaches to educational administration and leadership* (pp. 73–88). New York, NY: Routledge.

Grossman, D. (2007, March). Witness statement from Prof David Grossman. *Commission of Inquiry on Allegations Relating to Hong Kong Institute of Education.* Retrieved from http://www.commissionofinquiry.gov.hk/pdf/Witness%20Statement%20of%20Professor%20Grossman.pdf

Gulick, L., & Urlick, L. (1937). *Papers in the science of administration.* New York, NY: Institute of Public Administration.

Gunter, H. (2012). *Leadership and the reform of education*. Bristol, England: Policy Press, University of Bristol.

Gunter, H., & Thompson, P. (2009). The makeover: The new logic in leadership development in England. *Educational Review, 6*(4), 469–484.

Gurr, D., Drysdale, L., & Goode, H. (2007, April). *Findings from the survey phase of the International Successful School Principalship Project: Principals demographics and principals' perceptions of success*. Paper presented at the American Educational Research Association Conference, Chicago, IL.

Gusmao, X. (2005). On the occasion of the international conference on traditional conflict resolution and traditional justice in Timor-Leste. *East Timor Law Journal, 3*.

Habermas, J. (1984–1987). *The theory of communicative action*. Cambridge, England: Polity.

Habermas, J. (1992). *Between facts and norms*. Cambridge, MA: MIT Press.

Hampsher-Monk, I. (2000). History of political history. In *The concise Routledge encyclopaedia of philosophy* (p. 691). London, England: Routledge.

Handgraaf, M. J. J., Van Dijk, E., Vermunt, R. C., Wilke, H. A. M., & De Dreu, C. K. W. (2008). Less power or powerless? Egocentric empathy gaps and the irony of having little versus no power in social decision making. *Journal of Personality and Social Psychology, 95*(5), 1137.

Handy, C. (1976). *Understanding organizations*. London, England: Penguin.

Hardt, M., & Negri, A. (2000). *Empire*. Cambridge, MA: Harvard University Press.

Harris, C. E. (2008). Bourdieu's distinctions of taste, talent and power: Bridging political fields and administrative practice. In E. A. Samier & A. G. Stanley (Eds.), *Political approaches to educational administration and leadership* (pp. 89–108). New York, NY: Routledge.

Hatcher, R. (2005). The distribution or leadership and power in schools. *British Journal of Sociology of Education, 26*(2), 253–267.

Haufler, V. (2001). *A public role for the private sector: Industry self-regulation in a global economy*. Washington, DC: Carnegie Endowment for International Peace.

Herriman, N. (2009). The case to intervene and stop East Timorese killing witches. Retrieved from http://easttimorlegal.blogspot.com/2009/05/case-to-intervene-and-stop-east.html

Hobbes, T. (1914). *Leviathan*. London, England: Everyman.

Hodgkinson, C. (1978). *Towards a philosophy of administration*. Oxford, England: Basil Blackwell.

Hodgkinson, C. (1981). A new taxonomy of administrative process. *Journal of Educational Administration, 19*, 141–152.

Hodgkinson, C. (1983). *The philosophy of leadership*. Oxford, England: Basil Blackwell.

Hodgkinson, C. (1986). Beyond pragmatism and positivism. *Educational Administration Quarterly, 22*(2), 5–21.

Hodgkinson, C. (1991). *Educational leadership: The moral art*. Albany, NY: SUNY Press.

Hodgkinson, C. (1996). *Administrative philosophy: Values and motivations in administrative life*. Kidlington, England: Elsevier Science.

Hodgkinson, C. (1999). The triumph of the will: An exploration of certain fundamental problematics in administrative philosophy. In P. T. Begley & P. E. Leonard (Eds.), *The values of educational administration* (pp. 6–21). London, England: Falmer Press.

Hoffman, L. P., & Burrello, L. C. (2004). A case study illustration of how a critical theorist and a consummate practitioner meet on common ground. *Educational Administration Quarterly, 40*(2), 268–289.

Holmes, F. (1977). Lay and professional participation in educational administration in New Zealand. In J. Watson (Ed.), *Policies for participation: Trends in educational administration in Australia and New Zealand*. Wellington, New Zealand: New Zealand Council for Educational Research.

Honderich, T. (Ed.). (2005). *The Oxford companion to philosophy*. Oxford, England: Oxford University Press.

Hong Kong Institute of Education Council. (2007, June). Closing submission by Counsel Patrick Fung S C. *Commission of inquiry into allegations relating to the Hong Kong Institute of Education*. Retrieved from http://www.commissionofinquiry.gov.hk/pdf/Closing%20 submission-JSM.pdf

Howse, J., & Macpherson, R. J. S. (2001). New Zealand's educational administration policies 1984–1994 and the strategic management of its polytechnics. In P. Pashiardis (Ed.), *International perspectives on educational leadership* (pp. 125–139). Hong Kong: Centre for Educational Leadership, University of Hong Kong.

Hoy, W. K., & Miskel, C. G. (1978). *Educational administration: Theory, research, and practice* (1st ed.). New York, NY: McGraw-Hill.

Hoy, W. K., & Miskel, C. G. (1982). *Educational administration: Theory, research, and practice* (2nd ed.). New York, NY: McGraw-Hill.

Hoy, W. K., & Miskel, C. G. (2005). *Educational administration: Theory, research, and practice* (7th ed.). New York, NY: McGraw-Hill.

Hoyle, E. (1982). The micropolitics of educational organisations. *Educational Management and Administration, 10*(2), 87–98.

Hughes, M. (1980). Reconciling professional and administrative concerns. In T. Bush, R. Glatter, J. Goodey, & C. Riches (Eds.), *Approaches to school management: A reader* (pp. 238–251). London, England: Harper & Row, Open University.

Hulme, K. (1985). *The bone people*. Auckland, New Zealand: Hodder and Stoughton.

Hutton, W. (2007). *The writing on the wall: China and the West in the 21st Century*. London, England: Little, Brown.

Iannaccone, L. (1967). *Politics in education*. New York, NY: Center for Applied Research in Education.

Ikin, R. (2007a). Letter to the editor, all daily papers: Press release, Institute for Senior Educational Administrators, 15 April.

Ikin, R. (2007b). No pretence in Director-General's appointment: Press release, Institute for Senior Educational Administrators, 11 April.

Ikin, R. (2007c). Press release to all daily papers: Institute for Senior Educational Administrators, 15 April.

Ikin, R. (2007d). Press release to *The Australian*: Institute for Senior Educational Administrators.

Isaacson, W. (2011). *Steve Jobs*. London, England: Little, Brown.

Jesson, B. (1987). Behind the mirror glass: The growth of wealth and power in New Zealand in the eighties. Auckland: NZ: Penguin.

Johnson, B. L. (2003). Those nagging headaches: Perennial issues and tensions in the politics of education field. *Educational Administration Quarterly, 39*(1), 41–67.

Johnson, B. L., & Fauske, J. R. (2000). Principals and the political economy of environmental enactment. *Educational Administration Quarterly, 36*(2), 159–185.

Jones, A. (2007, 11 April). Michael Coutts-Trotter. *Editorial, 2GB Radio*

Jones, C. (1980). As if business ethics were possible, 'Within Such Limits' . . . *Organization, 10*(2), 223–248.

Jones, M. (1999). Strategic management. In L. Hall, T. Batley, G. Elkin, A. J. Geare, S. Johnston, M. T. Jones, J. W. Selsky, & A. Sibbald (Eds.), *Managing New Zealand organizations: Principles, practices and issues*. Auckland, New Zealand: Addison Wesley.

Justice Woo (2007, 16 March). Statement by Mr. Justice Woo. *Committee of inquiry into allegations relating to the Hong Kong Institute of Education*. Retrieved from http://www.info.gov.hk/gia/general/200703/16/P200703160280.htm

Kant, I. (1991). *Political writings* (H. Reiss & H. B. Nisbet, Trans.). Cambridge, England: Cambridge University Press.

Kaplan, R., & Norton, D. (2004). *Strategy maps: Converting intangible assets into tangible outcomes.* Boston, MA: Harvard Business School Press.

Kell, G. (2005). The global compact: Selected experiences and reflection. *Journal of Business Ethics, 59,* 69–79.

Kenway, J. (1990). *Gender and education policy: A call for new directions.* Geelong, Australia: Deakin University.

Kettl, D. F. (1997). The global revolution in public management: Driving themes, missing links. *Journal of Policy Analysis and Management, 16*(3), 446–462.

King, M. (1981). Between two worlds. In W. Oliver & B. Williams (Eds.), *The Oxford history of New Zealand* (pp. 179–301). Oxford, England: Clarendon Press and Oxford University Press.

Koehn, P. H. (2001). One government, multiple systems: Hong Kong public administration in transition. *Public Organization Review: A Global Journal, 1,* 97–121.

Kramnick, I. (1999). Edmund Burke. In R. Audi (Ed.), *The Cambridge dictionary of philosophy* (2nd ed., pp. 108–109). Cambridge, England: Cambridge University Press.

Kymlicka, W. (2002). *Contemporary political philosophy: An introduction.* Oxford, England: Oxford University Press.

Larue G. A. (1975) *Ancient myth and modern man.* Englewood Cliffs, NJ: Prentice-Hall.

Lather, P. (1991). *Feminist research in education: Within/against.* Geelong, Australia: Deakin University.

Lau, S.-K. (1984). *Society and politics in Hong Kong.* Hong Kong: Hong Kong University Press.

Law, F. C. F. (2007a). Fourth witness statement, 14 May, p. 57. *Commission of inquiry into allegations relating to the Hong Kong Institute of Education.* Retrieved from http://www.commissionofinquiry.gov.hk/pdf/4th%20witness%20statement%20-%20fanny%20law.pdf

Law, F. C. F. (2007b). Second witness statement, 11 April. *Commission of inquiry into allegations relating to the Hong Kong Institute of Education.* Retrieved from http://www.commissionofinquiry.gov.hk/pdf/2nd%20witness%20statement%20-%20fanny%20law.pdf

Law, F. C. F. (2007c). Statement of evidence, 23 March. *Commission of inquiry on allegations relating to the Hong Kong Institute of Education.* Retrieved from http://www.commissionofinquiry.gov.hk/pdf/witness%20statement%20-%20fanny%20law.pdf

Law, F. C. F. (2007d). Third witness statement, 11 April. *Commission of inquiry into allegations related to the Hong Kong Institute of Education.* Retrieved from http://www.commissionofinquiry.gov.hk/pdf/3rd%20witness%20statement%20-%20fanny%20law.pdf

Lee, E. W. Y. (1998). The political economy of public sector reform in Hong Kong: The case of a colonial-developmental state. *International Review of Administrative Sciences, 64,* 625–641.

Leonard, P. E. (1999). Future directions for the study of values and educational leadership. In P. T. Begley & P. E. Leonard (Eds.), *The values of educational administration* (pp. 246–253). London, England: Falmer Press.

Leung Kwok-Fai, T. (2007, 19 March). Witness statement of Leung Kwook-Fai, Thomas. *Commission of inquiry into allegations relating to the Hong Kong Institute of Education.* Retrieved from http://www.commissionofinquiry.gov.hk/pdf/witness%20statement%20-%20leung%20kwok%20fai.pdf

Levine, S., & Vasil, R. (1985). *Maori political perspectives.* Auckland, New Zealand: Hutchinson.

Levitt, T. (1958). The dangers of social responsibility. *Harvard Business Review, 36*(5), 41–50.

Li, A. K. C. (2007). Witness statement. *Commission of inquiry relating to the Hong Kong Institute of Education.* Retrieved from http://www.commissionofinquiry.gov.hk/pdf/Witness%20Statement_Professor%20Arthur%20Li%20.pdf

Li, A. K. C., & Law, F. C. F. (2007a). Executive summary, joint closing submission. *Commission of inquiry into allegations relating to the Hong Kong Institute of Education*. Retrieved from http://www.commissionofinquiry.gov.hk/pdf/CD_QGO1-900945-v1-HIKEd_case_-_Executive_Summary_(Finalized_Version).pdf

Li, A. K. C., & Law, F. C. F. (2007b). Joint closing submission. *Commission of inquiry into allegations relating to the Hong Kong Institute of Education*. Retrieved from http://www.commissionofinquiry.gov.hk/pdf/CD_QGO1-900361-v4-HKIE_-_Table_of_Contents_for_Closing_Submissions.pdf

Liebowitz, J., & Beckman, T. J. (1998). *Knowledge organizations: What every manager should know*. London, England: CRC Press.

Lindbloom, C. E. (1977). *Politics and markets*. New York, NY: Basic Books.

Lindle, J. C. (2004). William P. Foster's promises for educational leadership: Critical idealism in an applied field. *Educational Administration Quarterly, 40*(2), 167–175.

Lindle, J. C., & Mawhinney, H. B. (2003). Introduction: School leadership and the politics of education. *Educational Administration Quarterly, 39*(1), 3–9.

López, G. R. (2003). The (racially neutral) politics of education: A critical race theory perspective. *Educational Administration Quarterly, 39*(1), 68–94.

Luckcock, T. (2012a). Personal growth and spirituality in leadership development: A critical analysis of the construction of self in the LPSH. *Educational Management Administration and Leadership, 35*(4), 535–554.

Luckcock, T. (2012b). Spiritual intelligence in leadership development: A practitioner enquiry into the ethical orientation of leadership styles in LPSH. *Educational Management Administration and Leadership, 36*(3), 373–392.

Lugg, C. A. (2003). Sissies, faggots, lezzies, and dykes: Gender, sexual orientation, and a new politics of education? *Educational Administration Quarterly, 39*(1), 95–134.

Luk, B. (2007). Witness statement of Bernard Luk Hung Kay. *Commission of inquiry into allegations relating to Hong Kong Institute of Education*. Retrieved from http://www.commissionofinquiry.gov.hk/pdf/witness%20statement-bernard%20luk.pdf

Lumby, J. (2012). Leading organizational culture: Issues of power and equity. *Educational Management Administration and Leadership, 40*(5), 576–591.

Lumby, J., Crow, G., & Pashiardis, P. (Eds.). (2008). *International handbook on the preparation and development of school leaders*. London, England: Routledge.

Lyotard, J.-F. (1979). *The postmodern condition: A report on knowledge* (G. B. A. B. Massumi, Trans.). Minneapolis, MN: University of Minnesota Press.

MacBeath, J., & Dempster, N. (2009). *Connecting leadership and learning: Principles for practice*. London, England: Routledge.

Macey, J. (2007, April). NSW Libs call for sacking of education department head. *The World Today, ABC Radio*. Retrieved from http://www.abc.net.au/worldtoday/content/2007/s1894463.htm

Machiavelli, N. (1886). *The prince*. London, England: Routledge.

MacIntyre, A. (1984). *After virtue: A study in moral theory* (2nd ed.). Notre Dame, IN: University of Notre Dame Press.

Mackler, S. (2008). Hermeneutic leadership: Hannah Arendt and the importance of thinking what we are doing. In E. A. Samier & A. G. Stanley (Eds.), *Political approaches to educational administration and leadership* (pp. 109–122). New York, NY: Routledge.

Macpherson, R. (1980). *Role conflict and the role of deputy principals in Western Australian high schools*. Unpublished MEd Admin thesis, University of New England, Armidale.

Macpherson, R. (1983). The Western Australian peer process consultancy project: Action research as INSET for principals. *British Journal of Inservice Education, 9*(3), 141–149.

Macpherson, R. (1984a). *Being a regional director of education.* Unpublished PhD thesis, Monash University, Melbourne, Australia.

Macpherson, R. (1984b). On being and becoming an educational administrator: Methodological issues. *Educational Administration Quarterly, 20*(4), 58–75.

Macpherson, R. (1985a). Some problems encountered 'Boswelling' elite educational administrators. *The Canadian Administrator, 24*(4), 1–6.

Macpherson, R. (1985b). Structure and the action of regional directors. *The Administrator's Notebook, 31*(8), 1–4.

Macpherson, R. (1986a). Reform and regional administration in Victoria's education: 1979–1983. *Australian Journal of Public Administration, 45*(3), 216–229.

Macpherson, R. (1986b). Towards biographical and autobiographical research in educational administration. *Educational Administration Review, 4*(1), 14–28.

Macpherson, R. (1987a, December). *Equal power in adversity: An educational myth for post-Renwick policy making in New Zealand education.* Paper presented at the joint conference of the Australian Association of Researchers in Education and the New Zealand Association of Researchers in Education, University of Canterbury, Christchurch, New Zealand.

Macpherson, R. (1987b). The 'Scott Report' on the quality of teaching in New Zealand: A critical review. In J. F. Northfield, P. A. Duignan, & R. J. S. Macpherson (Eds.), *Educative leadership for quality teaching.* Sydney, Australia: NSW Department of Education.

Macpherson, R. (1988). Talking up organisation: The creation and control of knowledge about being organized. In D. Griffiths, R. Stout, & P. Forsyth (Eds.), *Leaders for America's schools: The report and papers of the National Commission on Excellence in Educational Administration* (pp. 160–182). Richmond, CA: McCutchan.

Macpherson, R. (1989). Radical administrative reforms in New Zealand education: The implications of the Picot Report for institutional managers. *Journal of Educational Administration, 27*(1), 29–44.

Macpherson, R. (1990). Creating administrative policy: Philosophy-in-action? *Australian Educational Researcher, 17*(2), 1–16.

Macpherson, R. (1991a). *Managing the myths of organisation.* Singapore: Singapore Asian Publications.

Macpherson, R. (1991b). The politics of Australian curriculum: The third coming of a national curriculum agency in a neo-pluralist state. In S. Fuhrman & B. Malen (Eds.), *Politics of Education Association Yearbook, 1990: The politics of curriculum and testing* (pp. 203–218). New York, NY: Falmer Press.

Macpherson, R. (1991c). Managing the myths of organisation. Singapore: Singapore Asian Publications.

Macpherson, R. (1992a, July). *Educative accountability policies for systems of 'self-managing' schools: Towards domesticating near-feral schools.* Paper presented at the Australian Council for Educational Administration Conference, Darwin.

Macpherson, R. (1992b). History, organisation and power: A preliminary analysis of educational management in Tasmania. *School Organisation, 12*(3), 269–288.

Macpherson, R. (1992c). Rebutting West to reassert the need for philosophical education for educational administrators and researchers. *Australian Educational Researcher, 19*(3), 87–90.

Macpherson, R. (1992d). The reconstruction of New Zealand education: A case of 'high politics' reform. In H. Beare & W. L. Boyd (Eds.), *Restructuring schools: An international perspective on the movement to transform the control and performance of school* (pp. 69–85). London, England: Falmer Press.

Macpherson, R. (1993a). Administrative reforms in the Antipodes: Self-managing schools and the need for educative leaders. *Educational Management and Administration, 21*(3), 40–52.

Macpherson, R. (1993b). Challenging 'provider-capture' with reforms to educational administration in New Zealand. In Y. M. Martin & R. J. S. Macpherson (Eds.), *Restructuring administrative policy in public schooling: Canadian and international studies* (pp. 219–242). Calgary, Alberta, Canada: Detselig.

Macpherson, R. (1993c). The radical reform of administrative policies in New South Wales school education: Surgery and genetic engineering. In Y. M. Martin & R. J. S. Macpherson (Eds.), *Restructuring administrative policy in public schooling: Canadian and international studies* (pp. 243–262). Calgary, Alberta, Canada: Detselig.

Macpherson, R. (1993d). The radical reform of administrative policies in New South Wales school education: Surgery and genetic engineering. In Y. Marton & R. Macpherson (Eds.), *Restructuring administrative policy in public schooling* (pp. 243–262). Calgary, Alberta, Canada: Detselig.

Macpherson, R. (1995a). Educative accountability policies for Tasmania's system of locally-managed schools: Tentative epistemological implications of cooperative policy research. *International Journal of Educational Research, 23*(6), 545–559.

Macpherson, R. (1995b). Generating educative accountability policies for systems of near-feral 'self-managing schools.' In K. M. Cheng & A. Wong (Eds.), *Educational leadership and change: International perspectives* (pp. 172–186). Hong Kong: Hong Kong University Press.

Macpherson, R. (1995c). Struggling for the soul of education: Towards accountability policy research. *International Journal of Educational Research, 23*(6), 561–566.

Macpherson, R. (1996a). Accountability: Towards reconstructing a 'politically incorrect' policy issue. *Educational Management and Administration, 23*(4), 139–150.

Macpherson, R. (1996b, September). *OFSTED school inspection and value adding: Educative and public accountability or symbolic politics?* Paper presented at the British Educational Research Association Conference, Lancaster University and University College of St. Martin's.

Macpherson, R. (1996c). Educative accountability policy research: methodology and epistemology. *Educational Administration Quarterly, 32*(1), 80–106.

Macpherson, R. (1996d, 12–15 September). OFSTED school inspection and value adding: Educative and public accountability or symbolic politics? Paper presented at the British Educational Research Association Conference, Lancaster University and University College of St. Martins.

Macpherson, R. (1997a). The Centre for Professional Development at the University of Auckland: Towards creating networks of moral obligations. *International Journal of Educational Management, 11*(6), 260–267.

Macpherson, R. (1997b). *Educative accountability: Theory, practice, policy and research in educational administration.* Oxford, England: Elsevier Science, Pergamon Press.

Macpherson, R. (1997c). Learning accountability in Tasmania: The move from command to neo-pluralist politics. *International Electronic Journal of Leadership and Learning, 1*(5).

Macpherson, R. (1998). Contractual or responsive accountability? Neo-centralist 'self-management' or systemic subsidiarity? Tasmanian parents' and other stakeholders' policy preferences. *Australian Journal of Education, 42*(1), 66–89.

Macpherson, R. (1999a). Building a communitarian policy of educative accountability using a critical pragmatist epistemology. *Journal of Educational Administration, 37*(3), 273–295.

Macpherson, R. (1999b). The methodology of a minor miracle: Killing a myth through strategic planning in the Elam School of Fine Arts. *International Journal of Educational Management, 13*(6), 272–280.

Macpherson, R. (1999c). More comprehensive evaluation of teaching systems. In P. Williams & D. Woodhouse (Eds.), *Achieving quality: Examples of good practice in New Zealand Universities* (pp. 84–88). Wellington, New Zealand: New Zealand Universities Academic Audit Unit.

Macpherson, R. (1999d). An organised anarchy or a community of diverse virtue ethics? The case of the Elam School of Fine Arts. *International Journal of Educational Management, 13*(5), 219–225.

Macpherson, R. (1999e). *The quality of teaching at the University of Auckland. Inaugural professorial lecture.* Auckland, New Zealand: University of Auckland, CPD.

Macpherson, R. (1999f). A review of the course evaluation questionnaire and implications for New Zealand universities. *New Zealand Journal of Educational Administration, 14*(10–13).

Macpherson, R. (1999g). Towards bicultural daughters of Picot: Nation building through 'low politics' educative leadership. *New Zealand Journal of Educational Studies, 34*(1), 222–233.

Macpherson, R. (2000a). Escaping to technology-based distributed faculty development: A case for reforming professional development in a knowledge organization. *International Journal of Leadership in Education: Theory and Practice, 3*(3), 275–291.

Macpherson, R. (2000b). A preliminary values audit of social issues in technology-based distributed learning: Implications for educational administrators. *Journal of Educational Administration and Foundations, 15*(1), 33–44.

Macpherson, R. (2008a). Critical management in knowledge organizations. *International Journal of Educational Management, 22*(7), 676–695.

Macpherson, R. (2008b). Teaching and learning at a Middle Eastern university: Scholarship, constructivism, educative leadership and autocracy. In S. Scott & K. C. Dixon (Eds.), *The 21st Century, globalised university: Trends and developments in teaching and learning.* Perth, WA: Black Swan.

Macpherson, R. (2009a). How secondary principals view New Zealand's preparation and succession strategies: Systematic professionalization or amateurism through serial incompetence? *Leading & Managing, 15*(2), 44–58.

Macpherson, R. (2009b). The professionalisation of educational leadership: The implications of recent international policy research in leadership development for Australasian education systems. *Journal of Educational Leadership, Policy and Practice, 24*(1), 53–117.

Macpherson, R. (2010a). Attitudes and intentions of New Zealand educators about preparing for and succeeding in educational leadership roles: Implications for a national professional leadership development strategy. *International Studies in Educational Administration, 38*(3), 115–152.

Macpherson, R. (2010b). Neophyte leaders' views on leadership preparation and succession strategies in New Zealand: Accumulating evidence of serious supply and quality issues. *Leading & Managing, 16*(1), 58–75.

Macpherson, R. (2011). Educational administration and management in Timor Leste: Language and capacity building challenges in a post-conflict context. *International Journal of Educational Management, 25*(2), 186–203.

Macpherson, R. (2013). Evaluating three school-based integrated health centres established by a partnership in Cornwall to inform future provision and practice. *International Journal of Educational Management, 27*(5, forthcoming, June).

Macpherson, R. (forthcoming). Senior leaders' views on leadership preparation and succession strategies in New Zealand: Time for a career-related professionalization policy and provisions. *International Electronic Journal for Leadership of Learning.*

Macpherson, R., Cibulka, J., Monk, D. H., & Wong, K. K. (1998a). Introduction to the politics of accountability: Challenges in retrospect. *Educational Policy, 12*(1–2), 5–17.

Macpherson, R., Cibulka, J. G., Monk, D. H., & Wong, K. K. (1998b). The politics of accountability: Challenges in prospect. *Educational Policy, 12*(1–2), 216–229.

Macpherson, R., & Cusack, B. (1996). John Dewey and educative leadership. *Leading and Managing, 2*(4), 267–283.

Macpherson, R., & Frielick, S. (2001). The Learning Improvement Strategies Questionnaire. *International Studies in Educational Administration, 29*(3).

Macpherson, R., Kachelhoffer, P., & Nemr, N. E. (2007). The radical modernization of school and education system leadership in the United Arab Emirates: Towards indigenized and educative leadership. *International Studies in Educational Administration, 35*(1), 60–77.

Macpherson, R., & Morrison, C. (2001). Boards of trustees' support for the Treaty of Waitangi and partnership in the governance and management of New Zealand secondary schools. In P. Little, J. Conway, K. Cleary, S. Bourke, J. Archer, & A. Kingsland (Eds.), *Learning partnerships: Research and development in higher education.* Newcastle, England: University of Newcastle, HERDSA.

Macpherson, R., Pashiardris, P., & Frielick, S. (2000). The quality of courses at the University of Cyprus: A case study and comparative analysis. *Teaching in Higher Education, 5*(2), 219–232.

Macpherson, R., & Riley, D. (1992). Coping tactics or strategic reform in NSW state schools? In D. Riley (Ed.), *Industrial relations in Australian education* (pp. 271–288). Wentworth Falls, NSW, Australia: Social Science Press.

Macpherson, R., & Sylvester, K. (2007, 24–27 June). *Demand for engineering professionals in the UAE: Development of an ABET-compliant program of engineering in Abu Dhabi.* Paper presented at the American Society for Engineering Education, Honolulu, Hawaii.

Macpherson, R., & Taplin, M. (1995). Principals' policy preferences concerning accountability: Implications for key competencies, performance indicators and professional development. *Journal of School Leadership, 5*(5), 448–481.

Macpherson, R., & Tofighian, O. (2007). Preparing and developing school leaders in the Middle East: Mediating Westernization with indigenous and evidence-based practice and theory of educative leadership. In G. Crow, J. Lumby, & P. Pashiardis (Eds.), *International handbook on the preparation and development of school leaders.* Oxford, England: Elsevier Science.

Macpherson, R., & Vann, B. (1996). Grief and educative leadership. *Journal of Educational Administration, 34*(2), 24–40.

Maddock, T. H. (1994). Science and subjectivity: On the relation of two non-foundational theories to educational administration. In T. Maddock & J. Woods (Eds.), *Theory, research and action in educational administration* (pp. 46–57). Victoria, Australia: ACEA.

Maddock, T. H. (1996). Three dogmas of materialist pragmatism: A critique of a recent attempt to provide a science of educational administration. In C. W. Evers & G. Lakomski (Eds.), *Exploring educational administration: Coherentist applications and critical debates* (pp. 215–237). Kidlington, Oxford, England: Pergamon.

Manning, B. (1977). Hyperlexis: Our national disease. *Northwestern University Review, 71.*

Marshall, C., & Anderson, G. L. (1995). Rethinking the public and private spheres: Feminist and cultural studies perspectives on the politics of education. In J. D. Scribner & D. H. Layton (Eds.), *The study of educational politics: The 1994 commemorative yearbook of the politics of education association (1969–1994).* London, England: Falmer Press.

Marshall, C., Patterson, J. A., Rogers, D. L., & Steele, J. R. (1996). Caring as a career: An alternative perspective for educational administration. *Educational Administration Quarterly, 32*(2), 271–294.

Martin, Y. (1993). Parental participation policy for schools: A comparative legislative analysis of reform and dynamic conservatism in British Columbia, Alberta and Quebec. In Y. Marton & R. Macpherson (Eds.), *Restructuring administrative policy in public schooling.* Calgary, Alberta, Canada: Detselig Enterprises.

Mathews, G. B. (2000). Augustine. *The concise Routledge encyclopedia of philosophy* (p. 63–65). London, England: Routledge.

Mawhinney, H. B. (2004). Deliberative democracy in imagined communities: How the power geometry of globalization shapes local leadership praxis. *Educational Administration Quarterly, 40*(2), 192–221.

Maxcy, B. D., & Nguyen, T. S. T. (2006). The politics of distributing leadership: Reconsidering leadership distribution in two Texas elementary schools. *Educational Policy, 20*(1), 163–196.

McCarthy, M. (2004). Reflections about Bill Foster. *Educational Administration Quarterly, 40*(2), 290–295.

McCornack, S. (2009). *Reflect and relate, an introduction to interpersonal communication* (2nd ed.). Boston, NY: Bedford St. Martin's.

McDougall, B. (2007, April). War over schools director. *The Daily Telegraph.* Retrieved from http://www.news.com.au/dailytelegraph/story/0,22049,21512397-5006009,00.html

McGregor, C. (2008). *Review of the Principal's Development Planning Centre.* Report of the PDPC Review Group, September, released under the Official Information Act, Wellington, New Zealand: Ministry of Education.

McGuinn, T. (1998). *East Timor: Island in turmoil.* Minneapolis, MN: Lerner Publishing Group.

McIndoe, K., & Macpherson, R. (2011). Tihei mauri ora: Becoming a primary school principal in New Zealand. In M. Cowie (Ed.), *New principals talking: Global perspectives.* London, England: Continuum.

McKenzie, D. (1981). The politics of non-planning: A review of the case for national education planning in New Zealand. In M. Clark (Ed.), *The politics of education in New Zealand* (pp. 27–42). Wellington, New Zealand: New Zealand Council for Educational Research.

Meacham, J. (2012). *Thomas Jefferson: The art of power.* New York, NY: Random.

Migone, A. (2008). Between foxes and lions: Machiavelli's discourse on power and leadership. In E. A. Samier & A. G. Stanley (Eds.), *Political approaches to educational administration and leadership* (pp. 23–26). New York, NY: Routledge.

Miles, M. B. (1993). 40 Years of change in schools: Some personal reflections. *Educational Administration Quarterly, 29*(2), 213–248.

Miliband, R. (1969). *The state in capitalist society.* New York, NY: Basic Books.

Mill, J. S. (1972). *Utilitarianism, on liberty, and considerations on representative government.* London, England: Everyman.

Millar, H. D. R. (1995). *The management of change in universities: Universities, state and economy in Australia, Canada and the United Kingdom.* Bristol, PA: Open University Press.

Miller, D. (1984). *Anarchism.* London, England: Dent.

Miller, D. (1998). Political philosophy. In E. Craig (Ed.), *Routledge encyclopedia of philosophy* (p. 687). London, England: Routledge.

Milley, P. (2008). On Jurgen Habermas' critical theory and political dimensions of educational administration. In E. A. Samier & A. G. Stanley (Eds.), *Political approaches to educational administration and leadership* (pp. 54–72). New York, NY: Routledge.

Milne, M. J., Tregidga, H., & Walton, S. (2007). The triple bottom line: Benchmarking New Zealand's early reporters. *The University of Auckland Business Review, 9*(2).

Ministry of Education. (2008). Teaching workforce statistics, personal communication, 4 July. Demographic and Statistical Analysis Unit.

Ministry of Education. (2009a, September). Collective agreements. Retrieved from http://www.minedu.govt.nz/NZEducation/EducationPolicies/Schools/SchoolOperations/EmploymentConditionsAndEvaluation/CollectiveAgreements.aspx

Ministry of Education. (2009b, September). Information for experienced principals. Retrieved from http://www.educationalleaders.govt.nz/Experienced-principals

Ministry of Education. (2009c, September). Professional development. Retrieved from http://www.minedu.govt.nz/NZEducation/EducationPolicies/Schools/Professional Development.aspx

Ministry of Education. (2009d, September). Professional leadership plan 2009–20010. Retrieved from http://www.educationalleaders.govt.nz/Leadership-development/Professional-Leadership-Plan

Morgan, G. (1980). Paradigms, metaphors and puzzle-solving in organisation theory. *Administrative Science Quarterly, 25*, 605–622.

Morgan, G. (1986). *Images of organization*. Newbury Park, CA: Sage.

Morris, P. (2007, March). Statement of evidence. *Commissioner of inquiry into allegations relating to the Hong Kong Institute of Education*. Retrieved from http://www.commissionofinquiry.gov.hk/pdf/Witness%20Statement-paul%20morris.pdf

Morte, M. V. L. (1997). Rights and responsibilities in the light of social contract theory. *Educational Administration Quarterly, 13*(1), 31–48.

Murphy, D. (1979). Essay review, *Education by Choice* by J. E. Coons and S. D. Sugarman. Berkeley: University of California Press.

Murphy, J. (2005). Unpacking the foundations of the ISLLC standards and addressing concerns in the academic community. *Educational Administration Quarterly, 41*(1), 154–191.

Murray H. A. (1960). *Myth and mythmaking*. New York: Braziller.

National Policy Board of Educational Administration. (2008). Educational leadership policy standards: ISLLC 2008. Retrieved from http://teal.usu.edu/files/uploads/asc/elps_isllc2008.pdf

Nettleship, R. L. (1935). *The theory of education in Plato's Republic*. London, England: Oxford University Press and Geoffrey Cumberlege.

New South Wales Legislative Council. (2007). *Extract from Full Day Hansard, 10 May (Proof)*.

New South Wales Premier's Department. (1998). *Code of conduct and ethics for public sector executives*. Sydney, Australia: Management Office, NSW Government. Retrieved from http://www.premiers.nsw.gov.au/our_library/ses/ses_code_of_conduct.html

New Zealand Treasury. (1987). *Government management. Volume Two: Educational issues*. Wellington, New Zealand: Government Printer.

Niner, S. (Ed.). (2000). *To resist is to win: The autobiography of Xanana Gusmao*. Melbourne, Australia: Aurora Books/David Lovell Publishing.

Norington, B. (2007, April). ALP faithful grow into mandarins. *The Australian*.

Norman, W., & MacDonald, C. (2004). Getting to the bottom of "triple bottom line." *Business Ethics Quarterly, 14*(2).

Northfield, J. R., Duignan, P. A., & Macpherson, R. J. S. (Eds.). (1987). *Educative leadership and quality teaching*. Sydney, NSW, Australia: NSW Department of Education.

Nozick, R. (1974). *Anarchy, state and utopia*. New York, NY: Basic Books.

O'Halloran, M. (2007). Director-general of education and training: Press release, NSW Teachers Federation.

Oliver, W. H., & Wiliams, B. R. (Eds.). (1981). *The Oxford history of New Zealand*. Oxford, England: Clarendon Press and Oxford University Press.

Organisation for Economic Co-operation and Development. (1983). *Review of national policies for education: New Zealand*. Paris, France: Author.

Otto W. F. (1965). *Dionysus, myth and cult*. Translated by R. B. Palmer. Bloomington, IN: Indiana University Press.

Palmer, G. (1979). *Unbridled power?* Wellington, New Zealand: Oxford University Press.

Parkyn, G. W. (Ed.). (1954). *The administration of education in New Zealand*. Wellington, New Zealand: New Zealand Institute of Public Administration.

Parliament of New Zealand. (1986). *The quality of teaching: Report of the Education and Science Select Committee*. Chairman Noel Scott MP. Wellington, New Zealand: Government Printer.

Patty, A. (2007, April). Della Bosca push for teacher merit pay. *Sydney Morning Herald*. Retrieved from http://www.smh.com.au/news/national/della-bosca-push-for-teacher-merit-pay/2007/04/04/1175366325690.html

Peckenpaugh, D. H. (1968). The contributions of William Claude Reavis to educational administration. Unpublished PhD dissertation, University of Chicago, p. 13, cited by R. F. Campbell (1972). Educational administration—A twenty-five year perspective. *Educational Administration Quarterly, 8*(1).

Perriton, L., & Reynolds, M. (2004). Critical management education: From pedagogy of possibility to pedagogy of refusal? *Management Learning, 35*(1), 61–77.

Peters, T. J., & Waterman, R. H. J. (1982). *In search of excellence: Lessons from America's best-run companies*. Sydney, Australia: Harper and Row.

Pettit, D., Duignan, P. A., & Macpherson, R. J. S. (Eds.). (1990). *Educative leadership and reorganising the delivery of educational services*. Canberra, Australia: ACT Department of Education.

Pippin, R. B. (1999). Georg Wilhelm Friedrich Hegel. In R. Audi (Ed.), *The Cambridge dictionary of philosophy* (2nd ed., pp. 365–370). Cambridge, England: Cambridge University Press.

Plant, R. (2000). Nature of political philosophy. *The concise Routledge encyclopaedia of philosophy*. London, England: Routledge.

Plato. (1963). *The last days of Socrates* (H. Tredennick, Trans.). Middlesex, England: Penguin.

Plato. (1974). *The republic* (D. Lee, Trans., 2nd ed.). London, England: Penguin Classic.

Pounder, D. G., & Johnson, B. L. (2007). Reflections of EAQ's past, present and future: Editor commentary. *Educational Administration Quarterly, 43*(2), 259–272.

Pratt, J. (1987). Education under adversity. *Educational Management and Administration, 15*(1), 19–22.

Prichard, C. (2002). Creative selves? Critically reading 'creativity' in management discourse. *Creativity and Innovation Management, 11*(4), 265–276.

Putnam, R. D. (1976). *The comparative study of political elites*. Englewood Cliffs, NJ: Prentice-Hall.

Quinn, M. (2008). Choosing languages for teaching in primary school classrooms. In J. Earnest, M. Beck, & L. Connell (Eds.), *Rebuilding education and Health in a post-conflict transitional nation: Case studies from Timor-Leste* (pp. 23–28). Rotterdam/Taipei, The Netherlands: Sense.

Ramsay, P. (1981). Decision-making in the New Zealand Institute of Education: Lead a horse to water. In M. Clark (Ed.), *The politics of education in New Zealand* (pp. 160–173). Wellington, New Zealand: New Zealand Council for Educational Research.

Ramsay, P., Sneddon, D., Grenfell, J., & Ford, I. (1983). Successful and unsuccessful schools: A study in southern Auckland. *Journal of Sociology, 19*(2), 272–304.

Randall, C. B. (1965). *Adventures in friendship*. Boston, MA: Little, Brown.

Raphael, D. D. (1970). *Problems of political philosophy*. London, England: Macmillan.

Rawls, J. (1987). The idea of an overlapping consensus. *Oxford Journal of Legal Studies, 7*(1), 1–25.

Rawls, J. (1993). *Political liberalism*. New York, NY: Columbia University Press.

Rawls, J. (1999). *Theory of justice* (2nd ed.). Cambridge, MA: Harvard University Press.

Rawls, J. (2005). *Political liberalism* (3rd ed.). New York, NY: Columbia University Press.

Renwick, W. L. (1986). *Moving targets: Six essays on educational policy*. Wellington, New Zealand: NZCER.

Rescher, N. (2005). American philosophy. In T. Honderich (Ed.), *The Oxford companion to philosophy* (2nd ed., p. 23). Oxford, England: Oxford University Press.

Reynolds, M. (1998). Reflection and critical reflection in management learning. *Management Learning, 29*(2), 183–200.

Reynolds, M. (1999). Critical reflection and management education: Rehabilitating less hierarchical approaches. *Journal of Management Education, 23*(5), 537–553.

Ribbins, P. (2006). History and the study of administration and leadership in education: Introduction to a special issue. *Journal of Education Administration and History, 38*(2), 113–124.

Ribbins, P., & Sherrat, B. (2012). Permanent secretaries, consensus in national policymaking—Sir David Hancock and the Reform Act 1988: A place for a humanistic research dimension. *Educational Management, Administration and Leadership, 40*(5), 544–558.

Richardson, L. (1997). *Fields of play (Constructing an academic life)*. New Brunswick, NJ: Rutgers University Press.

Rizvi, F. (1985). *Multiculturalism as an educational policy*. Geelong, Australia: Deakin University.

Rizvi, F. (1986a). *Administrative leadership and the democratic community as a social ideal*. Geelong, Australia: Deakin University.

Rizvi, F. (1986b). *Ethnicity, class and multicultural education*. Geelong, Australia: Deakin University.

Rizvi, F., Duignan, P., & Macpherson, R. (Eds.). (1990). *Educative leadership in a multicultural society*. Sydney, Australia: NSW Department of Education.

Rizvi, F., Duignan, P. A., & Macpherson, R. J. S. (Eds.). (1990). *Educative leadership in a multicultural society*. Sydney, NSW, Australia: NSW Department of Education.

Robinson, A. (1985). The political culture. In H. Gold (Ed.), *New Zealand politics in perspective* (pp. 12–26). Auckland, New Zealand: Longman Paul.

Robinson, V. M. J., Eddy, D., & Irving, E. (2006). Catering for diversity in a principal induction programme. *School Leadership and Management, 26*(2), 149–167.

Robinson, V. M. J., Irving, S. E., Eddy, D., & Le-Fevre, D. M. (2008). Capability in the leadership of teaching and learning in New Zealand: The validity and utility of a self-assessment tool. In M. Brundrett & M. Crawford (Eds.), *Developing school leaders: An international perspective* (pp. 155–172). Oxford, England: Routledge.

Romiszowski, A. (2005). *Fundamental school quality project: Consultancy report on teacher professional development and school-based performance management: Context; current situation; future strategies*. Dili: MECY.

Rorty, R. (1989). *Contingency, irony, and solidarity*. Cambridge, England: Cambridge University Press.

Rorty, R. (1989). *Continguency, irony, and solidarity*. Cambridge, England: Cambridge University Press.

Rorty, R. (1991). *Objectivity, relativism and truth: Philosophical papers*. Cambridge, England: Cambridge University Press.

Rosling, H. (2007). *Hans Rosling reveals new insights on poverty*. Paper presented at the Technology, Entertainment and Design Conference, Monterey, California. Retrieved from at http://www.ted.com/index.php/speakers/view/id/90

Rosser, A. (2009). Rebuilding governance in failed states: The case of Timor Leste. In W. Hout & R. Robison (Eds.), *Governance and the depoliticisation of development* (pp. 169–182). London, England: Routledge.

Rousseau, J. J. (1987). *The basic political writings* (D. Cress, Trans.). Indianapolis, IN: Hackett.

Ryan, J. (1999). The value of language and the language of value in a multi-ethnic school. In P. T. Begley & P. E. Leonard (Eds.), *The values of educational administration* (pp. 106–124). London, England: Falmer Press.

Sackney, L. (1993). Restructuring or state-contrived acquiescence? Curriculum reform in Saskatchewan. In Y. Marton & R. Macpherson (Eds.), *Restructuring administrative policy in public schooling: Canadian and international perspectives.* Calgary, Alberta, Canada: Detselig Enterprises.

Salm, T. (2009, April). *Measuring the outcomes: A literature review of interprofessional collaboration in schools.* Paper presented at the American Educational Researchers Association, San Diego, CA.

Samier, E. A. (2008a). Administration as a humanistic pursuit: Kant and Hegel on the political critique of educational administration. In E. A. Samier & A. G. Stanley (Eds.), *Political approaches to educational administration and leadership* (pp. 37–53). New York, NY: Routledge.

Samier, E. A. (2008b). Introduction. In E. A. Samier & A. G. Stanley (Eds.), *Political approaches to educational administration and leadership* (pp. 1–20). New York, NY: Routledge.

Samier, E. A., & Stanley, A. G. (Eds.). (2008). *Political approaches to educational administration and leadership.* New York, NY: Routledge.

Sankowski, E. (2005). History of political philosophy. In T. Honderich (Ed.), *The Oxford companion to philosophy* (2nd ed.). Oxford, England: Oxford University Press.

Schmidt, M. (2008). Risky policy processes: Accountability and school leadership. In E. A. Samier & A. G. Stanley (Eds.), *Political approaches to educational administration and leadership* (pp. 139–154). New York, NY: Routledge.

Schmuck, R. A., & Miles, M. B. (1977). *Organization development in schools.* La Jolla, CA: University Associates.

Schmuck, R. A., & Runkel, P. J. (1985). *The handbook of organization development in schools* (3rd ed.). Palo Alto, CA: Mayfield.

Schon, D. A. (1983). *The reflective practitioner.* New York, NY: Basic Books.

Schon, D. A. (1989). Dynamic conservatism. In D. Pettit, P. A. Duignan, & R. J. S. Macpherson (Eds.), *Educative leadership in the rationalisation of services.* Canberra, Australia: ACT Schools Authority.

Scott, B. (1989a). *Schools renewal: A strategy to revitalise schools within the New South Wales state education system.* Sydney, Australia: Management Review, NSW Education Portfolio.

Scott, B. (1989b). *TAFE restructuring: Building a dynamic vocational education and training enterprise for the 1990s.* Sydney, NSW, Australia: Management Review, NSW Education Portfolio.

Scott, B. (1990). *School-centred education: Building a more responsive state school system.* Sydney, Australia: Management Review, NSW Education Portfolio.

Scott, N., Fraser, A., Gregory, B., Marshall, D., & Richardson, R. (1986). *The quality of teaching: Report of the Education and Science Select Committee.* Wellington, New Zealand: New Zealand House of Representatives.

Scribner, J. D., Aleman, E., & Maxcy, B. (2003). Emergence of the politics of education field: Making sense of the messy center. *Educational Administration Quarterly, 39*(1), 10–40.

Scribner, J. P., Cockrell, K. S., Cockrell, D. H., & Valentine, J. W. (1999). Creating professional communities in schools through organizational learning: An evaluation of a school improvement process. *Educational Administration Quarterly, 35*(1), 130–160.

Selleck, R. J. (1982). *Frank Tate: A biography.* Melbourne, Australia: Melbourne University Press.

Sergiovanni, T. J. (1980). A social humanities view of educational policy and administration. *Educational Administration Quarterly, 16*(1), 1–19.

Sergiovanni, T. J. (1994). Organizations or communities? Changing the metaphor changes the theory. *Educational Administration Quarterly, 30*(2), 214–226.

Shapiro, J. P., & Stefkovich, J. A. (2011). *Ethical leadership and decision making in education: Applying theoretical perspectives to complex dilemmas* (3rd ed.). Abingdon, Oxon, England: Routledge.

Shields, C. M. (1999). Learning from students about representation, identity, and community. *Educational Administration Quarterly, 35*(1), 106–129.

Silmalis, L. (2007, April). I didn't think I would survive being in jail. *Sunday Telegraph*, p. 37.

Simpkins, T. (2012). Understanding school leadership and development in England. *Educational Management, Administration and Leadership*, 40(5), 621–640.

Singer, P. (2002). *One world: The ethics of globalization*. New Haven, CT: Yale University Press.

Smyth, J. (2008). Listening to student voice in the democratisation of schooling. In E. A. Samier & A. G. Stanley (Eds.), *Political approaches to educational administration and leadership* (pp. 240–251). New York, NY: Routledge.

Sorrenson, P. (1981). Maori and Pakeha. In W. Oliver & B. Williams (Eds.), *The Oxford history of New Zealand* (pp. 168–193). Oxford, England: Clarendon Press and Oxford University Press.

South China Morning Post. (1997, 24 November). President Jiang Zemin's speech at the handover ceremony, p. 21.

Spoonley, P., Macpherson, C., Pearson, D., & Sedgwick, C. (Eds.). (1984). *Tauiwi: Racism and ethnicity in New Zealand*. Palmerston North, New Zealand: Dunmore.

Sproul B. C. (1979). *Primal myths: Creating the world*. Sydney, Australia: Rider.

Starratt, R. J. (1993). *The drama of leadership*. London, England: Falmer Press.

Starratt, R. J. (2003). *Centering educational administration: Cultivating meaning, community, responsibility*. Mahwah, NJ: Lawrence Erlbaum Associates.

Starratt, R. J. (2004a). The dialogue of scholarship. *Educational Administration Quarterly*, 40(2), 259–267.

Starratt, R. J. (2004b). *Ethical leadership*. San Francisco, CA: Jossey-Bass.

Stefkovich, J. A., & O'Brien, G. M. (2004). Best interests of the student: An ethical model. *Journal of Educational Administration*, 42(2), 197–214.

Sterba, J. P. (2000). Political philosophy. In R. Audi (Ed.), *The Cambridge dictionary of philosophy* (2nd ed., pp. 718–720). Cambridge, England: Cambridge University Press.

Stone, M. (2007, 19 March). *Commission of inquiry into allegations about Hong Kong Institute of Education*. Retrieved from http://www.commissionofinquiry.gov.hk/pdf/witness%20 statement%20-%20michael%20stone.pdf

Strike, K. A. (1999). Can schools be communities? The tension between shared values and inclusion. *Educational Administration Quarterly*, 35(1), 46–70.

Supit, T. (2008). Initial steps in rebuilding the education sector in Timor-Leste following the September 1999 crisis. In J. Earnest, M. Beck, & L. Connell (Eds.), *Rebuilding education and Health in a post-conflict transitional nation: Case studies from Timor-Leste* (pp. 9–21). Rotterdam/ Taipei, The Netherlands: Sense.

Sydney Morning Herald. (2007a, 12 April). Issue is not drugs but know-how, Editorial, p. 10.

Sydney Morning Herald. (2007b, 12 April). Union backs new boss with drug past. Retrieved from http://72.14.253.104/search?q=cache:0wEoUUsvhaQJ:drugpolicycentral.com/ bot/article/smh.com.au8578.htm+coutts+trotter&hl=en&ct=clnk&cd=50&gl=nz

Taskforce to Review Education Administration. (1988). *Administering for excellence: Effective administration in education*. Report of the Taskforce to Review Education Administration, Chairman Brian Picot, Wellington, New Zealand: Government of New Zealand.

The Daily Telegraph. (2007, 11 April). New education boss has heroin conviction.

Trowler, P. R. (1998). *Academics responding to change. New higher education frameworks and academic cultures*. Philadelphia, PA: SRHE, Open University.

The Trustees Executors and Agency Co. Ltd v. Federal Commissioner of Taxation, 49 CLR 220, 234 C.F.R. (1933).

Tucker, R. (Ed.). (1978). *The Marx-Engels reader*. New York, NY: Norton.

University Grants Council. (2004). *Hong Kong higher education—Integration matters: Report of the institutional integration working party*. Hong Kong: University Grants Council, chaired by Professor Niland.

UNESCO. (1996). *The new global ethics.* World Commission for culture and development report to UNESCO and the United Nations. Retrieved from http://kvc.minbuza.nl/uk/archive/report/chapter1_intro.html

United Nations. (1987). *Our common future.* Report of the Brundtland Commission to the United Nations General Assembly: Oxford University Press.

United Nations Environment Programme. (2012). The global compact and the United Nations environment programme. Retrieved from http://www.unglobalcompact.org/ParticipantsAndStakeholders/un_agencies/un_environment_programme.html

Vogel, D. (1991). Business ethics. *Californian Management Review, 33*(4).

Walker, J. C. (1985). Materialist pragmatism and sociology of education. *British Journal of Sociology of Education, 6*(1), 55–74.

Walker, J. C. (Ed.). (1989). *Educative leadership and curriculum development.* Sydney, NSW, Australia: NSW Department of Education.

Wallace, J. (2008). At the service of the (restructured) state: Principal's work and neo-liberal ideology. In E. A. Samier & A. G. Stanley (Eds.), *Political approaches to educational administration and leadership* (pp. 223–239). New York, NY: Routledge.

Watkins, P. (1985). *Agency and structure: Dialectics in the administration of education.* Geelong, Australia: Deakin University.

Watkins, P. (1986). *A critical review of leadership concepts and research: The implications for educational administration.* Geelong, Australia: Deakin University.

Watson, T. J. (2001). Beyond managism: Negotiated narratives and critical management education in practice. *British Journal of Management, 12*(4), 385–396.

Webb, L. D., & McCarthy, M. (1998). Ella Flagg Young: Pioneer of democratic school administration. *Educational Administration Quarterly, 34*(2), 223–243.

Weber, M. (1947). *The theory of social and economic organizations.* Translated and edited by A. M. Henderson and T. Parsons. New York, NY: Free Press.

Webster, B. A. (1981). The politics of the Post Primary Teachers Association. In M. Clark (Ed.), *The politics of education in New Zealand* (pp. 174–206). Wellington, New Zealand: New Zealand Council for Educational Research.

Welch, D., & Patty, A. (2007, 11 April). Give me a chance: schools' chief. *Sydney Morning Herald.*

Wellington, M. (1985). *New Zealand education in crisis.* Milford, Auckland: Endeavour Press.

West-Burnham, J. (1994). Management in educational organizations. In T. Bust & J. West-Burnham (Eds.), *The principles of educational management* (pp. 9–32). Harlow, Essex: Longman, University of Leicester.

West, P. (1991). Politics and education in NSW 1988–91: Management or human values? *Australian Educational Researcher, 18*(3), 53–67.

Westheimer, J. (1999). Communities and consequences: An inquiry into ideology and practice in teachers' professional work. *Educational Administration Quarterly, 35*(1), 71–105.

Wheeler, T. (2004). *East Timor.* Victoria, Australia: Lonely Planet.

White, S. A. (2000). Marcus Tullius Cicero. *The concise Routledge encyclopaedia of philosophy.* London, England: Routledge.

White, S. K. (1991). *Political theory and postmodernism.* Cambridge, England: Cambridge University Press.

Williamson, J. (1990). What Washington means by policy reform. In J. Williamson (Eds.), *Latin American adjustment: How much has happened?* Retrieved from http://www.iie.com/publications/papers/paper.cfm?researchid=486

Willower, D. J. (1996). Inquiry in educational administration and the spirit of the times. *Educational Administration Quarterly, 32*(3), 344–365.

Wong, M., & Yvonne Tsui, Y. (2007, 25 March). Politics stands tall at bun festival: Fanny Law and Arthur Li provide satirical highlight of Cheung Chau parade. *South China Morning Post*.

Woods, P. (2005). *Democratic leadership in education*. London, England: Paul Chapman Publishing.

Woods, P. (2011). *Transforming education policy: Shaping a democratic future*. Bristol, England: Policy Press, University of Bristol.

Woods, P., & Woods, G. (2012, forthcoming). Degrees of school democracy: A holistic framework. *Journal of School Leadership, 24*(4).

Wootton, D. (Ed.). (1993). *The political writings of John Locke*. New York, NY: Mentor.

Wright, W. (2009). Witchcraft and murder in East Timor. *East Timor Law Journal, 6*(8 May).

Yates, L. (1990). *Theory/practice dilemmas: Gender, knowledge and education*. Geelong, Australia: Deakin University.

Yeung, C. K., & Lee, J. P. (2007). *Report of the commission of inquiry on allegations relating to The Hong Kong Institute of Education*. Hong Kong: Commission of Inquiry. Retrieved from at http://www.commissionofinquiry.gov.hk/eng/report/report.htm

Young, M. D., & López, G. R. (2008). Putting alternative perspectives to work in the politics of education. In E. A. Samier & A. G. Stanley (Eds.), *Political approaches to educational administration and leadership* (pp. 155–172). New York, NY: Routledge.

Index